DEMOCRACY & EDUCATION

2014

COLLECTED PERSPECTIVES

EDITED BY

VIKTORIA BYCZKIEWICZ

"Were all instructors to realize that the quality of mental process, not the production of correct answers, is the measure of educative growth something hardly less than a revolution in teaching would be worked."

John Dewey, *Democracy and Education*

Contents

Teaching for a Democratic World:
An Introduction to Democracy & Education, Collected Perspectives

It is a privilege to have been asked by the directors of the John Dewey Center for Democracy and Education to edit this first of what is envisaged to be a series of collections of papers addressing issues pertaining to and inspired by concepts well developed by the formidable scholar of educational philosophy, John Dewey. Although nearly a century has passed since Dewey first published *Democracy and Education*, his ideas remain relevant and certainly worthy of ongoing discussion, even more so on a universal scale today.

We find ourselves at a critical millennial juncture, when the fundamentals of how lives are lived, the precarious ecological balance of the Earth and its atmosphere, and the institutions that support our infrastructures have rapidly and radically changed over a century of astounding technologicization. Our daunting task is to adapt harmoniously as a universal front, and to salvage and repair the natural world's indisputably delicate web of interdependence. The only practical manner by which we can address these complex hurdles to creating a meaningful and dignified existence for all beings is to acknowledge the imperative of quality education, worldwide. For it is education and only education that levels the global playing field toward achieving the highest goal in modern and enlightened society: a truly universal democracy. It is only in a democratic framework that all beings may flourish.

How we teach, what we teach, and why we teach, the conditions of the environs in which schooling takes place, and the value societies confer on teachers are matters that should concern every educator, every education administrator, and every individual with a vested interest in the shape of the future. Bearing these concerns foremost in mind, the papers included here examine where we stand in terms of achieving democratic standards of education locally and globally, and enable us to envision the project of promoting education as our most precious tool toward achieving universal human rights.

Indeed, in some parts of the world, the central ideals of John Dewey (1859-1952), education philosopher extraordinaire, remain prone to controversy. These ideals include that education be accessible and available in service of individuals' interests, inclinations, and strengths, as well as in service of the needs and goals of the broader communities in which they live and work. Education is the primary means of socialization toward cultivating good and productive citizens, and an investment in the future of a healthy and robust world.

This collection begins with "Education and the Ninth Amendment," in which John Dewey Center for Democracy and Education co-founder Karl Rogers advocates for the right to education as a universal right of the people with reference to the unenumerated rights of the Ninth Amendment of the U.S. Constitution. Specifically, he explores the ongoing debate whether the government has an obligation to provide a free and public education. This is followed by Frank Schweigert's piece, "The Pragmatic Pursuit of the Good," on the need for a meaningful ethics in business education programs. Schweigert provides a Deweyan perspective on moral theory, applied ethics, and moral education, which he recommends as a philosophical foundation to heighten social consciousness and inform ethical, just, and socially responsible decision-making in the world of business and commerce. (Schweigert reserves a detailed delineation of his vision for a curriculum integrating Deweyan ideas of morality into business programs for a forthcoming paper.)

As a grounding clarification of the tenets of John Dewey's philosophy of education, Austin Volz gives us an in-depth modern interpretation of Dewey's seminal and timeless work, *Democracy and Education*. In "Beyond Commonplace Definitions," Volz unpacks in straightforward terms Dewey's framing of education as the reorganization of experience, which has consequences for social action and stimulates lifelong learning and growth. Education for Dewey is not an isolated endeavor, or rote or passive learning; education is a means of shaping thoughtful character, informing continual intelligent activity, inspiring curiosity, and awakening awareness of the self as a socially situated actor. Education informs possibilities for associated living, or true democracy, in which social boundaries are permeable and communications are open and fluid. A truly democratic community shares a wide variety of interests, supports an ample array of undertakings for mutual benefit, and freely engages in the exchange of ideas and information.

Laurel Cadwallader Stolte writes about her research in multicultural civics classes in the Boston area, drawing on interviews with teachers and students alike to present their perspectives on what it means to participate in local civics and community actions. The courses she describes in "Differentiating for Democracy: Social Processes and Civic Equality in Diverse Action Civics Classrooms" follow Deweyan or Freirean models of co-construction of knowledge and participatory democracy. In two case studies Stolte examines how students from different socioeconomic backgrounds respond to authoritative or authentic arrangements that are designed to serve as active laboratories for building a stronger sense of citizenship and community awareness.

Giridhari Pandit's paper on "Rebuilding Democracy, Rethinking Education" candidly examines ongoing discrepancies in the quality and quantity of education delivered to societies around the globe, with a focus on education in India, where the socially and politically undermined remain subjugated in part due to the failure of the system to deliver the resources necessary to educate, uplift, and thus emancipate the working and impoverished classes. Pandit connects the inequities in access to a fair and democratic education to longstanding pervasive or seemingly intractable economic conditions favoring privileged players in the global community. Pandit calls for a universal oath from among the members of the United Nations to provide education to all citizens of all nations in keeping with the Universal Declaration of Human Rights.

Alethea de Villiers provides an inside glimpse into the commitment of some South African educators today to continue toward transforming the education system formerly shaped by apartheid into one that is inclusive, democratic, and cosmopolitan in nature. In "Deweyan Democracy, Cosmopolitanism, and Music Education in South Africa," de Villiers describes the music education program that she oversees and teaches at Nelson Mandela Metropolitan University (NMMU) in Port Elizabeth as exemplary of embodying updated policies and standards in a nation gradually reinventing itself in accordance with democratic principles aligned with the South African concept of *Ubuntu*. Alon Serper, a guest scholar also at NMMU conducting post-doctoral research, provides a graphic historical account of "Bantu education" in the former apartheid South Africa; a system that engineered a mentality designed to reinforce race-based divisions, foster attitudes of suspicion and hostility, and thus justify in the collective mind the inequities so in opposition to the theoretical ideal of a participatory, democratic, and dialogic education. In "Democratic Education Practices in South Africa: A Critical Reflection on a Dialogic Perspective," Serper reflects on his experience of grappling to come to terms with an academic environment that he claims barely resembles the liberal milieu of institutions in other countries in which he has previously worked.

John Warner, in "Whole Systems Classroom Practices," describes his approach to education as a collective experience. He teaches from an organic model of evolution in a workshop-like setting driven by participants supportive of each other's learning and learning styles. Warner reflects on his long and edifying career teaching high school in Los Angeles. Currently, he is applying the same organic principles developed in the classroom to a farm community that he has created in retirement. Finally, Harvey Sarles, co-founder of the John Dewey Center for Democracy and Education, offers a vision of a flourishing future university guided by principles aimed at benefitting the real stakeholders in "A Vision: The Idea of a University in the Present Age."

To open these readings, Karl Rogers depicts the current discourse about public education in the U.S. as affected by a contingent of disproportionately vociferous Americans who are strongly opposed to the notion that education is a basic human right to be granted to citizens from within a publicly accountable framework. While these rogue voices may not represent those of the majority of Americans, the distorting nature of media propaganda amplifies such regressive and inherently divisive views – enough to win the proponents of expanding exclusive or significantly privatized education a tenable position at the bargaining table. This argument is being carried out among a populace either captivated by simplistic "philosophies" that preach extreme egocentrism and thus breed apathy and disdain for the public interest, or seemingly otherwise enthralled by the indulgences of consumerism that render them too benign to stand up to the 'conservative' bullies who persist in challenging democracy as a way of life.

In some nations, poor children, particularly girls or in rural areas or slums, do not have the option of receiving even a primary education by virtue of socioeconomic standing and longstanding culture- and class-based traditions. Giridhari

Pandit tells of the unfairly oppressive conditions in so-called developing countries where child labor and gender-based exclusion from access to school are common maladies. Alon Serper describes how South Africa, more than two decades following the fall of apartheid, as a nation continues to face the challenge of creating a society in which resources are allocated for and equitably distributed to Black students to the extent that they are for Whites. By openly embracing critical, reflective dialogue about history, equality, and access to education, Serper believes that the academic community can work toward empowering and restoring the dignity of those who still suffer the reverberations of colonial rule.

It is unfathomable that anyone in the sophisticated and technologicized world of this day and age would eschew the merits of a solid, well-funded, and generously supported participatory, or democratic, education for all. In defense of leveling – or eliminating – the playing field – Rogers clarifies how the Ninth Amendment to the U.S. Constitution technically affords the right to a public education to all Americans. He argues that the Department of Education, as envisioned in the 19th century, should remain extant as a neutral body to oversee the adequate distribution of education resources to individuals regardless of regional, familial, economic, or other categorical differences, yet that the content of such rigorous and substantive education should remain, as Dewey advocated, principally determined at local and community levels. At the very least the federal body guarantees citizens' choice to participate in public schools that observe standards deemed consistent with those of a modern, developed nation. Federal oversight is necessary as a safeguard because of a recent surge in the disputation of knowledge, as based on scientific rigor and fact, in favor of promoting a dogmatic or faith-based agenda. To stem the rise of dogmatic and ill-informed ideologies such as those that threaten democracy in education in America today or those that sullied South Africa under apartheid, democratic ideals encoded in systems of education ensure the free circulation and vital intersection of ideas and information.

But just what do we really mean by democracy and education? While each author offers insights into how democracy functions, or should function, in unique settings, we as representatives of the John Dewey Center for Democracy and Education mean the instillation and vigilant upholding of fairness, equity, and morality in every facet of the educational scheme. This means at the level of the classroom, among students, where each and every individual has the opportunity to develop into a critically thinking and creatively free individual in conditions that permit uncompromised integrity and encourage one's strengths, as well as within and emanating from the highest administrative offices and everything in between. What is most salient about a democratic education system is that even where infrastructural hierarchies inevitably remain in place and responsibilities are necessarily delegated according to mastery of skill and preparation, democracy guarantees *voice*.

In their separate contributions about classroom-specific practices and procedures, Laurel Cadwallader Stolte, Alethea de Villiers, and John Warner describe how teachers structure lessons with the aim of demonstrating and practicing inclusion, a necessary basis for building a democratic classroom, the laboratory for reproducing a democratic world. We might assert that the right to exercise one's voice is the most fundamental or defining feature of democracy. In the scenarios that both Warner and Stolte depict, one key to invigorating the high school classroom is to grant all students an entitlement to expression. Stolte's research on the teaching of action civics in Boston-area high schools to students from socioeconomically diverse or even diametrically opposed backgrounds enrolled side-by-side demonstrates how the presumption that one possesses the privilege to speak one's mind derives from social positioning or affiliation with prestige. Students automatically assumed the role that they had been conditioned to regard as natural. Those from affluent families were at the outset more assertive, whereas students unaccustomed to being "in charge" were likelier to readily assume a background role. Instructors creatively intervened by enabling different classroom configurations for association and communication. As I assure my own students, international graduate students at the University of Southern California hailing mostly from China and other parts of Asia, I – or we, as a fully attentive class – want to hear what they have to say. In order to engage in active dialogue in search of locating the good and the true, education must aim to illuminate myriad shades of perspective. As Rogers asserts, "education is embroiled in a class struggle, like it or not" (p. 15) – which means we have substantial work to do.

To cultivate the voice of agency and thereby train people to participate in constructing and maintaining a democratic or pluralistic world, it is important to encourage various approaches to discourse. During his decades as an innovative if not maverick high school teacher, while allowing ample time for the entire class to simultaneously engage in a variety of independent activities, mimicking a dynamic ecological community, Warner routinely gave his students controlled exercises in cultivating the voice by reading aloud. This practice functioned to bolster the physical assertion of the literate self and the building of self-esteem, with the guideline that everyone in attendance listen with full attention and gratitude for each contribution. Indeed, the attention that we are able to offer each other as cognizing, breathing individuals may be one of the great virtues of human capability to go by the wayside as electronic devices have hijacked the realm of the senses. We have become desensitized in service of the abstract and alienating demands of the gadgets and strategies perpetrated by the marketplace. At the same time, the Internet, social media, and new self-publishing technologies serve to democratize the dissemination of independent work. Curricula at all levels are swiftly incorporating a dizzying range of technologies, some of which are empowering and efficient, others that supplant direct forms of interaction and thus limit the stimuli of sharing physical space for the efficiency of virtual space. Sarles hopes that we can locate a balance so that the university retains its purpose in service of, for, and by the people.

A democratic environment is an environment that enables everyone; it is an environment of fairness; an ethical environment. A democratic environment values tolerance and diversity along the lines of the sophisticated concept of cosmopolitanism adopted as a definitive goal in the South African education system and, as defined by de Villiers, in which we are bound to each other by a sense of "conscious humanity." Unfortunately, the kind of crude and intentionally divisive debate that has become popular and rewards prowess for inciting intimidation and conflict is no model for a cosmopolitan, democratic world community that must thrive in order to empower the global citizenry with the knowledge and tools needed to promote universal peace, dignity, and equality as set forth among the grander goals of the body of United Nations. Giridhari Pandit paints this bigger picture in showing how democracy in education must be compulsory on an international scale in fulfillment of the UN's Millennium Development Goals. In his expansive piece, Pandit describes the bleak conditions contributing to unequal access to education in developing nations and posits a plan for the United Nations to implement a revised Universal Declaration of Human Rights that imposes sanctions on nations that fail to cooperate in practicing good neighborly and ethical relations. As Pandit writes,

> As citizens, either we are *all* free, enjoying universal human rights, or we are all *not* free at all if some are unable to enjoy basic human rights in their own countries. In our highly vulnerable and fragile world,

which is deeply divided between the rural and urban populations, on the one hand, and developed and developing nations, on the other, none of us can claim to be free so long as there remains even one single individual who is not able to enjoy basic human rights and economic choices. (p. 194)

Volz echoes this sentiment that free and democratic society rests on our inextricable common interests in that "when one's own interests match those of others then the success of one member has worth for another because it marks the achievement of similar goals" (p. 96). In other words, we are in this all together.

In "The Pragmatic Pursuit of the Good," Frank Schweigert discusses the necessity of teaching ethics in business schools to reinforce the primacy of a common social good and underscore the long-term value of democratic-minded decision-making. Whereas the doctrines of a competitive marketplace and self-interested profit tend to encourage "an atmosphere that legitimizes a culture of greed" (Mangan, as cited in Schweigert, p. 32) in which individuals justify short-term personal gain above all else, Dewey admonished that the business arena necessitate a collective approach to problem-solving in keeping with the goal of social betterment in all human activity. In deferring to a moral consideration of the socioeconomic ramifications of business dealings, decision-making is informed by reference to potential outcomes. The educator's task is to inculcate the habit of awareness of potential conflicts that might arise as a result of imprudent business decisions and to facilitate *deliberate* thinking about conflict avoidance and resolution. As Schweigert summarizes, "a shared process of deliberation is a powerful tool of moral education, which Dewey recognized and advocated at length in many of his writings on the unified purpose of democracy and education" (p. 52).

By uniting democracy and education – or more aptly, committing to democracy *in* education – we mean letting the entire diversity of voices within educational institutions be heard. Too often, in the domains where people study and learn and work, whether in the classroom, in meetings of teachers or administrators, or at the level of public policy deciding what education should be and how it should be delivered, the usual voices or ideologies dominate. We still do not have democracy in education because uneven power dynamics continue to reflect the "vested social interests and class disparities" described by Schweigert. By defaulting to these interests, decision-making processes are hardly collaborative. As Sarles laments, today's universities tend to be unhealthily invested in maintaining controlling bureaucratic hierarchies with a constant eye to competitive rankings or preoccupation with procuring celebrity faculty. Less consideration is given to the content of academic discipline in and of itself. The goal of education has apparently strayed from the art and practice of education!

So, it would seem that our main project is to build democracy. And we can *only* build democracy by drawing attention to existing power dynamics that *prevent* democracy by maintaining the status quo of inequity that furthers the dehumanization or impotence of large and small swaths of humanity. We can teach the uninitiated to reject the prevailing model and by showing them what democracy means and how it can optimally function. Again, our work begins in our classrooms, where the power struggles first manifest. Stolte provides evidence of these negotiations; of young minds coming to grips with the realities of a world divided into haves and have-nots. Warner demonstrates how even though students clearly display different strengths and abilities, the teacher takes on the task of teaching how the entire spectrum of style and ability is of value. De Villiers tells of music students uncomfortable with exercising their voice due to a history of cultural oppression conditioning them to adapt by staying silent. She uses modeling as a subtle means of teaching new, empowered, and respectful ways of interacting.

The status quo not only must change in the immediate classroom, changes in power dynamics must extend all the way to our international institutions, to the level of the United Nations, where Pandit calls for human rights as a universal goal to transcend its stagnant status as a lofty abstraction. All nations ought to be required to demonstrate compliance with standards of equality in education for women and children in order to keep in the company of the nations of a civilized world. Sarles envisions the future of higher education as a return to a focus on curricula and faculty, on knowledge and the quest for knowledge for the sake of it, and for its transformative capacities, rather than a focus on administration and attracting consumer-students and profits. The purpose of education must be enlightenment and edification, for all, so that all might lead full lives.

To further fulfill our pursuit of educating about how to implement democratic decision-making processes toward the goal of a common good, we can benefit from the careful examination of how talk reifies power relations. As scholars we can conduct discourse analyses of the myriad situations in which these dynamics are played out. That is, we can analyze the discourse of interactions in which decisions that impact our collectivity as humanity are being made. Once we plainly acknowledge how power is established in the often subtle and elusive ways that people employ and manipulate language, and how these power dynamics create our social realities, then we can actively and mindfully participate in reshaping our world into one that embraces democratic communicative practices.

Our call for a true democracy is nothing short of a call for truth.

Viktoria Byczkiewicz

An Open Letter on Democracy and Education from the Directors of the John Dewey Center for Democracy and Education

The connections between democracy and education are crucial to the future of a democratic world. Each new child; each new generation must be engaged in their own living experience and capable of acting as a democratic citizen. Education must be more than mere memorization; instead, the focus should be on observing the world and oneself, and learning how to better communicate and cooperate with others. Children need to be encouraged to think of themselves in the many contexts of teaching, schooling, understanding the world and what it means to be human, and exploring who one is (and will become).

Speaking as both teachers and directors of the John Dewey Center for Democracy and Education, we speak as persons who love people of all ages and love helping them engage with and ensure their own future through helping them develop and articulate meaningful life experiences that explore touching and examining the world and one's growing understanding of what it means to be a self in the world. Our understanding of education is that it is a means toward increasing children's ability to think and communicate what being a human being means to them.

Democracy depends on the ability of each person to see and participate in an increasingly globalized world. This is why we hope that education imparts a growing sense of humanity—of solidarity and inclusion—so we can learn how to share life on this planet with each other and with the other species that inhabit it.

John Dewey was deeply upset in 1944 by the destructive power of the two World Wars. In a later edition of his seminal Democracy and Education (first published in

1916), he included a section entitled "The Democratic Conception in Education" to explain how these wars had shown him that the very ideas of democracy and education had been rendered porous and dubitable.

Democracy is not guaranteed and it is very much at stake.

Dewey's 1944 writing on democratic faith and education shows that his once positive thinking had changed into fearful skepticism.

Even though the new technologies of mass media, planetary telecommunications, and the Internet available to us in the 21st century offer us great potential for democracy, education, and global inclusion, we would be wise to share something of Dewey's fearful skepticism. As he wrote:

> Let me return for the moment to my initial statement that the basic error of social idealists was the assumption that something called "natural law" could be trusted, with only incidental cooperation by human beings, to bring about the desired ends. The lesson to be learned is that human attitudes and efforts are the strategic center for promotion of the generous aims of peace among nations; promotion of economic security, and the worldwide cause of democratic institutions. Anyone who starts from this premise is bound to see that it carries with it the basic premise of education in creating the basis and outlook that are able and eager to secure the ends of peace, democracy, and economic stability.

It is for this reason that it is one of the central aims of the John Dewey Center for Democracy and Education to deepen our understanding of new technologies and possibilities and their impacts for human beings, citizenship, and democracy in this era of globalization. Will we develop these technologies and possibilities to realize their democratic potential and discover, share, and educate ourselves and each another in accordance with Dewey's original hopes?

As part of this ongoing analysis, we must direct ourselves back to the times in which Dewey was a big player in unraveling the Gilded Age of the "Robber Barons" of the early 20th Century. And we must remind and educate ourselves that we find ourselves – once again – in a Gilded Age in which globalization is being developed for the benefit of a wealthy few rather than everyone. Can we overcome this new Gilded Age? If we hope to do this, as a species, we must engage now in the task of moving towards a globally inclusive, democratic world.

We must expand our being to be conscious of the entire world. We need to be aware of all the people around the world who are now beginning to see us all, to see and think globally, and be seen "back" by others. We need to see ourselves as part of a planetary community, an ecology, within which we all have a stake in the future. Ideas are flowing from and to everywhere: from Eastern philosophies such as Buddhism, Hinduism (via yoga, for example), Confucianism, and Amerindian traditions, which have changed and broadened how we in the West think about human politics, health, and spirituality, and the human relationship to all other creatures and the whole universe. We have come to learn that the future rests particularly in the being and activities of women. Increasingly, women around the world are taking the lead in democracy, both at local and global levels. We have also come to learn that the future rests also on how we learn to live on this planet as an ecology. Western thought, which has been and continues to underscore the power of individuals and of history in framing the concepts of being human and how we understand existence, has also brought to the world ideas of equality, liberty, and democracy, along with an understanding of the power of science and reason. We need to see how all these ways of thinking from around the world – from all humanity – can help us understand the interconnectedness of our existence and how we all shape our shared future. How can these ideas be part of and elaborate on and extend our understanding of democracy in education?

Young(er) people – so invested in and aware of the new technologies and media to explore what and who we are, and may become – can speak to the entire world in an instant, at the speed of light. (Speaking and writing in English as an international language is not a small part of this, while opportunities to learn any of the languages of the world have never been greater.) The present age offers us the opportunity to study what it means to be a human being, and for all and any of us to communicate with anyone, anywhere, on this planet, who has access to a computer and a modem. Around the world an increasing proportion of the world's population has access to the Internet.

The current volume you are reading offers the reflections of a few people from several countries (India, South Africa, Israel, the United Kingdom, and the United States) about democracy and education, and how to move towards global inclusion in this current era. The authors in this volume all seek to help people to educate each other, to live more democratic lives and share in the creation of our future, very much in the spirit of Dewey's ideas of education and democracy for all.

Via education, we must move "past" this Gilded Age of money and power resting only in the hands of a few, and move towards a democratic world. Via democracy, we must move beyond the current ideas and practices of public education and the university system; beyond the ideas that success is most particularly cast in terms of monetary power and fitness for the job market. We need to broaden how children are educated to help them understand that this shared life and how we communicate our experiences are the foundations of democracy and education. What is an education for? What does it mean to live a good life? What does it mean to be a human being? We need to move toward the ideas that life and success will be cast in terms of an increasingly meaningful society and cooperative existence, among billions of people on a shared planet, who all have a great deal to learn from each other. We need to rediscover our wisdom traditions, learning how to respect aging and the experiences of people who have lived a long time, and learn from each other how to better live with each other.

The directors of the John Dewey Center for Democracy and Education would like to thank Viktoria Byczkiewicz of Trébol Press and the University of Southern California for all her insights and hard work putting together and editing this collection. We hope that you enjoy it.

Harvey B. Sarles

Karl A. Rogers

Jerry Timian

April 20, 2014

Education and the Ninth Amendment

Karl Rogers
The John Dewey Center
for the Study of Democracy and Education

Abstract

In America, it is often claimed by conservatives that there is no
constitutional basis for any federal involvement in education
and that education should be left to the states. Conservatives
also blame progressivism for declining standards in public
school education and promoting left-wing ideology. This paper
discusses both of these claims, defending progressive
education and federal involvement in education. Rogers also
argues that the U.S. Constitution obliges the government to
promote the general welfare and Congress to promote the
sciences and useful arts, under which categories education
clearly falls, and that these are not matters that should be left
to the states. However, the main thrust of his argument is that
education is a Ninth Amendment issue. He discusses this and
its implications for democracy and education.

Keywords: democracy and education, Dewey, media
misrepresentation, NCLB, Ninth amendment, public debate

Nowadays, it is a commonplace opinion among
conservative politicians and media pundits in America that
education is not a federal matter and should be left to the
states. They claim that there is no constitutional right to
education. Conservative "think-tanks," such as the Cato
Institute and FreedomWorks, have declared the Department
of Education or any federal involvement in education to be
unconstitutional.[1] This kind of opinion has been advanced by

---

[1] See the Cato Institute webpage at
http://www.cato.org/blog/yes-department-education-unconstitutional

various conservative organizations since the Department of Education (DoE) was created under the Carter Administration in 1980. For example, since its founding in 1983, the Home School Legal Defense Association (HSLDA) has called for the abolition of the DoE on the grounds that federal involvement in education is a violation of Tenth Amendment states' rights. This view has also become part of the Republican Party platform. During his presidential election campaign, Ronald Reagan ran on a promise to abolish the DoE and return control over education to the states. After Reagan reneged on his campaign promise, the Republican Party dropped the abolition of the DoE from its platform until Newt Gingrich became Speaker of the House and spokesman for the GOP opposition in 1994. By 1996, once again, the abolition of the DoE on the grounds of its unconstitutionality was central to the GOP platform.

Time and time again we hear from "conservatives" that public education is a failure and a colossal waste of taxpayers' money. We hear people blame governmental waste and mismanagement, teacher tenure and unmotivated teachers, classroom overcrowding, and also unmotivated and undisciplined students. However, while all these factors are serious concerns, it is rather simplistic to put the blame on the federal government and teachers' unions for a failed education system. We need to examine which goals, norms, and standards are being used to evaluate the success or failure of public education. When accusations of failure are more motivated by ideology than facts or reasoned argument, they are little more than anti-government and anti-union propaganda and sloganeering. Furthermore, it is not evident that public education is a failure, and certainly not to the extent that it is presented as being in right wing media. However, even if we

---

and the FreedomWorks website at
http://www.freedomworks.org/blog/jborowski/abolishing-the-department-of-education-is-the-righ

agree that public education is failing, we need to discover why this is the case. We also need to look at whether this state of affairs is national or whether it varies among different regions, cities, districts, and states, or among different socioeconomic or ethnic groups. Broad and sweeping declarations of failure are not at all helpful for the purpose of improving the situation. Before we can make the claim that public education is failing, we need to be clear what we consider its purpose to be. It is not at all evident that there is any national consensus on this and it is not clear how we could determine what the national consensus is.

America needs national debate and consensus on the definition and purpose of a good education. However, instead of public debate and consensus, we end up with scaremongering and discord. In large part, this discord has been deliberately engineered by the Republican Party propaganda machine and "conservative" media in general.

Interestingly, "conservative" arguments about the unconstitutionality of the DoE did not start in 1980. In 1867, after the Civil War and during the reconstruction period, Congress and President Andrew Johnson created the first federal Department of Education. The task of this bureau was to collect data on education (methods, practices, resources, and results) throughout the United States. During the congressional debates, the notion that this infringed on states' rights was raised by New Jersey Congressman Andrew Jackson Rogers, who argued that placing education under the jurisdiction of the federal government was the thin edge of the wedge towards federal government control over education. Once federal jurisdiction was established, he argued that it would be easy for Congress, via amendment to funding bills and laws, to increase the level of governmental control over any sphere, including education. Congressman Rogers also objected to Congressman Donnelly of Minnesota, who had argued that it was the failures of education in the southern states that had been responsible for ignorance, illiteracy, the continuation of slavery, and the ill-fated attempt to secede from the Union. Rogers responded that Donnelly's assertion thinly disguised an attempt by the federal government to create loyalty to itself by slowly taking control over education. Rogers argued that education must be left to the states rather than adopt the European "Napoleonic" model. He appealed to the U.S. Constitution, the Tenth Amendment and states rights, and "the natural right" of parents to educate their children however they deem fit and appropriate.

What sense can we make of this claim that the DoE is unconstitutional? If we look at the text of the Tenth Amendment, it reads, "The powers not delegated to the United States by the Constitution, nor prohibited by it to the States, are reserved to the States respectively, or to the people." Indeed, there is no mention of education in the Tenth Amendment, nor anywhere else in the U.S. Constitution. Does this mean that the DoE is unconstitutional? Well, no. What it means is that there is no constitutional mandate that places an obligation on Congress to fund education, but there is no constitutional prohibition either. It remains up to Congress, the states, and the people to decide what kind of role, if any, the federal government should take in funding, aiding, monitoring, or overseeing public education in America. Despite all the talk about states' rights, there has never been any serious court challenge to the federal funding of public education or to the 1979 Department of Education Organization Act that empowered the federal government to establish the DoE. The Supreme Court of the United States of America (SCOTUS) has consistently maintained a principle of *Expressio unius est exclusio alterius* ("the express mention of one thing excludes all others"), which means that anything that is not specifically mentioned in a list of rights and powers is assumed not to be covered by the statute or a contractual term. This principle that has been consistently understood by SCOTUS as being expressed by the Ninth Amendment of the

U.S. Constitution: "The enumeration in the Constitution, of certain rights, shall not be construed to deny or disparage others retained by the people."

The Ninth Amendment is in the Constitution to remind us that it is a social contract between the people, the states, and the federal government. The Ninth Amendment recognizes that the people, as beings with rights that were not created by signing the Constitution, are co-signatories, the "We the people" in the contract between the people, the states, the courts, and the federal government to form a union. Some rights – whether understood as natural rights or those established through English common law – pre-exist the Constitution.

Except in cases covering the right to privacy, such as abortion (*Roe v. Wade*, 1973), contraception (*Griswold v. Connecticut*, 1965), and private contracts (*Gibson v. Matthews*, 1991), the Ninth Amendment has only been invoked to point out that the powers and jurisdiction of the federal government are limited to those expressly mentioned in the Constitution, or in the case of *U.S. Public Workers v. Mitchell*, 1947, to prevent the federal government from employing communists and people actively seeking to overthrow the federal government. The Court concluded that the right of revolution rightly belongs to the people and not the federal government! The Supreme Court has said nothing about education—nor could it on the basis of the Constitution, given the Ninth Amendment.

On the one hand, it seems that there is nothing in the Constitution to stop the federal government from funding educational programs – providing that the government does not employ people at taxpayers' expense to promote revolution and its own overthrow – *or interfere with private contracts*. On the other hand, the federal government does not have any authority to prevent people from educating their own children, or dictate the methods and content of education within public schools.

The Ninth Amendment clearly leaves it to the people to decide for themselves how best to educate their children. The role of the federal government or whether education is left to the states, local districts, particular schools, or parents is a decision that must be left to the people to decide, and there is nothing within the text of Constitution that makes or mandates that decision for them. The DoE should be there to help the states fund and improve education. It could do this by providing schools and parents with resources and information, and leaving it to the schools and parents to decide for themselves how to use those resources and information. If the Ninth Amendment was applied consistently to education, the DoE would remain limited to distributing information and resources to schools and parents to educate children at home and in public schools, and collect and provide public information records and statistics on education, to help teachers and parents access and use public information services to learn from the successes and failures of other teachers and schools, but leave it to schools and parents to teach what they wish. Teachers and parents should be left to teach anything they wish, as a natural right and freedom left to them under the Ninth Amendment—and clearly also a First Amendment right of freedom of speech. It should be left to teachers, schools, parents, and students to decide the best content and methods of learning, and methods of evaluation and testing. The DoE would ideally largely focus all its efforts on maintaining public libraries and online services to help people find information and learn from the successes and failures of other schools and people around the country. The DoE could help the poorest states and people build, maintain, and access public education, schools, colleges, libraries, universities, records and archives all around America.

The problem is who will pay for it? Without federal taxes, there is no federal involvement in education. The likely outcome of this would be that education would become increasingly privatized and ghettoized almost to the point that there would be no public education, or education of any kind for the poorest people in America. Would local communities, towns and cities be able to fund their own public education? Richer communities would; poorer ones would not. It is as simple as that. The dissolution of public schooling would result in economic segregation and the reinforcement of a class-based society. Putting aside conservative Red-baiting and accusations of the federal funding of communists in government, the DoE and federal funding do indeed redistribute wealth in society to allow everyone to have access to public education, something from which the whole of society benefits. Who pays? Each generation pays for the education of the next generation. It is a matter of paying it forward. Educated people end up paying higher taxes after they are educated. Education creates wealth. Would this create greater economic equality among people? Yes, to some extent, it is inevitable that it would. Is this a good thing? I would say that it is.

One's answer to this question determines which side of the political fence they sit on when education becomes a political football, with each camp each trying to outdo the other in their struggle to use the term "class warfare" against the other. In recent years, and news cycles, the speeches of Republican Party presidential candidates have recycled the old call for the abolition of the DoE on the grounds of its unconstitutional "federal funding of class warfare" and "a redistribution of wealth," discontinuing the funding of public education on the grounds that it is theft from rich people. Ron Paul said that the public school system in America is failing due to the existence of federal funding, calling for the dissolution of the DoE and a return to private education (either by attending private for-profit schools or by home schooling)

(Paul, 2013). For Paul, taxpayer funded public education is on the slippery slope to the rise of one-world Communist government (Paul, 2011).

This kind of opinion has been repeated through the "conservative" media echo chamber. One such "conservative" voice heard on radio and on his Internet-based television channel is Glenn Beck.[2] Over and over again, listeners and viewers have been told that public education is failing and the DoE is an unconstitutional violation of states' rights. Beck has told us that 32 million Americans cannot read or write and that 63 percent of 18 to 24 year olds cannot find Iraq on a map (Beck, 2011, p. 62).[3] Of course, Beck has not told us why the DoE is to blame for this shocking level of illiteracy. After all, most American children have access to television, public libraries, books, magazines, and the Internet. An atlas costs less than the price of a computer game. Public school is not their only source of information. Is the inability of young adults to find Iraq on a map really the fault of the DoE and the public school system? Surely, some responsibility for the education of children must fall to their parents, and to the children themselves. Why is it that the Republicans call for "personal responsibility" but blame the government for all our failures? How is it the federal government's fault that 32 million Americans cannot read or write? Why didn't their parents teach them? In the United States of America, parents do have the option to homeschool their children, as well as many other options, and even if we acknowledge that in many families both parents have to work, and for the most part every single parent has to work such that homeschooling is not an option for these parents, surely even the hardest-working parents could find one hour per day to make sure that their children

---

[2] See Glenn Beck's website at http://www.glennbeck.com/
[3] This claim was taken from the 2006 National Geographic-Roper Public Affairs Geographic Literacy Study
http://www.nationalgeographic.com/roper2006/pdf/FINALReport2006GeogLit survey.pdf

are able to read and write. Even if public schools were failing to teach these children how to read and write, we would still need to ask whether the failure of the public schools to teach these 32 million Americans to read and write is really the fault of the federal government.

However, despite all the rhetoric, slogans, and sound bites, federal spending on education has continued to rise. After the turn of the century, the Bush Administration continued to involve the federal government in the standardization of testing and teacher training in accordance with the No Child Left Behind (NCLB) Act. Since the end of NCLB, the Obama Administration has further continued this direction with the development of Common Core. Are these federal programs really to blame for failures in public education? What about parents and students? Should they take some responsibility for failures in public schools?

Of course neither parents nor students like to hear that it might be even in part their fault that public education is failing in America. They need a scapegoat. Immigrants are a drain on resources, they claim. Or, as Glenn Beck (and Ron Paul) would have us believe, it is the fault of progressives and the teachers' unions! Of course, as I shall explain below, this opinion is not based on facts or reasoned argument, but on little more than a thinly veiled disguise for Beck's (and Paul's) resentment about having to pay taxes to educate other people's children. Pull away the veil and we can see that their ideological commitment to "the free market" and their guise of libertarianism are both masks to cover their selfishness with the gloss of legitimacy. Their criticisms of teachers' unions can be boiled down to two objections: (1) unions support teacher tenure and therefore support bad teachers; and (2) they are unions and therefore bad by definition. Instead, they appeal to the need for a traditional education—or a rather mythical image of what 1950s education was—but, at bottom, they both appeal to their own authoritarian views that they know best what American children should learn.

Let's start by taking a closer look at Beck (and Paul's) claims that unions are to blame for the failures in public school education:

With over three million members, the National Education Association (NEA)[4] is the largest teachers' union in America. The second largest is the American Federation of Teachers (AFT)[5] with over 850,000 members. (The AFT is affiliated with the American Federation of Labor and Congress of Industrial Organizations (AFLCIO), which is the largest federation of unions in the U.S.) How could these teachers' unions be to blame? Well, according to Beck, there are four ways that the teachers' unions are to blame: (1) They are to blame by being powerful and successfully lobbying the DoE and, by doing so, have managed to secure tenure which allows bad teachers to keep their jobs; (2) They are to blame by pushing left-wing political agendas and progressive ideologies in the classroom; (3) They have prevented parents from having any control over the content of their children's education; and (4) They are unions and thus by definition are bad, so somehow they must be to blame.

Let's start by looking at tenure. The reason why tenure is a bad idea seems quite obvious if it prevents teachers from being fired for not doing their job properly. It seems reasonable for a school to be able to fire a bad teacher. Why would anyone want to keep bad teachers in schools? Well, it is not so simple. The problem is: who decides what good teaching is? The Department of Education? The State Board of Education? The school board? The parents? The students? Other teachers? If Glenn Beck and Ron Paul had their way,

---

[4] See the National Education Association's website at: http://www.nea.org/
[5] See the American Federation of Teachers' website at: http://action.aft.org/

anyone who taught anything they disagreed with (i.e., progressive, liberal, or generally left leaning) or did not like (i.e., provided facts that did not fit their narratives) would be fired as a bad teacher. This is why the purpose of tenure should be to protect intellectual freedom and freedom of speech. A teacher should be able to dissent from mainstream norms, explore sensitive topics, or openly disagree with the authorities or popular opinion. Tenure should allow a teacher to disagree with parents or administrators without fear of losing their job. Tenure should afford teachers the same protection as is afforded university professors or judges with lifetime appointments. Without tenure, the tendency would be for schools to teach prevailing opinion and orthodoxy. It is also the case that tenure does not require good grades as a condition of continued employment, and, therefore, there is no motivation for teachers to lower standards or falsify test results in order to keep their jobs. This is the problem with so-called merit-based pay. Unfortunately, once teachers become financially motivated to secure good grades or results then corruption and deception will inevitably occur. Tenure secures impartiality. It increases the chance of problem areas and struggling students coming to public attention. The risk of lazy and unmotivated teachers is the price to pay for allowing good teachers the freedom to teach as they deem best and to teach what they deem to be important. It is the way to keep educational standards high. (It is also the case that, without tenure and without job security, teachers would demand higher salaries.) Tenure is not the reason why millions of Americans cannot read or write, or cannot find Iraq on a map.

Nobody wants children to be taught by bad teachers. Bad teachers are betraying the trust bestowed upon them, but parents need to take personal responsibility for their own children's education, and to make sure that their children are learning what they need to learn. However, the risk of bad teachers could be somewhat mitigated by having higher standards in teacher training and recruitment, and also by making sure that children only have the same teacher for a single school year or subject, at most, thereby allowing children the experience of being taught by several or many teachers. This is largely what happens in most public schools. Students also need to take personal responsibility for their own education. With access to the Internet, libraries, cable television, radio, magazines, newspapers, and books, students have many opportunities for learning outside of public schools. Students have a great deal of choice about how and what they learn, and they need to make their voices heard to teachers and parents. It has become a very convenient excuse to blame teachers, unions, or governments for the lack of student motivation and poor educational performance. The bottom line is that if we accept that education is a Ninth Amendment issue then we must accept that the people are responsible for education in America; there is no excuse for millions of Americans being unable to read or identify other nations on a map.

Most teachers are also parents who send their children to public schools. While the teachers' unions are there to protect their members' interests, the education of the members' children is an important interest. It is up to the members to make their voice heard through their union and ensure that their union delegates and leaders are accountable to them. If the unions are protecting the jobs of bad teachers at the expense of the public school system and students, then this phenomenon reflects the political choices of the membership. Teachers need to stand up and be counted. Their voices need to be heard about what they think a good education is and how it can be achieved. Through the unions, teachers have an opportunity to contribute to a national debate about public education and make it a political priority during elections. There have been plenty of opportunities to put public education higher on the list of national priorities. This current situation is the result of negotiations and political choices. If public education is failing due to a conspiracy between the teachers' unions and the DoE, as Paul and Beck have asserted, then the voters—as teachers, as parents, and as citizens—have been complicit in this too.

Of course, it is also worth mentioning that a great deal has been made by media pundits like Beck out of cases of teachers not being fired despite alleged sexual misconduct involving students. However, again, here tenure is important. Quite understandably, parents tend to be very concerned when there is even the suggestion of sexual misconduct by a teacher. Journalists are also attracted to such cases and seize upon them as an opportunity for sensationalist news. There is the tendency that a teacher can be subjected to a witch-hunt or lynch mob mentality based on accusation and rumor alone. Tenure protects a teacher from being forced from his or her job unjustly, due to false accusation. It must also be remembered that sexual misconduct involving a child is a crime and, as such, it is a police matter. If a teacher is convicted of any kind of sexual misconduct with a child, they can be fired immediately and face imprisonment. What we do not want is for teachers to be fired on the basis of a lower standard of evidence than that of a court. Conviction should precede dismissal. It is essential that firing a teacher require either a criminal prosecution or a strictly observed procedure involving people at many levels of oversight. We should respect due process and the burden of proof.

However, conservatives' real problem with tenure is that teachers can teach ideas that contradict their conservative ideology. They want schools to teach only what they think is right. If teachers teach something that they do not agree with or like, they want them fired. They are against intellectual freedom and freedom of speech in public schools. What they want is for teachers to reinforce their right-wing conservative view of the world, especially religious beliefs and myths about America. They want parents to have a mechanism by which they can pressure schools to fire teachers who do not teach the orthodoxy. To put it simply, the conservative right are concerned that leftist or liberal ideas might make their way into classrooms. This is why the so-called 'conservative' media spend so much time criticizing "liberal bias" in education.

Beck and Paul want the DoE to be closed down, an end to teacher tenure, and for all teachers' unions to be abolished. I shall not concern myself here with some of the more alarmist conspiracy theories; say Beck's crusade against the Common Core program's efforts to improve math scores and teach foreign languages, as if it were part of some United Nations strategy and secret Marxist indoctrination of American children.[6] Nor am I concerned here with Beck's generally slanderous tirades against progressivism. My response to these can be found elsewhere (Rogers, 2011).

My concern here is about democracy and education. In America, parents already have the choice whether to send their children to private schools or to homeschool them, so what is at the core of the objection to the federal funding of public education? One need only follow the money to answer this question. The objection to the federal funding of public education is primarily one of taxes being levied to pay for public school education. Proponents of this objection resent their money being spent on the education of other people's children. Hence they want education to be privatized. Their vision is that parents who cannot afford to send their children to private schools should either rely on charity or borrow the money. Alternatively, they have the option of homeschooling their children. Basically, in the "free market" vision of education they peddle, education would be a for-profit service industry, no different from beauty salons or dry cleaners. The best education would be available to those children fortunate to be born into a wealthy family. Whether any other children

---

[6] See Glenn Beck's website at http://www.glennbeck.com/2013/04/08/the-whole-story-on-common-core/

receive an education or not would depend on whether their parents are capable of finding a beneficent charity, using savings, or borrowing the money. If parents are unable to pay for the private education of their children then that is just their hard luck. If they have time, they will have to homeschool their children. Given that the parents of poor families often work long hours or have to do several jobs in order to make ends meet, it is unlikely that they will have time to homeschool their children. What kind of education are these children likely to receive?

Unsurprisingly the advocates of "private education" do not really care about the education of these children. After all, it is implicit to the vision of the "free market" that children from poor families don't really need an education; they will be needed by corporations in the future, as a low-paid workforce that can be hired or fired at will. A class-based society reproduces economic and political inequities by limiting the educational opportunities and experiences of children and favoring obedience training and other methods of child control. Ideologues suppress the fact that publicly funded education is the silver bullet to overcoming ignorance and poverty. Only an informed and enlightened people—capable of critical thinking, creative participation, and political participation—can provide the foundation for a genuine democracy in the United States of America. But this costs money. Improvements to the public education system, such as better teacher training, higher pay, and more books and buildings will require more taxes, and this is what the owners of the "free market" message are opposed to. Over and over again, people are told that public education is "a redistribution of wealth," as if that were a bad thing.

Sometimes we hear of the merits of the school voucher schemes. This is a means by which public funds can be rerouted into the for-profit private education system. It means that the best students can be siphoned off from the public education system, at taxpayers' expense, and go to private schools. Of course, this means less money for public schools and lower performance in comparison to private schools, which can further fuel to the message that the public school system is failing. Although the message masquerades as being based on a concern for the quality of children's education, it implies that most children would not have any education at all, of any kind, except perhaps what they learned from sitting at home watching television. Behind this "libertarian" message is the aim of dismantling public education and leaving the majority of parents in America facing massive debts, begging for charity, or educating their children at home. The concern for the liberty of the wealthiest Americans would leave most working Americans facing a lifetime of drudgery and hardship just to pay for their children to have a chance at a better life. Generations of uneducated Americans will be left facing either a lifetime of unemployment or low-paid labor. They will lack the skills and confidence necessary to participate effectively in politics at any level. Nor will they make any attempt at being good citizens and building healthy communities directed toward living good and healthy lives.

How shamelessly some people invoke the U.S. Constitution and the word "liberty" to justify these inequalities! Public education should be included as part of *the general Welfare and secure the Blessings of Liberty to ourselves and our Posterity,* in the Preamble to the Constitution, which reads:

> We the People of the United States, in Order to form a more perfect Union, establish Justice, insure domestic Tranquility, provide for the common defence, promote the general Welfare, and secure the Blessings of Liberty to ourselves and our Posterity, do ordain and establish this Constitution for the United States of America.

As long as we can agree that educating children is of benefit to *the general Welfare* of everybody—for each and every generation to discover afresh for itself what it means to have an equal right to life, liberty, and the pursuit of happiness, as well as determine what good government means and what it means to be a good citizen, and the practical and technical knowledge needed to exercise their rights, and the ability to cooperate with others to get things done, we can have a better chance of working out how best to do it.

That is what a progressive public education is all about! Can we find historical or traditional precedence for this view?

We can find precedence for this progressive view in the words of the North Carolina Legislature of 1789 when, on chartering the North Carolina University, they wrote

> Whereas in all well regulated Governments, it is the indispensable duty of every Legislature to consult the Happiness of a rising Generation, and Endeavour to fit them for an honorable Discharge of the Social Duties of Life, by paying strictest attention to their education. (November 12, 1789)

This was the same legislature that ratified the Constitution and Bill of Rights on December 11, 1789.

As Article I of the Constitution clearly states that Congress has the obligation "to promote the Sciences and Useful Arts" and that it can levy and spend taxes for "the general Welfare," we can argue that Congress does have a constitutional obligation to raise taxes to pay for public education, at least in the sciences and the useful arts, if we can acknowledge that education in the sciences and useful arts is required for there to be any sciences or useful arts to promote. It would be disastrous for public education to leave the funding of education to the states or to the private sector. Congress would be in dereliction of its Article I powers and duties. While the burdens of citizenship fall upon shoulders of the people—as they should—it needs to be generally acknowledged that an education helps people work out how to be good citizens and live good lives. There is nothing in the Constitution that says this should be left to the states. The claim that education is a Tenth Amendment states' right is arbitrary. Just as there is nothing in the Constitution that explicitly grants the federal government any authority over education, nor is this authority explicitly granted to the states. The Ninth Amendment makes it quite clear that unlisted matters should be left to the people. Education is a Ninth Amendment issue.

Herein lies the rub. The claim that the federal funding of education is unconstitutional is an example of their common tactic of cherry-picking. More often than not, the same "conservatives" who object to the unconstitutionality of federal funding of public school education want federal bans of same-sex marriage, flag burning, abortion, or the recreational use of narcotics, even though the federal government has no constitutional authority to ban any of these. Already Americans have the choice to send their children to private school, if they can afford it, or to homeschool them, if they have the time. What these "conservatives" want to do is *to take away* the people's choice to send their children to taxpayer-funded public school. The aim of this proposal is straightforwardly that of maintaining and reproducing the existence of an uneducated and poor underclass providing a cheap labor force for corporations. Education is embroiled in a class struggle, like it or not.

Once we see education as a Ninth Amendment right – as a natural or common law right that pre-exists the Constitution – it follows that the people can choose how to educate their children, as well as the level of political priority they want their government to give to education at either the national or state level. This comes down to a question of the kind of society that Americans want to live in and how they see themselves as organizers of that society. It importantly comes down to whether we can share a vision of a good society and navigate between different communities and peoples, all with their different experiences and perspectives. It is a question of democracy. Whose education is it? In a democracy, how education is organized and funded is a matter for the people to decide for themselves. Elected representatives at local, state, and federal levels of government are supposed to represent the people who elected them but need to be aware that they also should represent children and younger generations who do not have a voice in how their own education is being delivered to them.

If parents are unhappy with their children's education they can hold the state government and board of education accountable through the ballot box. Yet it would seem that many parents still seem happy to send their children to the local public school. Increasingly, more parents are choosing to send their children to charter schools or to homeschool their children. While the exact rules vary from state to state, in most states it is easy and straightforward to do so. States should be making it easier for people to set up their own schools for their communities. And, if they can afford it, parents can send their children to private school. No one is stopping them. Parents seem to have ample choice about how to educate their children in America.

Parents can run for election to their school boards. People could make public education into an election issue for both state and national elections. The quality of public school education reflects the political choices of the people. It remains up to the people whether they have a say about the content and level of funding of public education in their states and in the nation. If it is political suicide to suggest raising taxes to pay for better public education, then the electorate is to blame. If people want better public school teachers, then taxpayers must pay for higher standards of teacher training and higher levels of pay. If Americans are unsatisfied with the public education system then they have political routes by which they can change it.

We may well feel that a good education is the key to solving many national problems and is the key to personal success in life, but we need to ask deep questions about what an education is for. What is its purpose? We need to debate how education relates to our vision of society. Here, the DoE should help people to come together in local and national debates about the nature of a good education and make these debates accessible on public media and through public libraries. Americans need to take interest in local politics and ensure that their elected representatives are being held accountable for how state and federal funds are being spent. If politicians are not accountable to their constituents, this exposes a much deeper problem with the American political system than public education. People need to assemble— through school boards, town hall meetings, political parties, and unions—to make their voices and experiences known to each other, and through the ballot box by making public education an election issue when electing their school boards, mayors, governors, representatives, senators, and union leaders. Again, if elected leaders are not accountable to their constituents, this represents the deeper failure of the political system rather than that of public education.

Of course I do not claim that the DoE is above criticism. Federal funds do come with strings attached and the jurisdiction of the state governments and State Boards of Education, as well as the autonomy of schools, teachers, and parents, have been eroded as a result. By focusing on quantifiable testing methods, the 2001 No Child Left Behind Act and Common Core are more concerned with achieving bureaucratic convenience than helping teachers and parents teach children how to learn well (Granger, 2004). It is important that curricula and testing are left to teachers, parents, and students to determine. Schools should enjoy considerable autonomy over the content of public education, rather than being treated like bureaucrats and administrators of a "top-down" approach to education and the design of curricula. However, the states want federal funds, and parents want their children to go to public schools, and the teachers are left having to act like bureaucrats rather than like teachers.

Since passing NCLB in 2001, the federal government has mandated standardized testing in literacy, mathematics, and basic science. The DoE has also claimed that federal funding for public education in these areas has increased by almost 60 percent. Prior to this, it was left to the states to set their own standards, and there are not any national curricula or set of teaching methods imposed. NCLB was part of a nationwide drive to improve literacy, numeracy, and knowledge of basic science, which still leaves states and local districts with considerable control over public school education. This nationwide drive has been further developed as Common Core. Generally speaking this is a good thing, if it works and improves knowledge and skills in the targeted areas. However, there are problems associated with national standardized testing. Without necessarily doing it consciously, some teachers start "teaching to the test" rather than genuinely improving children's understanding of the subject matter; this has been termed as "washback" (Payne-Tsoupros, 2010; Wills, 2009). Of course, given that their jobs are at stake, teachers have a clear motive for consciously doing this and school principals may well put considerable pressure on teachers to teach so that students perform optimally on mandated tests. Determining the impact of NCLB or Common Core may well prove difficult, if not impossible. States that raised their standards may well have suffered lower scores in the early years as a result, while states that lowered their standards would likely show higher scores; any threat of punitive measures for failure encourages the lowering of expectations. And statistics can be manipulated in accordance with the desired result. It is also questionable whether the standardized testing of students is truly a valid way of measuring improvement. It is certainly the case that it is not a valid means of evaluating the quality of education. Furthermore, the funding for and focus on non-tested subjects (or "electives") has suffered as a result of NCLB and Common Core. Another problem with NCLB and Common Core is that, by focusing on standardized testing, it imposes a "one-size-fits-all" approach to education, ignoring cultural, economic, and individual differences. This standards-based education not only suppresses individual creativity, but could result in the segregation of schools along ethnic and class lines. Disabled children are also tested to the same standards as all other children, which has resulted in a poorer quality of education for them (Kayne Kaufman & Blewett, 2012).

Largely as a reaction to NCLB, there has been an increase in Charter Schools. Many of these schools have begun to adopt progressive teaching methods, and we are likely to see this trend continue as a result of Common Core. In my view, providing that they remain non-profit and do not charge tuition fees, receiving public funding on a per-student basis, Charter Schools offer a promising approach to public education. But the rules for setting up a Charter School vary among states, wherein some states only allow the State Board of Education to issue the charters, while in other states the charters are issued by the local school district. Still in some states charter schools are little more than a means of siphoning public money into the private sector. Some states allow state universities to issue charters. Some states allow any existing public school, by district petition and referendum among the parents of children attending that school, to be able to decide to convert that public school into a charter school. The advantage of charter schools is that they offer the possibility for local accountability and control over public school education, allowing curricula and teaching methods to be developed in accordance with local community needs and circumstances, and promising to further democratize public education. In my opinion, state government-imposed caps on the number of charter schools in the state should be lifted. The number of such schools should be determined by local demand.

Even taking NCLB and Common Core into account, the states and the people still have considerable say over public education. State legislatures and the residents of the state (via school boards and the ballot box) can have enormous say in how public schools are run and funded. How is it the fault of the DoE if a state accepts federal funds for public education, yet the public schools in that state perform poorly? Since 1980, the DoE has provided public schools across the U.S. with hundreds of billions of dollars. What have the states been doing with these additional funds? Even if we agree that there has not been any significant improvement in public school education as a result, how could anyone claim that the federal government has made the public education system worse by providing the states with more money? This claim cannot be made and substantiated by evidence-based narrative. Federal funding for public education is not responsible for millions of Americans not being able to read or write, or being unable to find Iraq on a map. The blame must lie elsewhere. Are the states and the people to blame? Could there be a social or cultural problem involved? Could it be possible that some Americans are to blame for neglecting the education of their own children? Dare we suggest that the lack of motivation for learning among students is the fault of their parents and the students themselves?

However, one of the problems faced by parents is that they have been excluded from participating in the design of curricula and the content of public education. The U.S. Ninth Circuit Court of Appeals has ruled that parents' fundamental right to control the upbringing of their children "does not extend beyond the threshold of the school door" and that a public school has the right to provide its students with "whatever information it wishes to provide, sexual or otherwise" (*Fields v. Palmdale School District*, 2005). I strongly disagree with this ruling, which strikes me as being in violation of the Ninth Amendment and fundamentally undemocratic. In my opinion, a progressive and democratic educational approach can only work in a decentralized education model, wherein schools have autonomy and different schools can try different approaches; some schools try experimental approaches, some traditional approaches, and others try mixed approaches, as each school deems best, in accordance with the hopes, experiences, and wishes of local teachers, students, *and parents*. While parents should not have absolute control over public education, they should be equal participants in deciding both the approach and content of education at their children's schools. After all, a progressive and democratic education involves teaching children how to live well within their community, which also includes their parents. To exclude parents is to exclude the wider community, which is itself not only an anti-democratic and regressive act, but also excludes a valuable pedagogic resource. After all, the vast majority of parents went to public school, and their experiences are valuable for learning how to improve educational methods and content. Teachers must learn from parents how to educate children, as well as guide parents towards understanding the methods and approaches being tried at schools. Students also need to participate in this process. There needs to be public dialogue between parents, teachers, and students about what a good education should be and how to achieve it. However, teachers should also have a high degree of autonomy to teach the content they deem important, using methods they deem appropriate. It is also important that the parents not be able to impose their views upon the schools either. If the teachers and students consider sex education or evolution theory, for example, to be important and they wish to discuss these, then parents should not be able to prevent their child from participating. Sometimes it is necessary for schools to teach children what their parents refuse to teach them, but these boundaries must be navigated at a local level, not imposed from above by the government and courts.

It is very important that the content of a progressive and democratic education is shaped and developed within local contexts; the application of its methods should be shaped in accordance with the experience and reflections of local students, teachers, and parents. It is also important that the practical, project-based aspects of the content of a genuinely progressive education are related to and integrated with community concerns, projects, and interests. In this way, a progressive education is an inherently democratic model of education that can be evaluated critically in relation to other approaches in different schools and communities. Any national curriculum and standardized teaching methods destroy this possibility.

If the Ninth Amendment protects the people from federal government overreach and violations of unenumerated rights, we could readily conclude that this amendment prevents the government from intruding on the content and methods of education. Programs like NCLB and Common Core set standards that provide a high degree of quantifiable results and bureaucratic convenience, but insofar as they dictate the content and methods of education, they constitute governmental overreach in areas that should be left to teachers, parents, and students to decide for themselves. Perhaps it is timely to return to the 1867 conception of the Department of Education as a bureau providing compiled statistics and information and as a resource for teachers, parents, and students rather than dictating to teachers what to teach and determining what students should learn? Should the DoE become a national center of educational research and data, rather than a center for social engineering and reform? How should teachers, parents, and students decide the content and methods of education? These are questions for the American people to decide.

The American philosopher John Dewey has already provided us with a wealth of thought to draw upon to help us develop progressive and democratic education models and practices. Unfortunately, there is not space here to do justice to the richness and depth of John Dewey's philosophy of education. This philosophy can be found in Dewey's formidable body of work including *My Pedagogic Creed* (1897), *The School and Society* (1900), *The Child and the Curriculum* (1902), *Democracy and Education* (1916), and *Experience and Education* (1938). The most that I can do here is to give a summary of Dewey's philosophy of education.

In his 1897 essay *My Pedagogic Creed*, Dewey wrote:

> Existing life is so complex that the child cannot be brought in contact with it without either confusion or distraction; he is either overwhelmed by a multiplicity of activities that are going on so that he loses his own power of orderly reaction, or he is so stimulated by these various activities that his powers are permanently called into play and he becomes either unduly specialized or else disintegrated.

Dewey said that children need guidance in how to live in wider society and it is essential that the school simplifies wider society by being a model of it—in order words, to provide an environment within which the child can learn how to act effectively within the broader society. It is the job of the teacher to provide this guidance. In the same essay, Dewey defined the role of the teacher:

> I believe that the teacher's place and work in the school is to be interpreted from this same basis. The teacher is not in the school to impose certain ideas or to form

certain habits in the child, but is there as a member of the community to select the influences which shall affect the child and to assist him in properly responding to these influences.

Dewey considered education and learning to be social and interactive processes situated within a community. Schools are social institutions from within which children should be guided through the process of learning how to think for themselves and live well within their community. Teachers are to act as guides and representatives of that community, rather than instructors or obedience trainers. In this way, children learn to become well-adjusted members of their community, and schools can act as a place wherein social reform can take place. Schools should have a civilizing influence on children. Dewey did not say that children should be left to do whatever they wanted or whatever they found to be fun. What he said was that students learn better when they are able to interact with the school's curriculum and play a part in deciding the content of their own education. He believed that students should have opportunities to participate actively in the directions and content of their education, while being guided by teachers in the process of doing this. His philosophy of education was not that of laissez-faire, child-centric education, which he considered to be tantamount to neglect, but instead, a careful, teacher-guided process based on child participation in learning how to be a good learner and a well-adjusted member of the school and wider society. Dewey considered this kind of education to be good for both the child and wider society. He argued that this was essential for the development of democracy, civic virtue, and good citizenship.

Education is not *only* about gaining knowledge and technical skills; it is *also* about learning how to learn and live well, how to participate in a democratic society, how to be a good member of the community, and how to become a good citizen. The acquisition of knowledge and technical skills is important, without doubt, but the traditional methods of instruction and discipline were thoroughly anti-democratic and damaging to the possibility of the emergence of well-adjusted, critical thinking, free and democratic citizens (which is possibly why Paul and Beck are in favor of a return to traditional methods). It was for this reason that Dewey argued that education should *not* be focused on the acquisition of a predetermined curriculum, but *instead* should be focused on helping the student realize their full potential, think critically about how society could be better, and put to use their skills and knowledge to work towards achieving those goals. The aim of education should be to help the student prepare for the future by fully developing her capacities as a human being and a democratic citizen.

Education is the process by which children come to develop social consciousness. The adjustment of individual behavior in relation to this process is the best way to achieve social reform. This cannot be achieved using traditional methods of instruction and discipline without turning education into a form of brainwashing and obedience training. Dewey rejected such traditional methods because they force the student into a passive relationship with their own education. He argued that the content of education must be presented to students in terms of their own experiences, deepening their connection with the new knowledge. This kind of dialectical and dialogic education finds its roots in the Ancient Greek philosopher Plato's Dialogue entitled *Meno*. In this Dialogue, Socrates shows how an uneducated slave boy could deduce the first principles of geometry by being guided dialectically, through questions and answers. It is interesting that in this Dialogue the Greek word *mathesis* means both teaching and learning simultaneously. The role of the teacher is to learn from the student how to teach the student to be able to learn how to see the new knowledge for himself. For example, a child cannot be taught the general concept of the number three by being passively shown three chairs, three apples, or three cats, then being instructed to grasp the concept of the number three. This cognitive step must be taken by children for themselves, and the role of the teacher is to guide children through the process by which they will come to realize the concept at hand.

Dewey criticized "child-centric" approaches to education (often developed by people who considered themselves to be followers of Dewey) because *too much* reliance on the child was detrimental to learning and *neglected* their education. Education should seek a balance between the student and the teacher, wherein the teacher has an important responsibility as a guide through which the student properly engages with their own education. Hence Dewey believed that the best method of education is one of guided interaction with real objects in the world through active "hands on" approaches that placed the focus on both the activity and the child's own experience of the activity in question. Rather than being "child-centric," this is *experiential education*. This does not mean that children should do whatever they want or think is fun but that teachers and students should interact within a learning environment that allows the student, guided by the teacher, to learn actively from direct experience and reflection upon those activities. Put simply, the idea is that children learn by thinking about what they are doing and why they are doing it.

There are two basic aims to this approach: (1) to help the student learn in ways that are meaningful to the student; and (2) to promote freedom of thought (and critical thinking). Dewey believed the student should be able to judge the meaning and quality of their experience for themselves, in their own terms. Hence, he was opposed to both authoritarian and laissez-faire forms of education insofar as both approaches stunt or distort the development of students' ability to learn and think.

What is a progressive education? It is not finger-painting, being indoctrinated by Marxist propaganda, or reading lovely poems and discussing feelings, as many so-called conservatives would have us believe. Rather, a progressive education is an interactive, social approach that is influenced by Dewey's model of learning which suggests that learners (1) become aware of the problem; (2) define the problem; (3) propose hypotheses to solve it; (4) evaluate the consequences from one's past experiences; and (5) test to find the most plausible solution. This seems more like common sense than radical doctrine.

Following this model, progressive education emphasizes the importance of active "hands on" learning by doing, with a strong emphasis on problem solving and critical thinking. Instead of testing the ability of children to memorize and recall rote knowledge, the progressive assessment of learning involves the evaluation of project work in terms of participation and productivity. Hence, a progressive education tends to de-emphasize the importance of textbooks (and reading, writing, and textual analysis) in favor of the social, practical project-based, and experimental use of varied learning resources and media. While reading and writing, as well as textual analysis and interpretation, are important skills, it is also necessary to place these in context and achieve a more balanced approach to learning. It also focuses on the needs of the students' community, selecting subject content according to estimations of those needs, and aims at anticipating the future of society. It hopes to achieve these goals through an integrated curriculum. The focus on group work and cooperation is to help children see *for themselves* the value of social skills—leading towards helping children gain social skills and capacities for lifelong learning, democratic participation, and adapting to changes in future society.

Arguably, only someone with a vested interest in preserving the status quo or promoting an anti-democratic agenda would have a problem with a Deweyan approach to education. However, who decides which varied learning resources are selected? Who estimates the needs of society? Who anticipates the future of society? Who designs the curriculum? These decisions should not be based on the directives of the Department of Education, by using strings attached to funded federal programs such as NCLB or Common Core. Nor should they be based on dictates from the leadership of teachers' unions or the State Board of Education. Regardless of how well intended they might be, these kinds of authoritarian directives and dictates are based on political criteria and aims rather than educational criteria and aims, and are detrimental to teacher-student relationships to the extent of making any kind of progressive education quite impossible. Any imposition of a curriculum and methods upon teachers and students unavoidably results in a return to the traditional and authoritarian model, even if the content of the curriculum is seemingly progressive. This kind of education is not progressive at all, and is, in fact, damaging to both teacher and student motivation. Education based on an imposed curriculum taught using seemingly progressive methods not only fail to achieve the goals of a genuinely progressive education, but it also fails to teach children basic knowledge and skills through traditional methods as well. It is the worst of both worlds.

Insofar as a progressive education has been in any sense damaging to public education, it is to the extent that it has been badly implemented and developed by politicians and bureaucrats, and in fact is not a progressive education at all. The imposition of a seemingly progressive education results in a lazy form of pedagogy, wherein an *ad hoc* and conflicting mishmash of educational methods and policies are imposed from above without any degree of feedback from teachers. However, a progressive education simply cannot be imposed from above nor properly implemented and developed through any centralized policy, agenda, or curriculum without distorting and destroying it. A genuinely progressive education can only happen if schools have autonomy, and the content and methods used in that school are developed by teachers in relation with the students.

In this essay I have argued that the future and purpose of education in America is a democratic matter that needs to be raised in public debates. It is something that should be something that each generation discovers or rediscovers for themselves. Is the purpose of future education to be constrained to serving the needs of the market? Or does it have intrinsic value? What role does education have in the development of intellectual, moral, personal, and civic character? The public debate about these questions has wider and deeper implications than the benefits of public education for individuals. It also involves more than questions about the constitutional duty of government to promote "the progress of science and the useful arts" and "the general Welfare." This is more than "a redistribution of wealth." It is a question of how *to invest* public funds and resources to improve society by empowering its citizens not only to better adapt to the changing circumstances and complexities of the world, but more importantly, to improve the quality of public debate upon the public good, and enhance the power of the citizenry to realize it through democratic action. It is an investment in the possibility of democracy.

References

Beck, G. (2011). *Arguing with idiots: How to stop small minds and big government.* New York, NY: Threshold Editions.

Dewey, J. (1897/2011). *My pedagogic creed.* Ann Arbor, MI: University of Michigan Libraries.

Granger, D. A. (2008). No Child Left Behind and the spectacle of failing schools: The mythology of contemporary school reform. *Educational Studies, 43*, 206–228.

Kayne Kaufman, A., & Blewett, E. (2012). When good enough Is no longer good enough: How the high stakes nature of the No Child Left Behind Act supplanted the *Rowley* definition of a free appropriate public education. *Journal of Law and Education,41*(1), 5-23.

Paul, R. (2011). *End the fed.* Washington. DC: Grand Central Publishing.

Paul, R. (2013). *The school revolution: A new answer for our broken education system.* Washington DC: Grand Central Publishing.

Payne-Tsoupros, C. (2009). No Child Left Behind: Disincentives to focus instruction on students above the passing threshold. *Journal of Law and Education, 39*(4), 472-501.

Rogers, K. (2011). *Debunking Glenn Beck: How to save America from media pundits and propagandists.* Santa Barbara, CA: Praeger.

Wills, J., & Haymore Sandholtz, J. (2011). Constrained professionalism: Dilemmas of teaching in the face of test-based accountability. *Teachers College Record, 4*, 1065-1114.

The Pragmatic Pursuit of the Good

Francis J. Schweigert
College of Management, Metropolitan State University,
Minneapolis, Minnesota

Abstract

The best-known approaches to moral education can be broadly described as the cognitive-developmental approach associated with Lawrence Kohlberg, character or virtues education, and values clarification. To these a fourth should be added, based on the extensive contributions of John Dewey, to be called the *pragmatic pursuit of the good.* The pragmatic approach fosters and guides moral learning in the context of a moral community that is engaged in building a better world through democratic processes. In the pragmatic pursuit of the good, the moral community plays a vital role in nurturing moral character, moral values, and a recognition of the good to be achieved—including the public good, which requires going beyond the moral community in cooperation with other communities and the public at large. Defining and achieving the public good requires the cultivation of democratic participation and open, empirical investigation. In keeping with John Dewey's philosophy of education, the overall aim is movement toward growth in opportunity, unity, and harmony: every deliberate choice is a moral opportunity to choose the good—the better option in view—and thus a moment of moral growth and achievement.

Keywords: moral character, moral education, pragmatic pursuit of the good, participatory democracy, virtues education

John Dewey's commitment to social betterment pervades his work. In true progressive spirit, he remained convinced throughout his career that the introduction of scientific thinking and experimentation in social situations would increase human control over social processes and lead to improved conditions, in the same way that the natural sciences had expanded control over the natural environment and transformed industry, transportation, communications, warfare, medicine, and agriculture. What stood in the way of this progress were old habits of thinking in regard to human nature that obstructed clear and objective thought and—not entirely innocently—protected vested social interests and class disparities. Classical and medieval philosophies had bequeathed to the modern age two divisions in thought that were no longer defensible but were locked into place in habits of discourse and education, perpetuating class interests and obstructing human betterment: (a) the separation of morals from other areas of knowledge and practice, and (b) the separation of the human individual from human nature as a social being. In the first section of this paper, these two divisions in moral theory are explored as they arise in the teaching and practice of business ethics. The second section provides a brief summary of the origins and persistence of the separation of morals from other areas of life, concluding with Dewey's argument for a practical morality. In the third section, Dewey's philosophy of the human person is presented as a way to recover the social significance of morals in action. The fourth section returns to the question of education, exploring how Dewey's practical moral theory could ground a more effective approach to ethics education that would support the knowledge and practice of a pragmatic pursuit of the good.

Locating the Disconnect in Business Ethics Education

The belief that all genuine education comes about through experience does not mean that all experiences are genuinely or equally educative. Experience and education cannot be directly equated to each other. For some experiences are mis-educative. Any experience is mis-educative that has the effect of arresting or distorting the growth of further experience. An experience may be such as engenders callousness; it may produce lack of sensitivity and of responsiveness. Then the possibilities of having richer experience in the future are restricted. (Dewey, 1938/1963, pp. 25-26)

This inquiry into moral education arose not from a general pessimism about the quality of our schools nor from a chronic lament about the sorry state of the world, but rather from a specific recognition of educational failure: teaching ethics in business schools. Reflecting on the financial meltdown in 2008, Kelley Holland noted that all of the major figures contributing to the crisis held M.B.A. degrees. She quoted Ángel Cabrera, a management school dean:

It is so obvious that something big has failed. We can look the other way, but come on. The C.E.O.s of those companies, those are people we used to brag about. We cannot say, 'Well, it wasn't our fault' when there is such a systemic, widespread failure of leadership. (2009, para. 5)

The instructors Holland interviewed offered two explanations for business schools' contributions to this failure: the schools are successfully teaching students that their primary responsibility is to maximize shareholder value, and at the same time they are not succeeding in teaching ethics.

To be clear, ethics *is* being taught. As Daniel Baer has observed, the commitment to teaching ethics is "proclaimed at alumni dinners, advertised to prospective students...And business school deans and university presidents claim...that ethics matters, that it is integral to their business schools, that it is foundational to their missions" (Baer, 2009, p. A27). A 2007 study reported that 84.1% of the top 50 business schools in the country (as rated by the *Financial Times* 2006) require students to study ethics and/or corporate social responsibility (Christensen, Peirce, Hartman, Hoffman, & Carrier, 2007). Baer also noted, however, that these same schools have not invested in ethics instructors and research as they have in other areas of the curriculum: "most top business schools have done little to build a core presence of tenure-track faculty members in ethics" (2009, p. A27). John Quelch, writing before the financial crisis, saw the same lack of priority for ethics and same commitment to the high priority on financial success:

> Most business schools pay lip service to teaching ethics, but few professors can or want to follow up. As a result, research in this area still falls short relative to its importance. It may well be, as Milton Friedman contends, that "the business of business is business," but the slavish dedication of many business-school academics to studying how to increase short-term shareholder value, and reward managers in such a way that encourages them to do so, borders on myopia. Increasingly, business leaders recognize that solving social problems is critical to long-term business success.... (2005, p. B19)

Mr. Khurana and Mr. Gintis put it more starkly, that the theory of shareholder primacy taught in business schools "creates an atmosphere that legitimizes a culture of greed in which managers are encouraged to care about nothing but personal gain, and in which such human character virtues as honesty and decency are deployed only contingently in the interests of personal material reward" (as cited in Mangan, 2006, p. A15). To say that personal greed is legitimized is not to claim it is taught directly; it is fostered in more subtle and indirect ways.

> The documentary [*A Dangerous Business*, PBS Frontline, 2003] was effective because it demonstrated clearly that when companies or individuals act unethically, people

can be harmed. Why don't students generally see this connection? In part, because few examples of unethical behavior are as extreme as those in the McWane case...But another reason is that this is how students are taught to think in business school. Across most curricula, students learn to consider the financial implications of unethical acts, such as the risk of fines, penalties, lawsuits, and damaged reputations. Their professors show how these actions negatively affect organizational outcomes, such as profitability. But little time is spent teaching students that unethical behavior can actually harm employees in tangible, nonmonetary ways. (Promislo & Giacalone, 2013, p. 22)

By recasting ethical issues as monetary issues, students learn that the real world standard for business operations is financial success. Ethical issues are real but subordinate. This subordination of ethics to finances can also make it more difficult for employees to speak up when ethical concerns might conflict with business, compounding the social pressures employees feel to minimize negative information when reporting to superiors or, indeed, to avoid being labeled a troublemaker by questioning organizational priorities (Milliken, Morrison, & Hewlin, 2003).

Thus, the lack of educational impact in business ethics can be seen as two sides of one coin: students correctly grasp the centrality of corporate and personal success on one side and the subordinate role of ethics on the other. This lack of impact is compounded, however, by the kind of ethics taught and the way it is taught. The typical curriculum is well summarized by Julian Friedland, who described his successful students as learning to apply "canonical ethical theory to contemporary business dilemmas, wrestling with their values and reconsidering the proper role of business in society" (Friedland, 2009, p. A26). One is prompted to ask how values clarification and canonical ethical theory—the moral theories of Kant and Mill—can be expected to change behavior given the clear priority on business success. The educational priority echoes a social priority, and the actual role of business in society carries more weight than ethical qualms.

The educational problem therefore appears to be located at the intersection between the very real world of business and the theoretical and individualized constructs of ethics. It is not a simple problem to address: a real-world ethical theory is needed, articulated as a theory of applied morals and carried forward as education through increasing use in the real world. For someone familiar with the writings of John Dewey, the problem and directions for addressing it clearly echo his long campaign to redeem ethics from its isolation in the individual conscience and from its marginalization in fixed ideals, in order to incorporate it into human activity as a practical social science for the betterment of society: a pragmatic pursuit of the good.

Recovering a Practical Theory of Morals

> The foremost conclusion is that morals have to do with all activity into which alternative possibilities enter. For wherever they enter a difference between better and worse arises. Reflection upon action means uncertainty and consequent need for decision as to which course is better. The better is the good; the best is not better than the good but is simply the discovered good. (Dewey, 1922/2008, p. 187)

Morality, for Dewey, referred to all human activity that requires a choice among alternative possibilities, for all such choices raise the question of which course of action would be better (Dewey, 1922/2008, p. 187). Human existence, as Dewey saw it, was "precarious and perilous" and "fundamentally hazardous" (Dewey, 1929, pp. 38, 40). Therefore, "man fears because he lives in a fearful, an awful world" (Dewey, 1929, p. 39), and the precarious character of existence requires every organism to steer its way through the hazards of the situation toward what enhances its life. All living things must maintain themselves through continual renewal, acting on their environment and readapting their lives to succeed in it (Dewey, 1916/1966, pp. 1-2). The quality of life and indeed survival itself depend upon the quality and direction of adaptations: at times changing the environment, and at times changing one's own place and practice within the environment. Humans have no choice but to act, and in order to survive must adapt, just as every part of nature must adapt to the other parts (Dewey, 1929, p. 335).

Faced with a precarious existence, human beings from the beginning sought ways of acting and thinking that would increase their sense of security. These elements of knowledge appeared at the dawn of history in the symbolic practices of religion, drama, and poetry—preserved through many generations as social habits of thought and performance. The first major shift in Western European thinking occurred among the Greek philosophers at a time when traditional religious practices were being questioned. Prompted by a conservative impulse to save traditional thinking under a different form, Socrates and Plato offered knowledge as a substitute for tradition, logic and proof as substitutes for religious certainty, and universal comprehensive concepts as substitutes for the eternal gods (Dewey, 1920/1948). For the next 1500 years, their conceptual framework persisted, sometimes conceived as unchanging and eternal divinity, sometimes as unchanging truth as in Aristotle's "Being which never changes" (Dewey, 1929, p. 44).

As persistent as this conceptual framework was in religion and morals, however, European societies continued to expand their control over the natural environment with innovations in engineering, transportation, architecture, and manufacturing and to expand the reach of social institutions through banking, exploration, and education (Stark, 2005). This gradual progress exploded forward in the 16th and 17th centuries with accelerated control of the natural environment and the simultaneous expansion of geographical knowledge, posing new challenges to longstanding thought about social conditions and human destiny and propelling a crisis of division and development in Christianity. Instead of abandoning the old conceptual framework for morals, however, Dewey saw a struggle to preserve the old language of unchanging certainty in new forms—leaving in place, in many cases, social stratification and human miseries. Dewey pointed to Immanuel Kant's work in moral theory, which replaced eternal divine commands with the regularity and universality of reason as a basis for moral law, explicitly separating moral duty from empirical investigation and the chaos of sensation (Dewey, 1922/2008, pp. 162-163; 1929, p. 45). In social theory, Dewey noted Herbert Spencer's conversion of Darwin's discovery and demonstration of continual evolution through natural selection into a "fixed and universal equilibrium" (Dewey, 1929, p. 45)—confirming the superiority of those in wealth and power as a fact of nature and a binding natural law (Dewey, 1922/2008, p. 202).

Morals were thus exempted from scientific investigation and knowledge, so that the possibility of progress in human welfare and justice was slowed or deferred. Dewey protested that "our science of human nature in comparison with physical sciences is rudimentary, and morals which are concerned with the health, efficiency and happiness of a development of human nature are correspondingly elementary" (Dewey, 1922/2008, p. xxi). Nevertheless, Dewey saw tremendous potential for growth in understanding through the new sciences of psychology and sociology, and he pressed forward with a reform agenda for education that would incorporate this new knowledge into greater freedom: increased efficiency in action, increased capacity to change the course of human affairs, and increased personal choice in pursuit of human desires (Dewey, 1922/2008, p. 203). "Morals must be a growing science," he argued, seeking new principles to guide human behavior based on "methods of inquiry" rather than fixed moral laws, employing scientific hypotheses rather than rigid formulas, seeking new empirical generalizations rather than remaining content with inherited eternal truths (Dewey, 1922/2008, pp. 158-160).

It was especially clear to Dewey that a renewed morality was needed in business affairs to challenge the fallacy that all economic activity was driven by self-love and a fixed acquisitive instinct (Dewey, 1922/2008, pp. 86, 90). The key question in regard to business, he thought, required going beyond admiration for the ingenuity and energy of commercial enterprises to ask

> why it is that so much of creative activity is in our day diverted into business, and then ask why it is that opportunity for exercise of the creative capacity in business is now restricted to such a small class, those who have to do with banking, finding a market, and manipulating investments; and finally ask why creative activity is perverted into an over-specialized and frequently inhumane operation. (Dewey, 1922/2008, pp. 92-93)

Sentimental appeal to moral ideals carried very little weight in the face of "love of power, of desire to impress fellows, to obtain prestige, to secure influence, to manifest ability, to 'succeed' in short under the conditions of the given regime" (Dewey, 1922/2008, p. 92). These powerful sentiments prompted many thinkers to assume that self-interest drove all human decisions and that moral progress was unrealizable in human life. At most, morals might dampen the power of self-interest from time to time, but the inherent drives and general course in human activity would be toward individual advantage and acquisition.

Dewey strongly objected to this view of human nature as contrary to empirical observation; rather, it was a self-serving creed supported only by old habits of thought and long-standing social stratification, especially in economic life:

> There is doubtless some sense in saying that every conscious act has an incentive or motive. But this sense is as truistic as that of the not dissimilar saying that very event has a cause. Neither statement throws any light on any particular occurrence. ... Those who attempt to defend the necessity of existing economic institutions as manifestations of human nature convert this suggestion of a concrete inquiry into a generalized truth and hence into a definitive falsity. They take the saying to mean that nobody would do anything, or at least anything of use to others, without a prospect of some tangible reward. (Dewey, 1922/2008, p. 74)

Dewey refused to accept this portrayal of human economic activity as merely a "calculated pursuit of gain," arguing instead that economic decisions were part of the complete fabric of life and responsive to "a complex social environment involving scientific, legal, political and domestic conditions" (Dewey, 1922/2008, p. 146). To say that the impulse to survive was inherent in human life did not mean all activity was self-interested as opposed to socially cooperative or generous. It meant instead that the morality of self-interest, cooperation, and altruism could be understood through empirical investigation into the social conditions that supported these orientations, opening the way to a moral program of social invention, experimental engineering, and education leading to effective reform (p. 94) and a continual renewal of the human situation that was capable of challenging vested interests (p. 107).

Rather than considering morality to be on the periphery of life as a largely ineffective guard against errors or a vain hope for perfection, Dewey insisted that morals lay at the center of life: all decisions that required reflective intelligence were moral decisions, for all such decisions ultimately would bear on improvement or expansion of the quality of life. To those who objected that this approach would replace traditional moral values and virtues with "whatever works," Dewey responded that "the good" – to be meaningful in a realistic sense – did indeed have to "work," rectifying present troubles, harmonizing present incompatibilities, and expanding meaning in human activity for all those affected by the situation at hand (Dewey, 1922/2008, p. 139). It was pointless to enshrine traditional values as fixed infinite ideals that were in fact overlooked in practical affairs and had no power to improve practices or change social habits that preserved privilege for the few. Morals had to be seen as embedded in human activity, in "every act that is judged with reference to better and worse and that the need of this judgment is potentially coextensive with all portions of conduct" (Dewey, 1922/2008, p. 188).

Restoring the Social Dimension of Human Conduct

Current philosophy held that ideas and knowledge were functions of a mind or consciousness which originated in individuals by means of isolated contact with objects. But in fact, knowledge is a function of association and communication; it depends upon tradition, upon tools and methods socially transmitted, developed and sanctioned. Faculties of effectual observation, reflection and desire are habits acquired under the influence of the culture and institutions of society, not ready-made inherent powers...Habit is the mainspring of human action, and habits are formed for the most part under the influence of the customs of a group. (Dewey, 1927, pp. 158-159)

The starting point for Dewey in understanding human nature was recognizing the power of social membership, interaction, and nurture. Each person exists as a member of a group or society which imparts to its members vital directions for actions and means to control their environment. All members share language, institutions, morals, technical skills, and a complex set and sense of relationships with other persons and the natural environment, summarized by Dewey as *habits*, "a form of executive skill, of efficiency in doing...an ability to use natural conditions as means to ends...an active control of the environment through control of the organs of action" (Dewey, 1916/1966, p. 46). Dewey considered these habits to be "decisive because all distinctively human action has to be learned, and the very heart, blood and sinews of learning is creation of habitudes" (1927, p. 160).

This approach to human nature emphasizes the practical value of social life in the continual building up of knowledge and power to improve the quality of living. It is a social heritage that is obvious in such things as language and agriculture and subtle in forms of thought and patterns of perception. So pervasive are these habits that they penetrate to what is usually considered the sacred private center of the person—one's free will.

> The essence of habit is an acquired predisposition to *ways* or modes of response, not to particular acts except as, under special conditions, these express a way of behaving. Habit means special sensitiveness or accessibility to certain classes of stimuli, standing predilections and aversions, rather than bare recurrence of specific acts. It means will. (Dewey, 1922/2008, pp. 20-21; emphasis in original)

Morals, as part of this social heritage, are clearly objective modes of action that incorporate the environment as surely as the habit of walking incorporates the terrain and legs into movement. At the same time, morals become subjective when conflicts between habits or changes in the environment present the individual person with a choice or problem to solve (Dewey, 1922/2008, p. 29). Most importantly, morals are useful; they are practical habits of thought and action directed to improvement in quality of life.

In Dewey's analysis, Western society has established a set of moral values, virtues, and principles that are locked away from practical affairs and attached to the salvation or integrity of a separate individual self—in religious terms, an immortal soul; in secular terms, the personal inner tribunal of conscience. Classical and medieval psychology is assumed today in the assumption of independent minds, each separate from other minds and from the environment and each complete in itself. Morality was located in the free will of the private inner self or soul as a matter of private integrity or a personal quality or degree of perfection rather than as "acts which have public meaning and which incorporate and exact social relationships" (Dewey, 1922/2008, p. 50). The consequence of this individualized notion of moral integrity, in Dewey's view, was that only this mind or soul could be moral or immoral by integrity or failure of individual will, by excellence or corruption of character, or by pursuit or perversion of good ends. Even though it was recognized that perfect integrity was a "practical impossibility," it was still "conceived as the ideal" and moral progress was "defined as approximation to it" (Dewey, 1922/2008, p. 114). This sets up precisely the challenge addressed in business ethics curricula such as *Giving Voice to Values* (Gentile, 2010), in which individuals are instructed on how they might intervene in external business affairs on the basis of their personal set of inner values. In such scenarios, failures of integrity are understandable and even acceptable in the face of social pressures and practical concerns, for human nature is weak and variable in contrast to fixed moral ideals, and moral perfection is mitigated by extenuating circumstances of employment loyalties and career trajectories.

Dewey registered a fundamental challenge to the notion of a fixed self with an independent and solid moral character.

> Inconsistencies and shiftings in character are the commonest things in experience. Only the hold of a traditional conception of the singleness and simplicity of soul and self blinds us to perceiving what they mean: the relative fluidity and diversity of the constituents of selfhood. There is no one readymade self behind activities. There are complex, unstable, opposing attitudes, habits, impulses which gradually come to terms with one another, and assume a certain consistency of configuration, even though only by means of a distribution of inconsistencies which keeps them in watertight compartments, giving them separate turns or tricks in action. (Dewey, 1922/2008, pp. 87-88)

A morality of principles and values grounded in personal moral integrity is bound to be ineffective because no such complete and solid self exists. In relation to the natural environment, the human being is one organism among many, pervaded by the environment and interacting as part of the environment. "Environmental energies constitute organic functions" (Dewey, 1917/1960, p. 24), not only in the food we eat and the air we breathe, but also in the qualities of experience and social relations that inform and shape our thoughts and feelings. Even our innermost experience—the language of our thoughts—is already an environmental and social product, the presence of the other within us (Dewey, 1929, p. 143). The subjective mind is not separate and distinct from surroundings but an intermediate function or position constituted in a "system of beliefs, recognitions, and ignorances...instituted under the influence of custom and tradition" (Dewey, 1929, p.

180), not a fixed entity but a "course of action" (Dewey, 1916/1966, p. 130). Morals are "working adaptations of personal capacities…which incorporate objective forces," meaningful and effective not as inner possessions but as patterns of interaction between the individual and society that affect the quality of personal and social existence in observable and material ways (Dewey, 1922/2008, p. 4).

Morals understood as habits are instituted in language, family, property, and religion (Dewey, 1922/2008, pp. 44-46), not chosen by each individual upon birth but instead discovered to be already in us when we become conscious of ourselves; already shaping our perceptions and guiding our actions. The quality of these habits is of paramount importance for morality, for they can be oriented to originality of thought capable of coping with new forces and information, or they can be oriented to routine and blind conformity (p. 36).

Renewing Moral Education as Pursuit of the Good and the Practice of Justice

> The meaning of justice in concrete cases is something to be determined by seeing what consequences will bring about human welfare in a fair and even way. (Dewey, 1908/1980, p. 107)

The preceding sections lay the groundwork for a fourth approach to moral education as the *pragmatic pursuit of the good,* building on John Dewey's moral theory and philosophy of the human person. This social and philosophical foundation includes five facets: *First,* the pursuit of the good is a general aim in life that appears whenever a decision must be made to choose the best course of activity among alternatives. *Second,* the pursuit of the good draws upon the social fund of experience, relationships, and habits of thought and action built up in every society to inform exactly such decisions (Bellamy, 1897; Farr, 2004), and at the same time every decision contributes to this social fund. Pursuit of the good is therefore a shared human effort that shapes the lives of those involved as well as achieves some experienced good, so that one of the goods to be achieved in this pursuit is the cultivation of a habit of pursuing the good, which in turn is available as a social tool for future pursuit. *Third*, the process of reflection required in choosing among alternatives can be a shared process of deliberation among persons involved in the decision, which is a normal and advantageous act of democracy. *Fourth*, the good being pursued is experienced in the means of pursuit as well as in the ends-in-view and should be expected to yield tangible progress in human affairs—that is, its effectiveness should be, at least in theory, measurable. *Fifth*, the preceding four elements can contribute directly to developing a program of moral education with components of moral learning, moral theory, applied morality, public deliberation, and assessment of the good—including critical appraisal of just distribution and preservation of liberties.

Pursuit of the Good as a Pervasive Human Activity and Social Aim

John Dewey's starting point for morals and moral education was the inescapable fact that human life demands decision-making. We are inevitably confronted with problematic or confusing situations or with alternative courses of action that require determination of problems and choices among possible solutions. One of Dewey's great contributions to philosophy and education was his careful analysis of thinking and problem-solving and the effect of this demand on the human person. "The situation," according to Dewey, "forms man as a desiring, striving, thinking, feeling creature," engaged in active pursuit of purposes both personal and social (Dewey, 1929, p. 65). These characteristics of striving, thinking, and choosing locate morality within the ordinary decision-making and practicalities of human life:

The reason for dividing conduct into two distinct regions, one of expediency and the other of morality, disappears when the psychology that identifies ordinary deliberation with calculation is disposed of. There is seen to be but one issue involved in all reflection upon conduct: The rectifying of present troubles, the harmonizing of present incompatibilities by projecting a course of action which gathers into itself the meaning of them all. The recognition of the true psychology also reveals to us the nature of the good or satisfaction. Good consists in the meaning that is experienced to belong to an activity when conflict and entanglement of various incompatible impulses and habits terminate in a united orderly release in action. (Dewey, 1922/2008, p. 139)

The essential task of moral education is therefore growth in problem-solving ability, guiding the natural functions of desiring, thinking, and deciding toward the pragmatic pursuit of the good. The aim of moral education is practical improvement in the conditions affecting human life by modifying the factors that shape future results (1922/2008, p. 6). For Dewey, this could not be a matter of moral indoctrination, which would limit the range and power of these human faculties. Rather, to be truly educative "implies attention to the conditions of growth...the power to retain from one experience something which is of avail in coping with the difficulties of a later situation...creat[ing] a desire for continued growth and...means for making the desire effective in fact" (Dewey, 1916/1966, pp. 10, 44, 53). Education must aim to enhance the entire process of apprehending the problematic situation, determining the problem and working through options for action, and culminating in action.

Pursuit of the Good as Cultivation of Positive Social Habit

According to John Dewey's psychology, "the formation of habits of belief, desire, and judgment is going on at every instant under the influence of the conditions set by men's contact, intercourse, and associations with one another. This is the fundamental fact in social life and in personal character" (Dewey, 1922/2008, p. 216). Every human being is therefore engaged in a process of creating, strengthening, or weakening habits of human striving, thought, and action, not in isolation but as interwoven social assets and processes, each affecting and affected by the others, so that "the strength, solidity of a habit is not its own possession but is due to reinforcement by the force of other habits which it absorbs into itself" (Dewey, 1922/2008, p. 18).

Because habits are working tools, they are retained and strengthened when they produce the consequences desired, and they are weakened when they fail to result in the desired consequences. This constant modification of habits can be enhanced by conscious attention, but it proceeds unnoticed in many cases, entirely shaped by the reinforcement of consequences. Even when consciously trying to change habits, it is not a matter of simply deciding and then trying to act differently. Habits are embedded in the body and in experience; they precede thought and condition what is possible. Dewey (1922/2008) used the example of a man with a habit of bent posture who decides to stand up straight; he can make a conscious attempt squaring his shoulders and arching his back, but by this momentary awkward effort he cannot change his posture (p. 13). That would require changing the conditions that have produced his current bent stature. Dewey pointed out that "to change the working character or will of another we have to alter objective conditions which enter into his habits"—the demands of the workplace, the habits of sleep and exercise, and the habits of social enjoyment or distraction—as well as "our own schemes of judgment, of assigning blame and praise, of awarding punishment and honor" (Dewey, 1922/2008, p. 6). To cultivate the habit of pursuing the good would therefore require changes in what is actually valued among a person's workmates and family, as well as what is rewarded and punished in the surrounding culture.

> To increase the creative phase and the humane quality of these activities is an affair of modifying the social conditions which stimulate, select, intensify, weaken and coordinate native activities. The first step in dealing with it is to increase our detailed scientific knowledge. We need to know exactly the selective and directive force of each social situation; exactly how each tendency is promoted and retarded. ... A study of the educative effect, the influence upon habit, of each definite form of human intercourse, is prerequisite to effective reform. (Dewey, 1922/2008, p. 94)

Daunting as this may seem, Dewey considered it a realistic endeavor given the growing power of the social sciences. He emphasized this as a more optimistic doctrine than the fatalistic acceptance of human character as it was, either virtuous or vicious, solidly formed and sequestered within each individual conscience. "Honesty, chastity, malice, peevishness, courage, triviality, industry, irresponsibility are not private possessions of a person" (Dewey, 1922/2008, p. 4), and such vices and virtues could be changed with adequate attention to causes and consequences, fostering modifications with conscious attention to improvements. Dewey refused to accept the theory of the self-centered rational calculator assumed in economic theory:

> Deliberate unscrupulous pursuit of self-interest is as much conditioned upon social opportunities, training, and assistance as is the course of action prompted by a beaming benevolence. The difference lies in the quality

and degree of the perception of ties and interdependencies, in the use to which they are put. Consider the form commonly assumed today by self-seeking; namely command of money and economic power. Money is a social institution; property is a legal custom; economic opportunities are dependent upon the state of society; the objects aimed at, the rewards sought for, are what they are because of social admiration, prestige, competition, and power. If moneymaking is morally obnoxious it is because of the way these social facts are handled... (Dewey, 1922/2008, p. 212)

One could add, as well, that to justify moneymaking as a personal aim requires supportive social structures of reward and reinforcement (Shiller, 2012; Smith, 2012; Veblen, 1899/1953). It is critical to note that Dewey's attention was on the conditions of thought and perception actually in use that produced results as desired or designed. Results were necessarily both external in material or social consequences and internal in personal patterns of thought and perception. Yet the target of these changes was not a special internal faculty of moral knowledge—the individual's conscience—but instead simply good judgment:

The moral is to develop conscientiousness, ability to judge the significance of what we are doing and to use that judgment in directing what we do, not by means of direct cultivation of something called conscience, or reason, or a faculty of moral knowledge, but by fostering those impulses and habits which experience has shown to make us sensitive, generous, imaginative, impartial in perceiving the tendency of our inchoate dawning activities. Every attempt to forecast the future is subject in the end to the auditing of present concrete impulse and habit. Therefore the important thing is the fostering of those habits and impulses which lead to a broad, just, sympathetic survey of situations. (Dewey, 1922/2008, p. 137)

To cultivate good judgment requires changing the patterns of activity that reward, punish, and support these skills of impartial perception and empirical investigation. Dewey was especially firm that

> no amount of preaching good will or the golden rule or cultivation of sentiments of love and equity will accomplish the results. There must be change in objective arrangement and institutions. We must work on the environment not merely on the hearts of men. (1922/2008, p. 8)

To illustrate Dewey's point, we can recall the patterns of action and reward in financial institutions leading up to the 2008 banking crisis, clearly summarized by Robert Jackall (2010). The investment bankers involved were educated at the top business schools, where "they are drilled in the imperative of increasing the value of the assets in their care in as short a time as possible" (pp. 236-237). This short-term gain was good for them personally and was rewarded with substantial bonuses; it was good as well for their superiors and other members of their team. That this strategy of investment might be detrimental to investors over the longer term was not considered the bankers' problem, for investors are smart people who should be watching out for themselves. This pattern of action fostered a moral climate to support it, regardless of what the espoused rules of the profession or organization may have been, for

> Only those men and women who allow peers and superiors to feel morally comfortable in the ambiguous muddles of the world of affairs have a chance to survive and flourish in big organizations when power and authority shift due to changes in markets, internal

power struggles, or the need to respond to external exigencies. (Jackall, 2010, p. 237)

Given this environment, it would be pointless to lecture students of high finance on the morality of putting the investor's benefits first without at the same time taking some action to change the practices and priorities in the banks. Greg Smith (2012) was especially clear on documenting how a shift in priorities at Goldman Sachs was reinforced by the informal systems of moral support among traders and sales staff through team loyalty, respectful submission to superiors, mutual advocacy and protection, shared enthusiasm for common goals, and mutual leverage for success. Smith's portrayal of the moral qualms among some banking personnel affirms Dewey's view that most business professionals were specialists conforming to social pressures rather than opportunists merely pursuing their own calculated self-interest. The needed change was not a moral reformation of conscience but instead the "objective conditions which provide the resources and tools of action, together with its limitations, obstructions, and traps" (Dewey, 1927, p. 162).

Dewey fully recognized that the social pressures turning business against the common good could not be corrected by converting people to an ideal notion of right or duty. Indeed, he questioned what the priority of Right that ethicists hallowed could be, other than "the totality of social pressures exercised upon us to induce us to think and desire in certain ways" (Dewey, 1922/2008, p. 218). One's sense of right and justice was not an inherent endowment of conscience but rather the cumulative result of personal perceptions inevitably shaped by what those around us acted upon and insisted upon as right and just. Moral learning is always in process as long as we are alive and engaged in society, for "not only is social life identical with communication, but all communication (and hence all genuine social life) is educative" (Dewey, 1916/1966, p. 5). Although this realization might discourage some educators with a never-ending task, Dewey embraced the pervasiveness of moral learning as increased opportunities and means for improvement, if only such changes were seriously and scientifically pursued. "There is every reason in other words for cultivating another enjoyment, that of the habit of examining the productive potentialities of the objects enjoyed" (Dewey, 1922/2008, p. 169).

Recognition of how morals are shaped enables us to consciously shape them by understanding and altering the conditions, causes, and consequences of current behavior. Certainly this could mean challenging established ways of thinking and acting and would require a genuine organized and persistent effort of inquiry and experimentation with attention to results over time. Dewey believed this could be achieved through the social sciences, not through the application of immutable laws and in pursuit of fixed goals as was possible in the natural sciences, but rather through ongoing analysis and regulation of social conditions, continually testing and improving working hypotheses in pursuit of releasing the potentialities for the good in human society (Dewey, 1927, pp. 196-202). This experimentation and coordination were, in Dewey's view, the task of the educator who was specially delegated responsibility to assess the impacts of social conditions and the competing claims of habits of thought and action, and then to coordinate the relevant factors of the situation to invoke recognition of the conflicts and deliberation on solutions (Dewey, 1922/2008, p. 129).

Pursuit of the Good as Shared Deliberation—an Exercise in Democracy

Even though each person has his or her own moral responsibility in responding to the confusions or conflicts in any given situation, each person faces these responsibilities and challenges equipped with habits of thought, value, and behavior that are shaped by prevailing social conditions and consequences. This opens the way to expand the personal process of reflection and deliberation to include interpersonal deliberation and social cooperation in problem solving. Indeed, a shared process of deliberation is a powerful tool of moral education, which Dewey recognized and advocated at length in many of his writings on the unified purpose of democracy and education.

> A democracy is more than a form of government; it is primarily a mode of associated living, of conjoint communicated experience. The extension in space of the number of individuals who participate in an interest so that each has to refer his own action to that of others, and to consider the action of others to give point and direction to his own, is equivalent to the breaking down of those barriers of class, race, and national territory which kept men from perceiving the full import of their activity. These more numerous and more varied points of contact denote a greater diversity of stimuli to which an individual has to respond; they consequently put a premium on variation in his action. They secure a liberation of powers which remain suppressed as long as the incitations to action are partial, as they must be in a group which in its exclusiveness shuts out many interests. (Dewey, 1916/1966, p. 87)

Shared processes of moral reflection are powerful in prompting and nurturing individual moral learning and at the same time in fostering a stronger sense of community. Dewey saw such reflection as necessary in order to keep up with continual changes in the conditions affecting moral decisions, because the concepts and beliefs *with* which we think change more slowly than the social and natural conditions *in* which we live; shared moral reflection increases congruity (Dewey, 1927, pp. 141-142). As a fact of modern life, Dewey admitted that the time demands and intellectual attention required for individuals to stay informed on complex issues affecting their community were too high. Without a programmatic approach to engagement, the public is eclipsed and shared moral decision-making is left to a policy elite (Dewey, 1927, p. 138) or relegated to government agencies (Christie, 1977). Yet such policy choices are moral choices and a route to moral improvement too important and pervasive to be ignored.

When personal and social moral beliefs are disconnected from the social conditions responsive to these beliefs, the moral authority of the larger community is scattered and eroded, decreasing a sense of shared interests and values and leaving individuals less equipped to reflect reasonably upon moral choices—and thus more vulnerable to the most immediate pressures of the workplace, neighborhood, vigilante posse, religious congregation, or any other social group. In response to this situation, shared deliberation has the potential to build common interest among individuals and to strengthen their skills in critical reflection and reasonable choice, while at the same time building the same skills and intelligence as a function of community. Experience has shown that civic deliberation and attention to consequences can strengthen democracy once the violence of war subsides even in places of poverty such as Nicaragua (Anderson & Dodd, 2005), Sierra Leone, Burundi, Serbia, Georgia, and Ukraine (Diamond, 2008). Studies on the local level have shown similar effects on moral learning and civic deliberation through the practice of restorative justice, which requires ordinary citizens affected by a crime to assess the harm done and work out responses and reparations to repair the damage done (Braithwaite, 1989; Christie, 1977; Schweigert, 1999; Schweigert, 2000; Umbreit, 1994).

John Braithwaite pursued these connections further to identify specific lessons from restorative justice that could inform democracy, all of which are relevant to the moral deliberation-democracy connection: *first*, "bringing into a

59

[restorative justice] circle a multiplicity of people who are affected in different ways" reduces power imbalances due to gender and positional bias; *second*, "it is better to put the problem rather than the person in the centre of the circle"—focusing, as Dewey indicated, on solving the problem at hand rather than accommodating participant affections or prejudices; *third*, "material reparation was less important than symbolic or emotional reparation," a clear indication of Dewey's concern about habits of thought as part of the conditions needing to be addressed and his assertion that symbols promote communication and foster shared meanings (Dewey, 1927, p. 153); *fourth*, "democracy is something that must be taught," or, more accurately, learned through listening, caring and shared deliberation; and *fifth*, learning occurs through taking responsibility for the process and outcomes, not through passive observation (1999, "Democracy Renewed" section). These lessons have been affirmed by multiple assessments outside restorative justice, such as Skocpol's observation that membership and active participation are essential for democracy (2004) and Goetz and Jenkins's call for greater public accountability through raising citizens' expectations and providing formal institutions for public oversight (2004).

All moral choice involves deliberation as Dewey defined it because morality means "recognizing facts and using them as a challenge to intelligence to modify the environment and change habits" (Dewey, 1922/2008, p. 202). Whether deliberation proceeds as a "dramatic rehearsal of possible lines of action" as Dewey described it (1922/2008, p. 126) or according to some other method of weighing facts, values, possible actions, and likely results (Gutmann & Thompson, 1996), the potential for moral learning is high. Indeed, deliberation is the preeminent means of moral learning: "Actually then only deliberate action, conduct into which reflective choice enters, is distinctively moral, for only then does there enter the question of better and worse" (Dewey, 1922/2008, p. 187). The same is true for shared deliberation.

It is important to emphasize that deliberation and democracy, as Dewey understood them, were not compatible with what he saw as a marketplace for votes amidst widespread apathy or ignorance regarding the issues at hand (1927, esp. "The Eclipse of the Public," pp. 110-142). It was not merely a matter of bargaining to advance one's own interests or compromising to reach some mutually acceptable conclusion. He insisted, rather, that "the office of deliberation is not to supply an inducement to act by figuring out where the most advantage is to be procured. It is to resolve entanglements in existing activity, restore continuity, recover harmony, utilize loose impulse and redirect habit" (Dewey, 1922/2008, p. 132). This is a challenging expectation to implement, but it is essential to Dewey's conception of a practical morality with just outcomes.

First, the "function of reflective thought is to transform a situation in which there is experienced some obscurity, doubt, conflict, disturbance of some sort, into a situation that is clear, coherent, settled, harmonious" (Dewey, 1933, pp. 100-101). Note that it is the *quality of the present situation* that is the criterion for completion of the process, not some ideal end as judged against an external standard or a convenient end as agreed by the parties involved. In looking forward to consequences of various lines of action, the aim is not to predict the future but to try to determine which activity in the present can unify the conflicting elements in the situation (Dewey, 1922/2008, p. 136). The qualitative outcome achieved should be evident to observers and participants alike in the present situation and empirically verifiable.

Second, deliberation is by definition deliberate rather than hurried, "an attempt to uncover the conflict in its full scope and bearing...to reveal qualitative incompatibilities by detecting the different courses to which they commit us, different dispositions they form and foster, the different situations into which they plunge us" (Dewey, 1922/2008, p. 143). The process aims toward a decision, but much of its value lies in increasing knowledge of the facts of the situation, including the dispositions and values of the participants. "This continuous interaction of the facts disclosed by observation and of the suggested proposals of solution and the suggested methods of dealing with conditions goes on till some suggested solution meets all the conditions of the case and does not run counter to any discoverable feature of it" (Dewey, 1933, p. 104).

Third, the resolution achieved should unite, in some sense, the various lines of inquiry and differences in viewpoint, thus bringing a determinate shape and direction to an indeterminate situation (Dewey, 1938/1960, p. 116). By this Dewey did not mean an ideal or final whole, for "all deliberation is a search for a way to act, not for final terminus" (Dewey, 1922/2008, p. 128). Rather, it should be seen as an end-in-view that does justice to the various concerns raised, at least in the action to be taken. In that sense, the action represents a unity of purpose.

> Nothing is more extraordinary than the delicacy, promptness and ingenuity with which deliberation is capable of making eliminations and recombinations in projecting the course of a possible activity. To every shade of imagined circumstance there is a vibrating response; and to very complex situation a sensitiveness as to its integrity, a feeling of whether it does justice to all the facts, or overrides some to the advantage of others. Decision is reasonable when deliberation is so conducted. (Dewey, 1922/2008, p. 128)

A variety of practical means have been developed to serve these purposes, such as tools for defining community, mapping land use, visualizing growth, and constructing shared scenarios (Snyder, 2006). All these means coincide with Dewey's criteria that all citizens share responsibility for group cohesion and direction, each according to his or her capacity, and exercising these responsibilities can develop these capacities further and increase the potential for shared responsibility and understanding of the common good (Dewey, 1927, p. 147).

Fourth, a growing sensitivity to this kind of integrity would be one very real benefit of shared deliberation, since "the thing actually at stake in any serious deliberation is not a difference in quantity, but what kind of person one is to become, what sort of self is in the making, [and] what kind of a world" (Dewey, 1922/2008, p. 143). Every process of deliberation is forward-looking, not only in the sense of foreseeing consequences to the action taken but in preparing those involved to increase the quality and scope of their deliberations in the future. Dewey believed that democracy should stimulate original thought to address new situations rather than attempt to affirm previous ways of thinking and acting. (Dewey, 1922/2008, pp. 36-37).

Pursuit of the Good in Means, Ends, and Evidence of Progress

One of the great challenges in moral philosophy is the diversity of understandings of the Right and the Good as overarching, perennial, secure ideals. Because life is complex and ever adapting to changing conditions, the formulae for the Good and the Right must be stated abstractly. In some traditions, for example, the Right is identified with obedience to the commands of the deity and the Good is salvation or union forever with the deity. Other traditions follow the Stoics in identifying the Good and Right with what is natural for humanity, requiring conformity to a natural law inherent in every person and consistent with the entire natural environment—a view originating with Plato and continuing in some lines of Christian and Western rationalism. Enlightenment philosophers, skeptical of sources outside human experience, sought to articulate the same ideals as outcomes of rational reflection. Thus, Immanuel Kant focused on the Right as prior to the Good, identifying duty as an act of good will logically consistent with universal moral law— analogous to natural law but discoverable in purely formal, logical terms (1985/1956). Jeremy Bentham (1789/1961), followed by John Stuart Mill (1861/1979), articulated an alternative rational morality giving priority to the Good as an outcome providing for the greatest happiness for the greatest number.

Nietzsche (1887/1956) objected that these ideals did not in fact arise from divine origins or pure reason, but instead had to function within "a system of purposes" serving the ends being pursued by the elite in power, with the inevitable result that those more powerful imposed their ends and values on those less powerful (p. 210). Morals, in this view, were constructed through positive acts in history, always serving those interests that predominated in any age: acts of "adaptation" rather than eternal truths or laws (Nietzsche, 1887/1956, p. 211). According to Richard Rorty, Dewey moved from attempting a systematic philosophy of morals to a similar view as he "came to see his earlier effort as self-deceptive" and instead sought a theory of morals that could be "therapeutic rather than constructive, edifying rather than systematic" (1979, p. 5). However accurate this characterization of Dewey's development may be, Dewey was indeed explicitly attempting to unhook moral philosophy from abstract ideals and relocate it in human affairs as a practical enterprise for individual and social improvement. Similar to Nietzsche, Dewey referred to virtues as "working adaptations of personal capacities with environing forces" (1922/2008, p. 4). His focus was consistently on the utility of morals in resolving real situations of confusion, conflict, and injustice.

Drawing upon this insight, he was especially concerned with reorienting moral philosophy in two respects: the bearing of human action and the capacities of human nature.

Central to Dewey's moral philosophy was his insight that "...ends are not strictly speaking ends or termini of action at all. They are terminals of deliberation, and so a turning point *in* activity" (Dewey, 1922/2008, p. 148; emphasis in original). This is why he preferred the term *ends-in-view*, which communicated the practical bearing of ends as giving purpose to action and at the same time serving as a means or pivot in further activity.

Dewey consistently sought to redirect human attention away from abstract, ultimate, and ultimately unachievable ends such as human perfection or eternal salvation—not because such ends were theoretically impossible but because they lacked specific bearing in concrete situations and distracted persons from concerns at hand. His objection to fixed ends was practical:

> The doctrine of fixed ends not only diverts attention from examination of consequences and the intelligent creation of purpose, but, since means and ends are two ways of regarding the same actuality, it also renders men careless in their inspection of existing conditions. (Dewey, 1922/2008, p. 154)

He preferred the term *ends-in-view*, which communicated the practical role of ends as

> foreseen consequences which arise in the course of activity and which are employed to give activity added meaning and to direct its further course. They are in no sense ends *of* action. In being ends of deliberation they are redirecting pivots *in* action." (Dewey, 1922/2008, p. 150; emphasis in original)

Dewey insisted on a continuity of means and ends. Since "all effects are also causes" (Dewey, 1939, p. 43), every end-in-view is also a means for something else, so that all ends are means. At the same time, every means that is chosen, simply in being chosen, is an end of that choice, so all means are thus ends. *End-in-itself* is therefore a contradictory term, since every end is such only because it is related to the means that are involved in reaching it. Nothing could be an end apart from its being the result of means. "Means are means; they are intermediates, middle terms. To grasp this fact is to have done with ordinary dualism of means and ends. The 'end' is merely a series of acts viewed at a remote stage; and a means is merely the series viewed at an earlier one" (Dewey, 1922/2008, p. 15).

This did not mean that Dewey treated ends lightly. Ends were critically important in morals as "that object which were it present would link into an organized whole activities which were it present would link into an organized whole activities which are now partial and competing" (Dewey, 1922/2008, p. 166). Rather, he consistently sought to redirect human attention away from abstract, ultimate, and ultimately unachievable ends such as human perfection, complete justice, or eternal salvation—not because such ends were theoretically impossible but because they lacked specific bearing in concrete situations and distracted persons from concerns at hand.

> The doctrine of fixed ends not only diverts attention from examination of consequences and the intelligent creation of purpose, but, since means and ends are two ways of regarding the same actuality, it also renders men careless in their inspection of existing conditions. (Dewey, 1922/2008, p. 154)

Dewey was also keenly concerned that human nature be recognized as active and purposeful with the potential for achieving real progress in human affairs, rather than being denigrated as a fallen creature incapable of real goodness. He was frustrated by moral theories that "put the blame exclusively on a person as if his evil will were the sole cause of wrongdoing" (1922/2008, p. 5), because such characterizations distracted attention from the habits and conditions that shaped human choices and therefore left those conditions in place without challenge. In regard to the detrimental conditions of employment and the inordinate focus on accumulation of wealth, Dewey charged that we

> satisfy ourselves cheaply by preaching the charm of productivity and by blaming the inherent selfishness of human nature, and urging some great moral and religious revival. The evils point in reality to the necessity of a change in economic institutions, but meantime they offer serious obstacles to the change. (Dewey, 1922/2008, p. 80)

Rather than accept such conditions as inevitable results of industrialization or as unchangeable evidence of human failings, he argued for directing the new sciences of psychology and sociology to investigation of the social causes of these sufferings. Dewey admitted that these social sciences lagged far behind the natural sciences, and as a consequence our understanding of morals and human development was also rudimentary (Dewey, 1922/2008, p. xxi). But he saw this state of the social sciences as temporary, if only attention were given to the antecedent conditions of social problems and a rigorous accounting of effects of remedial actions.

To those who might object that Dewey was giving up on the human potential for goodness, he countered with a call for empirical verification of positive results of moral action:

> There are plenty of negative elements, due to conflict, entanglement and obscurity, in most of the situations of life, and we do not require a revelation of some supreme perfection to inform us whether or not we are

making headway in present rectification. We move on from the worse and into, not just towards, the better, which is authenticated not by comparison with the foreign but in what is indigenous. Unless progress is present in reconstructing, it is nothing; if it cannot be told by qualities belonging to the movement of transition it can never be judged. (Dewey, 1922/2008, p. 189)

This would call for a science of moral evaluation in terms of the actual ends-in-view achieved in each situation rather than in comparison to an abstract and unchanging notion of the good.

The good is never twice alike. It never copies itself. It is new every morning, fresh every evening. It is unique in its every presentation. For it marks the resolution of a distinctive complication of competing habits and impulses which can never repeat itself. (Dewey, 1922/2008, p. 140)

Each round of activity would have to be evaluated on its own terms. Progress in human conditions could not be accurately defined in advance, beyond expressions of desire for certain qualities of outcomes and environments. Rather, progress would have to be recognized as it happened in regard to specific improvements. There was no general formula for human progress (Dewey, 1922/2008, p. 190).

Indeed, progress might not always look like progress. As Dewey (1922/2008) observed, "from the side of what has gone before achievement settles something. From the side of what comes after, it complicates, in introducing new problems, unsettling factors" (p. 191) Dewey dismissed a theory of social evolution that society was developing in some definite directions and accumulating a growing stock of firm and lasting accomplishments. The focus of evaluation had to remain tied instead to the quality of present conditions and the quality of habits of thought and desire. If real change was being achieved, it would be disturbing as well as comforting, forcing us to

> recognize the truth that in fact we envisage the good in specific terms that are relative to existing needs, and that the attainment of every specific good merges insensibly into a new condition of maladjustment with its need of a new end and a renewed effort. (Dewey, 1922/2008, p. 193)

What Dewey called for, as outlined above, was a social habit of pragmatic pursuit of the good:

> Positive attainment, actual enrichment of meaning and powers, opens new vistas and sets new tasks, creates new aims and stimulates new efforts. The facts are not such as to yield unthinking optimism and consolation; for they render it impossible to rest upon attained goods. New struggles and failures are inevitable. The total scene of action remains as before, only for us more complex, and more subtly unstable. But this very situation is a consequence of expansion, not of failures of power, and when grasped and admitted it is a challenge to intelligence. Instruction in what to do next can never come from an infinite goal, which for us is bound to be empty. It can be derived only from study of the deficiencies, irregularities and possibilities of the actual situation. (Dewey, 1922/2008, pp. 193-194)

Pursuit of the Good as Moral Education—Theory, Application, and Learning

Up to this point in Western European societies, the common approaches to moral education have been broadly identified as character education, values clarification, and the cognitive-developmental approach. Although their elements overlap in education and in daily life, each of these approaches was designed to respond to a different concern and builds on a distinct theory of individual development and ethics.

The *cognitive-developmental approach* is based on Piaget's theory that childhood moral judgment develops in stages (1965), and it is the educator's role to stimulate a child's natural progress from a pre-conventional egoistic stage to conventional thinking based on affective attachments and social norms. At adolescence and beyond, individuals can progress to a third stage of post-conventional moral reasoning in accord with universal principles "centering on principles of justice" (Kohlberg, 1980, p. 71) in accord with universal moral principles as represented by Immanuel Kant's "categorical imperative" (1785/1956). This last stage can be stimulated through the use of moral dilemmas carefully designed to aid development of moral reasoning. The focus is both individual and social, since new stage is an elaboration of the previous one in a progressive ability to organize cooperation (Rest, 1994, p. 5).

Character education is rooted in Aristotle's observation that moral virtue cannot be taught like a science (*epistome*) nor built through training like a skill (*techne*) but must be learned by bearing the responsibility of deciding and acting on the best course using practical reason (*phronesis*). By doing the right thing in the right way for the right reasons, the individual acquires a habit of virtuous action and a virtuous character (*Nicomachean Ethics*, Bk. VI. 1103a). The educator's role is thus to foster a moral community that can provide direction, practice, role models, and support in cultivating positive virtues, to the point that these become habitual (Lickona, 1991; Ryan, 1996).

The *values clarification* approach is designed to help students sort through conflicting moral imperatives in a culturally diverse world, respecting differences yet recognizing and holding firmly to their own core values (Fletcher, 1966). It focuses especially on the emergence of critical thinking at adolescence when youth are naturally inclined to question received beliefs, to help them move through questioning to settled moral views.

The *pragmatic pursuit of the good* as outlined in preceding sections of this paper incorporates some elements of these approaches to moral education. Similar to Kohlberg, Dewey saw an important role for moral reasoning, not as a means to foster individual development according to pre-determined stages but more broadly: to assess social conditions and the bearing of habits of thought in constructing practical solutions to current problems. Similar to values clarification, Dewey advocated a critical approach to morality by seeking different perspectives and rationales to articulate the good to be achieved, including changes to current moral assumptions if called for—but always, as well, going beyond individual clarification to social action and results. Similar to virtues education, Dewey saw the critical role played by the moral community in the workplace and elsewhere in the civic arena, including mutual accountability, but he also saw that sometimes the virtues espoused by the community would need to be revised.

A program of moral education, like all education in Dewey's view, requires discerning among experiences and supporting those that are oriented to growth and directed to "create conditions for further growth" (Dewey, 1938/1963, p. 36). To support the aim for continual growth in the ability to create a better life—to achieve social progress in real terms—does not require that we have

> formulated a definite ideal of some better state. An educational enterprise conducted in this spirit would probably end merely in substituting one rigidity for another. What is necessary is that habits be formed

which are more intelligent, more sensitively percipient, more informed with foresight, more aware of what they are about, more direct and sincere, more flexibly responsive than those now current. (Dewey, 1922/2008, p. 81)

We thus reach a technical definition of education: It is that reconstruction or reorganization of experience which adds to the meaning of experience, and which increases ability to direct the course of subsequent experience. (Dewey, 1916/1966, p. 76)

It goes beyond the scope of this study to design a curriculum or program for moral education in pursuit of the good. It may be helpful, however, to recast the preceding discussion of social and philosophical foundations in a framework for moral action, using the Four Component Model proposed by James Rest and based on his review of research on morality and social learning (1994, pp. 22-25). Employing a social scientific approach similar to Dewey's, Rest asked "What must we suppose happens psychologically in order for moral behavior to take place? We wind up with at least four distinct processes" (p. 23).

Component 1. Moral Sensitivity: Interpreting the Situation

"Moral sensitivity is the awareness of how our actions affect other people" (Rest, 1994, p. 23). This necessarily includes perceiving who is involved and who cares about what is happening, empathy for those involved, and seeing oneself with certain role-related responsibilities (role-taking skills). It would also include awareness of possible lines of action and how these might affect others, imaginatively constructing various scenarios action could take, the cause-consequence relationships among events (D. Narvaez, personal communication, Spring 1996).

This view of moral sensitivity is very similar to what Dewey outlined as the "dramatic rehearsal" that takes place in moral reflection (1922/2008, p. 119). Cultivating moral sensitivity (as proposed by Rest) would involve deliberation from perception of a difficulty, through awareness of the bearing and direction of the difficulty, to institution and naming of the problem to consideration of alternative courses of action—working with actual social factors and pending decisions. Dewey (1909/1975) called attention to the need to cultivate "a prompt and almost instinctive sensitiveness to conditions, to the ends and interests of others, [without which] the intellectual side of judgment will not have proper material to work upon" (p. 52). Given the social nature of perception, this kind of sensitivity would be fostered by increasing group awareness of actual conditions, review of previous courses of action, and evaluation of results in terms of the good done. This kind of study or learning would be synonymous with the social sciences and evaluation studies but would proceed beyond investigation and assessment to choosing and implementing the best choice available.

Perception of contributing conditions would be central to moral education in learning to identify "that antecedent which if manipulated regulates the occurrence of this consequent" (Dewey, 1929, p. 92). In this way, the pragmatic nature of morality would be reinforced. It is difficult to imagine this kind of learning occurring outside of actual moral situations. Similar to the learning that occurs among participants actively engaged in restorative justice, the most powerful moral learning would involve engagement in and reflection upon the process of actually solving problems in the pursuit of the good.

Component 2. Moral Judgment: Selecting the Most Moral Action

"Once the person is aware of possible lines of action and how people would be affected by each line of action

(Component I), then Component II judges which line of actin is more morally justifiable" (Rest, 1994, pp. 23-24). It is noteworthy that Rest made no attempt to justify actions in accord with some overarching moral Right or final and complete Good; rather, he looked for specific criteria that might be good reasons for pursuing the action in mind: meeting the demands of authority or reciprocity, contributing to social harmony, building consensus and cooperation (D. Narvaez, personal communication, Spring 1996).

These are precisely the kinds of justifications that Dewey espoused as reasonable. He declared it "false that every person has a consciousness of the supreme authority of right and then misconceives it or ignores it in action." Rather, what persons did have was "a sense of the claims of social relationships as those relationships enforce in one's desires and observations." If moral sensitivity worked to bring awareness of these relationships, including awareness of how various lines of action would affect parties involved, then moral judgment could work to determine which line of action would be most reasonable and supportable. "The belief in a separate, ideal, or transcendental, practically ineffectual Right" would not be necessary or even useful; it would only get in the way, "a reflex of the inadequacy with which existing institutions perform their educative office" which should be directed instead toward "generating observation of social continuities" (Dewey, 1922/2008, p. 219).

Component 3. Moral Motivation: Prioritizing Moral Values Relative to Other Values/Concerns

Rest asked how "we are we to account for the most notoriously evil people in the world" (1994, p. 24). He did not consider their moral failure as "due to deficiencies in awareness of what they were doing (Component I), or because they couldn't figure out what would be the fair thing to do (Component II)." Rather, he saw their failure as putting other values or ends ahead of what was right and good for the people to be affected, both in the implementation and in the effects of the action (D. Narvaez, personal communication, Spring 1996).

Dewey was highly concerned with the question of motivation, which he preferred to address as a modification or cultivation of habits of thought—that is, addressing it from a social perspective. He thought it of little use to preach to individuals that they should buck up and do their duty:

> If the standard of morals is low it is because the education given by the interaction of the individual with his social environment is defective. Of what avail is it to preach unassuming simplicity and contentment of life when communal admiration goes to the man who 'succeeds'—who makes himself conspicuous and envied because of command of money and other forms of power? (Dewey, 1922/2008, p. 213)

Therefore, he sought to generate social support for giving higher priority to pursuing the good. The paramount example would be Dewey's commitment to cultivating the habit of pursing the good4—which he considered every bit as achievable as the habit of pursuing wealth.

Component 4. Moral Character: Ability to Implement Values and Decisions

"This component involves ego strength, perseverance, backbone, toughness, strength of conviction, and courage" (Rest, 1994, p. 24). Even if a person or group is sensitive to the moral dimensions of the issue at hand, can articulate good reasons for pursuing a particular course of action, and give high priority to good means and results, the person or group might still lack the ego strength to persevere in the face of fear, weariness, lack of social support, or outright opposition. It might also be the case that they lack the skills to complete the action—or are not aware that they have the capacities and abilities to do so (D. Narvaez, personal communication, Spring 1996).

Dewey understood well that individual moral strength rested upon social commitments to do the good and reward the good. Perhaps a program of moral education could hold some examples of this kind of strength high, as a way to encourage others to follow suit; yet the more telling influence would be the informal affirmation, working in the way that virtues always have, through meaningful support, admonition, advancement, trust, and honor.

Applications to Professional Ethics

We can return here to the educational problem posed at the end of the first section (above) regarding the intersection between the very real world of business and the theoretical and individualized constructs of ethics. As outlined in this paper, the pragmatic pursuit of the good would be a program of applied morals bridging this divide: it would be assumed in management science as part of professional decision-making at all levels with consideration for seeking and achieving the good, and it would be a program of systematic reflection on professional behavior with attention to social conditions that comprise the context for action along with critical assessment of alternative assumptions, perspectives, and habits of thought. That is, the pragmatic pursuit of the good would stand as a real world ethical theory, educationally and practically. The pursuit of the good as applied would in its application also be educative. Indeed, for Dewey, "morals is education. It is learning the meaning of what we are about and employing that meaning in action" (Dewey, 1922/2008, p. 188). In this way, ethics would be incorporated it into human activity as a practical social science for the betterment of society. "Moral science" so defined "is not something with a separate province.

It is physical, biological and historic knowledge placed in a human context where it will illuminate and guide the activities of men" (Dewey, 1922/2008, p. 199).

This is the meaning of education; for a truly humane education consists in an intelligent direction of native activities in the light of possibilities and necessities of the social situation. (Dewey, 1922/2008, p. 60)

References

Anderson, L. E., & Dodd, L. C. (2005). *Learning democracy: Citizen engagement and electoral choice in Nicaragua, 1990-2001.* Chicago, IL: University of Chicago Press.

Aristotle. (1962). *Nicomachean ethics* (M. Ostwald, Trans.). Englewood Cliffs, NJ: Prentice Hall. (Original published c. 330 BCE)

Baer, D. (2009, November 13). By the numbers, business schools barely care about right and wrong. *The Chronicle of Higher Education*, p. A27.

Bellamy, E. (1897). *Equality.* New York, NY: D. Appleton.

Bentham, J. (1961). An introduction to the principles of morals and legislation. In R. B. Brandt (Ed.), *Value and obligation* (pp. 176-189). New York, NY: Harcourt, Brace & World. (Original published 1789).

Braithwaite, J. (1989). *Crime, shame, and reintegration.* New York, NY: Cambridge University Press.

Braithwaite, J. (1999). *Democracy, community and problem solving.* Available from the International Institute for Restorative Practices at http://www.iirp.edu/article_detail.php?article_id=N Dgz

Christensen, L. J., Peirce, E., Hartman, L. P., Hoffman, W. M., & Carrier, J. (2007). Ethics, CSR and sustainability education in the *Financial Times* top 50 global business schools: Baseline data and future research directions. *Journal of Business Ethics, 73*(4), 347-368.

Christie, N. (1977). Conflicts as property. *The British Journal of Criminology, 17*(1), 1-15.

Dewey, J. (1927). *The public and its problems.* Denver, CO: Alan Swallow.

Dewey, J. (1929). *Experience and nature* (2nd. ed.). LaSalle, IL: Open Court Publishing Co.

Dewey, J. (1933). *How we think: A restatement of the relation of reflective thinking to the educative process.* New York, NY: D. C. Heath and Company.

Dewey, J. (1939). *Theory of valuation.* In O. Neurath (Ed.), *International encyclopedia of unified science* (Vol. II. No. 4). Chicago, IL: University of Chicago Press.

Dewey, J. (1948). *Reconstruction in philosophy* (enlarged ed.). Boston, MA: Beacon Press. (Original published 1920)

Dewey, J. (1960). The need for a recovery of philosophy. In R. J. Bernstein (Ed.), *On experience, nature, and freedom: Representative selections* (pp. 19-69). New York, NY: Random House. Original published as *Creative intelligence: Essays in the pragmatic attitude,* 1917.

Dewey, J. (1960). The pattern of inquiry. In R. J. Bernstein (Ed.), *On experience, nature, and freedom: Representative selections* (pp. 111-132). New York, NY: Random

House. (Original published as *Logic: The theory of inquiry*, 1938).

Dewey, J. (1963). *Experience and education.* New York, NY: Macmillan. (Original published 1938).

Dewey, J. (1966). *Democracy and education.* New York: Macmillan, Inc. (Original published 1916).

Dewey, J. (1975). *Moral principles in education.* Carbondale, IL: Southern Illinois University Press. (Original published 1909)

Dewey, J. (1980). *Theory of the moral life.* New York, NY: Irvington Publishers, Inc. (Original published 1908)

Dewey, J. (2008). *Human nature and conduct.* New York, NY: Barnes & Noble. (Original published 1922)

Diamond, L. (2008). *The spirit of democracy: The struggle to build free societies throughout the world.* New York, NY: Henry Holt and Company.

Farr, J. (2004). Social capital: A conceptual history. *Political Theory, 32*(1), 6-33.

Fletcher, J. (1966). *Situation ethics: The new morality.* Philadelphia, PA: Westminster Press.

Friedland, J. (2009, November 13). Where business meets philosophy: The matter of ethics. *The Chronicle of Higher Education*, pp. A26-A27.

Gentile, M. (2010). *Giving voice to values.* Available from Babson College at www.givingvoicetovalues.org.

Goetz, A. M., and Jenkins, R. (2004). *Reinventing accountability: Making democracy work for the poor.* London: Palgrave.

Gutmann, A., & Thompson, D. (1996). *Democracy and disagreement.* Cambridge, MA: Harvard University Press.

Holland, K. (2009, March 15). Is it time to retrain b-schools? *New York Times.* Retrieved May 28, 2012 at http://www.nytimes.com/2009/03/15/business/15school.html?pagewanted=all

Jackall, R. (2010). *Moral mazes: The world of corporate managers.* New York, NY: Oxford University Press.

Kant, I. (1956). *Groundwork of the metaphysic of morals* (H. J. Paton, Trans.). New York, NY: Harper & Row. (Original published 1785)

Kohlberg, L. (1980). Stages of moral development as a basis for moral education. In B. Munsey (Ed.), *Moral development, moral education, and Kohlberg* (1-98). Birmingham, AL: Religious Education Press.

Lickona, T. (1991). *Educating for character: How our schools can teach respect and responsibility.* New York, NY: Bantam Books.

Mangan, K. (2006, June 23). Agents of fortunes. *The Chronicle of Higher Education,* A14-A16.

Mill, J. S. (1979). *Utilitarianism.* Cambridge, MA: Hackett Publishing Company. (Original published in 1861)

Milliken, F. J., Morrison, E. W., & Hewlin, P. F. (2003). An exploratory study of employee silence: Issues that employees don't communicate upward and why. *Journal of Management Studies, 40*(6), 1453-1476.

Nietzsche, F. (1956). *The genealogy of morals: An attack* (F. Golffing, Trans.). New York, NY: Doubleday. (Original published in 1887)

Piaget, J. (1965). *The moral judgment of the child* (M. Gabain, Trans.). New York, NY: Macmillan Publishing Co.

Promislo, M. D. (2013, January/February). Sick about unethical business. *BizEd*, pp. 20-26.

Quelch, J. (2005, December 2). A new agenda for business schools. *The Chronicle of Higher Education*, B19.

Rest, J. R. (1994). Background: Theory and research. In J. R. Rest & D. Narváez (Eds.) *Moral development in the professions: Psychology and applied ethics* (1-26). Hillsdale, NJ: Lawrence Erlbaum Associates.

Rorty, R. (1979). *Philosophy and the mirror of nature*. Princeton, NJ: Princeton University Press.

Ryan, K. (1996). Character education in the United States. *Journal for a Just and Caring Education, 2*(1), 75-84.

Schweigert, F. J. (1999). Learning the common good: Principles of community-based moral education in restorative justice. *Journal of Moral Education, (28)*2, 163-183.

Schweigert, F. J. (2000). Mending the moralnet: Moral education in strengthening personal and family networks. *Journal of Research and Development in Education, 33*(2), 74-84.

Shiller, R. J. (2012). *Finance and the good society*. Princeton, NJ: Princeton University Press.

Skocpol, T. (2004). *Diminished democracy: From membership to management in American civic life*. Norman, OK: University of Oklahoma Press.

Smith, G. (2012). *Why I left Goldman Sachs: A Wall Street story*. New York, NY: Grand Central Publishing.

Snyder, K. (2006, July). Putting democracy front & center: Technology for citizen participation. *Planning* (American Planning Association), pp. 24-29.

Stark, R. (2005). *The victory of reason: How Christianity led to freedom, capitalism, and Western success.* New York, NY: Random House.

Umbreit, M. S. (1994). *Victim meets offender: The impact of restorative justice and mediation.* Monsey, NY: Willow Tree Press.

Veblen, T. (1953). *The theory of the leisure class.* New York, NY: The New American Library. (Original published in 1899)

Beyond Commonplace Definitions:
Dewey's Conceptions of Democracy and Education

Austin Volz
Harvard Graduate School of Education

Abstract

This paper is an in-depth analysis of John Dewey's *Democracy and Education*. The paper begins by examining the connection between educational and societal forms. The paper then shows that Dewey's conception of education resembles that of experimentation and consists of both action and observation. That Dewey's conception of democracy centers on a mode of associated living which does not necessarily exist in all political structures of democracy follows. Lastly, combining these two concepts, the exact meaning of democratic education is identified and its quality is evaluated according to the established definition of the aims of education.

Keywords: democracy, education, Dewey

Educated citizens improve every nation or society. The availability of better doctors, politicians, scientists, teachers, and businessmen increases the health, industry, and wealth of the society. Education makes the advancement of these professions possible, thereby aiding the nation as a whole.

No one doubts the importance of education. Every society has some sort of education. Whether it be learning traditional stories in an African tribe or respecting one's elders in China, being a member of society requires certain learning.

In *Democracy and Education* Dewey investigated the exact relationship between a society and education.[7]

The variety of forms education may take in different societies are a reflection of the society itself. As Dewey wrote, "a criterion for educational criticism and construction implies a particular social ideal" (Dewey, 2004, p. 95).[8] Just as the criteria for the success of the educational system in a society cannot be separated from the society itself, so the society to a large extent determines the aims of education. Each society has an education most appropriate to it. Different societies will conduct education differently, have different social groups as participants, and utilize different curricula and pedagogies. Concentrating on a democratic society, this paper asks what education is most appropriate to a democracy and why.

The paper first explains Dewey's concept of education and the importance of experience therein. Second, it analyzes the relationship between society and education and how some form of education is necessary to form a society. The third section synthesizes the preceding two sections to characterize democratic education. Lastly, I argue that given Dewey's depiction of education, the democratic form in fact constitutes a particularly effective form of education.

Education

Since Dewey's concept of education differs so distinctly from other conceptions, it facilitates this inquiry to first define education before pursuing why and how democratic education differs from that appropriate to other

---

[7] As part of the establishment of The John Dewey Center for Democracy and Education this paper seeks to explicate Dewey's definition of the terms 'democracy,' 'education,' and 'experience' and accordingly operates fully within Dewey's system of thought as expressed in *Democracy and Education*. Existing objections to and analyses of Dewey's thought lie outside of the aims of this paper.

[8] All quotations taken from Dewey, J. (1916/2004). *Democracy and Education*. New York, NY: Dover Publications.

societies, such as aristocracies. Should we call educated someone who can remember historical dates? Someone who can do calculus without difficulty? Someone who can fix a car with ease? Apart from these particulars the question essentially concerns what sort of person an educational system aims to produce.

As this paper focuses on clarifying Dewey's conceptions, it begins with his concise statement of education as "that reconstruction or reorganization of experience which adds to the meaning of experience, and which increases ability to direct the course of subsequent experience" (p. 74). Education thus always reorganizes experience and results in an increased ability to achieve subsequently desired experiences. Experience, rather than the institution of school, is at the core of Dewey's educational concept.

What is experience? Experience—in Dewey's conception—does not constitute every moment of our lives. Nor does he find experience as synonymous with perception.[9] Seeing a bird fly overhead, tripping on a stone, hearing cars pass outside the bedroom window; none of these properly form experiences. They all remain simple perceptions. Rather,

> The nature of experience can be understood only by noting that it includes an active and a passive element peculiarly combined. On the active hand, experience is trying—a meaning which is made explicit in the connected term experiment. On the passive, it is undergoing. When we experience something we act upon it, we do something with it; then we suffer or undergo the consequences. (p. 133)

The examples above lack the active element of trying. Seeing that an object appears black or that something feels hot does

---

[9] Throughout this essay, perception and observation are used to mean sense experiences that are isolated and not experienced as consequences of prior action.

not resemble an experiment in that it can neither succeed nor fail—and Dewey reminds us that trying links experience and experiment. Taking note of objects' characteristics lacks the purpose that an experiment has: in that case observing is not undergone as the consequence of an action – it is purposeless. Experience, in contrast, has a goal.

Similarly, action is only one half of experience. Impulsively acting in order to achieve an end without noting the consequences also does not constitute experience according to Dewey. Going sky diving or bungee jumping, while exciting, does not constitute an experience unless one notes the consequences of the action in relation to the end for which one was *trying*. Experience requires both elements: trying and undergoing. A process of acting with a purpose (trying) and perceiving the consequences of that action (*undergoing*) forms experience. As Dewey wrote using a different example:

> It is not experience when a child merely sticks his finger into a flame; it is experience when the movement is connected with the pain which he undergoes in consequence....Being burned is a mere physical change, like the burning of a stick of wood, if it is not perceived as a consequence of some other action. (p. 134)

Mere physical changes include things like dropping a plate, getting a tattoo, or hitting one's elbow. Insofar as these occur as isolated from an individual's aim they do not constitute experiences. One may notice that drinking milk that has been left out and tastes sour makes one feel ill, but analogous to Dewey's example, this does not constitute a full experience unless that illness is connected as a consequence of drinking sour-smelling milk. When these events are disconnected from aims or not seen as the consequence of prior action they no more constitute experiences than the child burning his finger.

Since the element of trying plays such an important role, this concept of experience becomes much more similar to that of an experiment. One perceives an object's traits or an event's parts, but cannot properly said to be undergone. Without intentional purpose, one's perceptions of this kind are not situated and lack reference to other parts of one's life:

> Experience is no longer a mere summarizing of what has been done in a more or less chance way in the past; it is a deliberate control of what is done with reference to making what happens to us and what we do to things as fertile as possible of suggestions (of suggested meanings) and a means for trying out the validity of the suggestions. (p. 262)

Taking the classic example, a child puts his hand near the stove with the intention of warming it. Let us express this event using the vocabulary of the previous quotation. The child puts his hand near the stove to test the suggested meaning of the stove as an object that gives warmth when near the hand. From the consequence of the experience the child may acquire many suggestions, such as that distance from the stove determines degree of warmth or that the stove may cause pain. Similarly, in an experiment one hypothesizes and tests certain suggested meanings. Based on the results of the experiment one's experience is reorganized. Based on this reorganization, another experiment may be conducted so as to clarify the relationship between one's action and the results. Likewise, the child may continue to test suggested meanings of the stove, learning about turning it on and off and how different foods are cooked. Ultimately, the continuity of suggested meanings exemplifies experience.

Experience, however, does not necessarily have to be firsthand, but can be transferred through language as well. A historical event, although not properly experienced (since not produced as the result of trying), might still play a part in experience by means of its suggestions. Were the historical event the success of a given political move, or the failure of a certain business venture, it suggests changes in one's own attempts as a politician or businessman. Studying historical events suggests actions that succeeded or failed at achieving an objective. When deeply engaged with this study, these suggestions modify experience's element of activity so that one may act differently in an attempt to achieve what was already desired or alter one's goals entirely. Thinking back to the concise definition of education given as "that reconstruction or reorganization of experience which adds to the meaning of experience, and which increases ability to direct the course of subsequent experience" (p. 74) shows that studying the historical event has produced such a reorganization of experience.

Dewey's conception of experience is intricately linked with that of education. Without explicit instruction in an educational institution we still learn from our experiences: experimenting, testing, and clarifying the suggested meanings of things. This conception of experience implies that any experience can be educational, but mere perception or mindless activity cannot. Education as the reorganization of experience is dynamic, concerned more with actions (trying) and consequences (undergoing) than abstract facts. Education increases one's understanding of consequences: actions and consequences that previously seemed related may now appear as independent and, conversely, actions previously thought of as isolated now appear to have had interrelated consequences. However, describing education solely in terms of a new organization of actions and consequences neglects the fact that education itself generates new actions. As opposed to simply memorizing the dates of the Civil War, the truly educational approach to this event produces suggestions in the life of the student. He or she may begin acting differently as a member of society: trying out the suggestions of this event in his or her own social group. As education rearranges experience it also affects its constituent elements of trying and undergoing. Trying and undergoing both change through education.

An example may help illustrate how trying and undergoing both change in education. The trying element is constructing a miniature boat. At first one may select the lightest materials, believing that the weight of a boat is most important. If an excessively tall boat is constructed the boat-maker will undergo the discovery that despite the material's weight, the boat sinks deep into the water. Noticing that the boat only sinks partially and then is able to float may suggest a redirection of activity. He may try different materials or make different sizes for the boat's bottom. Through various instances of experimenting the boat maker may discover that the weight of the displaced water must at least equal the weight of the boat for it to float. The entirety of the experience, the combination of the trying and undergoing elements, has been reorganized.

Through being based in the trying element of experience, education responds to a tendency or interest that already exists. Abstract information cannot be educational precisely because it is abstract. What is truly learned fits into one's present experience:

> Of course if geography and history are taught as ready-made studies which a person studies simply because he is sent to school, it easily happens that a large number of statements about things remote and alien to everyday experience are learned. Activity is divided, and two separate worlds are built up, occupying activity at divided periods. No transmutation takes place; ordinary experience is not enlarged in meaning by getting its connections; what is studied is not animated and made real by entering into immediate activity. (p. 200)

Although this statement focuses on the study of history and geography, its criticism applies to any subject learned in this way. Education aims to increase the perceived connections between one's actions and their consequences. When teaching results in two worlds: that of the school and that of everyday experience, teaching actually undermines a fundamental aim of education. Teachers school by having their students sit in a classroom and 'learn' arithmetic without reference to problems that arise naturally in the course of their experience.

The 'two worlds' to which Dewey refers arise from different motivations for learning. The crucial point here is that the subject is studied out of an intrinsic motivation in the student. Whether the subject is useful or not is not so important: if a student is interested in music, poetry, or mathematics then that is sufficient for the education to which Dewey refers. An abstract world does not necessarily arise when a subject lacks a direct application, but rather when the subject is, in Dewey's words, 'ready-made' and has no connection to the student's experience. In this case the trying element of experience has been left out and education does not occur as a natural outgrowth of experience. In contrast to schooling, teachers educate by introducing arithmetic as a suggested way to satisfy the student's desire to achieve some end. In contrast to education, schooling neither enhances the meaning of experience, nor redirects it. Implied in the contrast with school, education does not necessarily require an institutionalized or formalized component. The most essential thing – experience – is already present as an intrinsic part of life.

Two consequences arise from this notion of education as the reorganizing of experience. First, it means that education has no end except education itself. Dewey defines education as the reorganization of experience. The reconstruction of experience changes one's activity, and a change in activity means greater opportunity for new stimuli and further learning.

The connections between one's activity and its consequences as well as the suggested meanings of an object or action continually increase. Education enhances the meaning of each subsequent experience, adding layers and increasing opportunities for later experiences. For Dewey, education's aims are not static. Rather,

> ... [T]here is nothing to which education is subordinate save more education. It is commonplace to say that education should not cease when one leaves school. The point of this commonplace is that the purpose of school education is to insure the continuance of education by organizing the powers that insure growth. The inclination to learn from life itself and to make the conditions of life such that all will learn in the process of living is the finest product of schooling. (p. 49)

By basing education on experience, Dewey has ensured that his conception of learning remained distinct from training. Training has a static end by which to judge its success. In weight training, for instance, one either can or cannot lift the desired weight, and when one succeeds the purpose of the training has been achieved. Education not only contains no such static achievements but remains antithetical to such things.[10]

The second consequence is that education results in a different kind of person, not just the same person in possession of different information. This second implication follows from the fact that education necessarily results in a change in activity. As a consequence of education one will better foresee the consequences of his or her actions and act accordingly.

---

[10] See Hildreth (2011), *What Good is Growth? Reconsidering Dewey on the Ends of Education Education & Culture* 27(2) (2011): 28-47 for further discussion regarding Dewey's conception of education's purpose.

Dewey characterizes the change in activity by calling it intelligent activity. Intelligent activity does not mean an increase in academic preoccupations, but rather an expanded awareness of the meaning of one's actions:

> When I hear a noise and run and get water and put out a blaze, I respond intelligently; the sound meant fire, and fire meant need of being extinguished. I bump into a stone, and kick it to one side purely physically. I put it to one side for fear someone will stumble upon it, intelligently; I respond to a meaning which the thing has. (p. 29)

This quotation shows that intelligent activity stems from knowing both the consequences of one's actions and the meaning of present circumstances, which include events and objects. Since an object's meaning does not consist in a list of properties but rather "it is the characteristic use to which the thing is put, because of its specific qualities, which supplies the meaning with which it is identified" (p. 28). It follows from this notion of meaning, and the notion of intelligence as the identification of meaning, that intelligence requires using things and acting. Taken as such, intelligence most accurately describes the result of education.

This notion of intelligent activity sheds light on the second part of Dewey's definition of education: that it "increases the ability to direct the course of subsequent experience" (p. 74). In this way, education increases intelligence, for

> The other side of an educative experience is an added power of subsequent direction or control. To say that one knows what he is about, or can intend certain consequences, is to say, of course, that he can better anticipate what is going to happen; that he can, therefore, get ready or prepare in advance so as to

secure beneficial consequences and avert undesirable ones. (p. 74)

The ability to better anticipate what will happen occurs as a result of an increased awareness of the consequences of our actions. Education enables actions as simple as choosing the appropriate width for the bottom of a toy boat and as complicated as navigating different social contexts after realizing the implied meanings of one's behavior. The direction of experience results in building boats that can carry things or forming a broader community of friends. Education, stemming from present experience, enables one to affect later experiences as well.

While some may think of such control as merely functional and distinct from intelligence, Dewey here shows that it in fact depends upon an intellectual element. Acting efficiently to achieve a certain end requires acknowledging the great number of relationships between one's actions and their consequences—one cannot accomplish it haphazardly. Since education results in an increased awareness of the relationships involved in a particular action, such effective action requires education. In basing education on experience Dewey makes it difficult to maintain a complete separation between intelligence and activity. Activity, as a part of an experience, leads to increased awareness of connections and this awareness similarly changes the course of one's actions.

Education and Society

Returning to the quote at the start of this paper, in Dewey's conception, society determines the form of education because the very existence of society depends on shared ends and meanings.[11] Society is a kind of community, not only a group of people who share a language, land, and leader, and a

---

[11] "a criterion for educational criticism and construction implies a particular social ideal" (p. 95).

community means a unity amongst individuals who may even be quite distanced from one another physically. As Dewey wrote,

> Individuals do not even compose a social group because they all work for a common end. The parts of a machine work with a maximum of cooperativeness for a common result, but they do not form a community. If, however, they were all cognizant of the common end and all interested in it so that they regulated their specific activity in view of it, then they would form a community. (p. 5)

Education enables both the awareness of this common end and the ability to act with it in mind. The members of a society must know the meaning of this end; especially they must share this end as a goal and know its relevance to and influence on their own actions. A sports team desires to win a competition. The successful completion of this end necessitates that the team members share this goal. It also requires that the members understand the consequences of their actions; that is to say that through education they know the rules of the game, previously successful and unsuccessful strategies, or how the ball will respond when handled a certain way. In Dewey's words, success requires intelligent action. Through education, society's members become able to regulate their behavior intelligently in reference to a common end.

Needing to understand the consequence of actions in society entails that becoming a member of a social group means developing a certain kind of intelligence. For Dewey, social development and intellectual development are not strictly separable. Intelligence identifies a thing's meaning and "it is the characteristic use to which the thing is put, because of its specific qualities, which supplies the meaning with which it is identified" (p. 28). Objects have a particular social use and so have different meanings in different societies. Accordingly, intelligence takes on a different form. For instance, the meaning of a book in a society without a system of writing would differ: perhaps the society would use it to start a fire or prop something up. The society might even come to integrate it as a commonplace item for starting fires. Despite the physical similarity of the book in each society, it would have a different meaning. The intelligence of the object, or what it means to know about it, would correspondingly differ.

The same can be said even about things such as the knowledge of mathematics or reading. Mathematics has a social relevance. We can use calculus to determine the rate at which a disease spreads and arithmetic to keep track of spending. We can also think back in history when the opportunity to learn to read was largely confined to the upper class. The education of the society and the resulting intellect would reflect the social dynamic produced by this profession.

Experience consists in both trying and undergoing. Different instances of trying produce different instances of undergoing. Since the social aims of a community encourage different instances of trying, the whole of experience also differs. For example, a society that values large families because of the labor provided by numerous children will have increased interactions between siblings and the reorganization of experience that arises from those interactions. The social aim of large families changes the experience of its members. Inasmuch as the aims of society largely, though not completely, determine what kind of experiences its members will have, education, or the reorganization of experience, also differs.

Returning to the earlier definition of intelligence as an awareness of a thing's meaning, which is to say the uses to which it is put (p. 29), it becomes clear that society generates a different kind of intelligence in its members. Since trying involves the use of objects, and society will largely determine an object's use, different meanings for objects are established. In the previous example, a society that values large families will give a meaning to marriage that includes subsequently having many children. Intelligence amounts to knowing this meaning and being aware of the connection between marriage and the family structure. Due to the aims provided by society, insofar as meanings differ between societies, so does intelligence.

Since the possession of common ends and the ability to act in accordance with those ends constitute the essence of society, society's existence requires a shared awareness of the connections between actions and consequences. The possession of this common understanding in an individual makes him a member of the society:

> To have the same ideas about things which others have, to be like-minded with them, and thus to be really members of a social group, is therefore to attach the same meanings to things and to acts which others attach. Otherwise, there is no common understanding, and no community life... If each views the consequences of his own acts as having a bearing upon what others are doing and takes into account the consequences of their behavior upon himself, then there is a common mind; a common intent in behavior. (pp. 29-30)

This notion of a common mind does not preclude the existence of an individual mind. Although all the members of a particular society may attach the same meaning to, say, the act of gift giving, this does not amount to brainwashing, where every person would decide on the same gift under the same circumstances. Whereas in one culture giving a gift may be an act of generosity or kindness, in another it could be insulting and imply inferiority in the recipient. In both cases there are still the individual tastes of the recipient and the decision-making process of the giver. Nor does a common intelligence and interest mean that every person will wish to pursue the same career and have the same personal interests or tendencies. Rather, a common mind means a common understanding as to the potential consequences of one's actions and the common meanings suggested by objects, such as what constitutes success, what counts as a polite or impolite action, or what a book is for.[12]

Dewey's argument may seem circular to some because society produces a common intelligence and yet common intelligence also serves as a condition of already participating in society. One might ask which comes first, being in a society or having a common understanding. The importance of the objection lies in its ability to call into question the validity of the relationship between intellect and society. If Dewey contradicts himself, and establishes the relationship between intellect and society based on this contradiction, then that whole relationship is called into question.

Dewey responds to this objection of primacy by referring to the process of imitation. Children will unavoidably grow up around others. The helplessness of the child ensures that even in the case of being orphaned one will have others around him or her. However, the child becoming part of the society depends on its relations with those around:

> Within even the most social group there are many relations which are not as yet social. A large number of human relations in any social group are still upon the machine-like plane...So far as the relations of parent and child, teacher and pupil, employer and employee, governor and governed, remain upon this level, they form no true social group, no matter how closely their respective activities touch one another. (p. 5)

A truly social society is not guaranteed by the proximity of people and likewise proximity does not guarantee that child becomes part of the society. Rather, the child becomes part of society when the relations of her activities to members of the

---

[12] See Brick, B., John Dewey and the New Definition of Individual Responsibility. (2008) *American Educational History Journal*, v35 n1 p117-130 for more on the individual and society.

society move beyond a phase of machine-like automation to become more closely interrelated.

Imitation serves as the means for a community's relations to be more closely connected. Even when the group lacks a shared end that results in a common intelligence the pressure of success and failure still applies. For an individual "to get happiness or to avoid the pain of failure he has to act in a way agreeable to others... In this case, his original impulse is modified. He not merely acts in a way agreeing with the actions of others, but, in so acting, the same ideas and emotions are aroused in him that animate others" (p. 13). When first entering the community he desires not to appear a failure within the social group and so acts in a kind of mechanical imitation of the others in the society. In Dewey's conception this acting ultimately forms corresponding mental and emotional dispositions.

Dewey outlines the process of the transformation from imitation to the formation of intelligence as follows:

> A tribe, let us say, is warlike. The successes for which it strives, the achievements upon which it sets store, are connected with fighting and victory. The presence of this medium incites bellicose exhibitions in a boy, first in games, then in fact when he is strong enough. As he fights he wins approval and advancement; as he refrains, he is disliked, ridiculed, shut out from favorable recognition. It is not surprising that his original belligerent tendencies and emotions are strengthened at the expense of others, and that his ideas turn to things connected with war. Only in this way can he become fully a recognized member of his group. Thus his mental habitudes are gradually assimilated to those of his group. (p. 13)

The concern of an immature member in seeking approval eventually changes into sharing the same concerns as the group of which he or she will become a part. When a member only wants to appear a certain way he or she acts less successfully. A member will not as effectively solve challenges that arise (such as persevering through a difficult fight in Dewey's example) when he only appears to care. To the extent that he only goes through the motions so as to achieve acceptance he will ultimately perform less successfully. And the opposite is equally true: to the extent that his interest is genuine he is more likely to achieve success.

The objection that intelligence comes from society and that society depends on the existence of intelligence fails to recognize the transformation of mechanical action into intelligent action. When a society means merely a group of people who cooperate solely out of a desire to benefit themselves their actions remain mechanical and the true social element is absent. When, however, each begins to value others' opinions of him or herself, his actions begin to share the common interest of recognition and success. The more superficial interest develops into an actual sharing of ends and thus a common intelligence. From the common intelligence the group becomes more than mechanical cooperation: it becomes an actual, genuine society.

Looking to the second element of education, the ability to direct later experiences, we see that differences in intelligence result in different abilities to affect later experiences. While the members of one society may be aware that their actions will have certain consequences, they may also lack an awareness of how to direct other experiences. While able to bring a raincoat on a cloudy day, one might be unable to start a fire without matches. Conversely, one who is able to start a fire without matches may not know the consequences of trying to turn on a blender without plugging it in. Usually the ignorance of such consequences does not cause any problems because the member of the respective society so rarely encounters them: primitive societies do not use blenders and Americans can buy matches. These difficulties arise primarily when one tries to do something outside the common aims of his or her society.

Democracy and Association

Having followed Dewey beyond the commonplace definitions of education, experience, and society, it is now time to turn to the democratic theme of this volume and explain Dewey's notion of democracy. This section will first describe the interactions between social groups within a democracy and then generalize to discuss a democratic country. In the course of the explanation frequent contrasts to other social forms, particularly aristocracy, will be used.

The characteristic traits of political democracy are clear: political power originates among the people, often by some form of representation.[13] Political democracy focuses on the extent and origin of governing power. While important, Dewey's idea of democracy is more societal than political, as shown in his description of democracy as primarily a form of associated living (p. 83). Inasmuch as democracy constitutes a mode of associated living, the daily interactions between people characterize the essence of democracy more than the method of legislation.

Not all political systems rest as heavily on the mutual associations of its people as democracy does. Dewey, by distinguishing democracy as a mode of associated living, implies that other forms of government do not depend on their people being mutually associated with another but instead they

---

[13] The CIA *World Factbook* defines democracy as "a form of government in which the supreme power is retained by the people, but which is usually exercised indirectly through a system of representation and delegated authority periodically renewed." Democracy. (n.d.). In *The World Factbook*. Retrieved from https://www.cia.gov/library/publications/the-world-factbook/fields/2128.html

may largely live in isolated social groups. Education enables this association:

> The devotion of democracy to education is a familiar fact. The superficial explanation is that a government resting upon popular suffrage cannot be successful unless those who elect and who obey their governors are educated. Since a democratic society repudiates the principle of authority, it must find a substitute in voluntary disposition and interest; these can be created only by education. But there is a deeper explanation. A democracy is more than a form of government; it is primarily a mode of associated living, of conjoint communicated experience. (p. 83)

Here Dewey implies that many other forms of government rely on the principle of authority—those in power make policy decisions on the basis of authority. In contrast, democracy entails a common intelligence where people can freely share their experiences, hold many purposes in common, and where reliance on social authority is at a minimum.[14]

Associated living exists primarily in the two traits of having a variety of shared interests and minimizing the boundaries between social groups. As Dewey wrote, "these two traits are precisely what characterize the democratically constituted society" (p. 83).

We will first look at what it means to have a variety of common purposes in a social group. Taking the family as an iconic example of sharing interests we see that it usually requires interest not only in each individual's success but in common values and goals: "If we take. . .the kind of family life which illustrates the standard, we find that there are material, intellectual, aesthetic interests in which all participate and that

---

[14] See Narey, D., Democratic Visions/Pluralist Critiques: One Essential Conversation for 21st Century Philosophy of Education. *Philosophical Studies in Education* 43 (2012) for further discussion of conceptions of democracy.

the progress of one member has worth for the experience of other members..." (p. 79). Since the progress of each member has value for the others, society is not simply an effective way to achieve one's personal interests. When one's own interests match those of others then the success of one member has worth for another because it marks the achievement of similar goals.

Looking now at the country level, while the variety of shared purposes in a democracy may produce a kind of nationalistic pride through which one finds worth in another's success, it also encourages group – as opposed to individual - undertakings. In a democracy, "In order to have a large number of values in common, all the members of the group must have an equable opportunity to receive and to take from others. There must be a large variety of shared undertakings and experiences" (p. 80). In this quotation, the importance of the variety of shared undertakings shows that one group or individual should not dictate the actions of another. A true democracy eliminates such isolated interests and slavish subservience. Conversely, this quotation also highlights the importance placed on group undertakings as the common mode of operating in a democracy. When one wishes to get something done in a democracy one finds others with the same common interest rather than finding others willing to serve. This method enhances the variety of interests present in a democracy.

Common purpose leads to the second characteristic of democracy: free interchange between social groups. This interchange does not mean an absence of separate social groups, but rather the absence of social isolation. One sees the opposite of democratic association

> wherever one group has interests "of its own" which shut it out from full interaction with other groups, so that its prevailing purpose is the protection of what it has got, instead of reorganization and progress through

wider relationships. It marks nations in their isolation from one another; families which seclude their domestic concerns as if they had no connection with a larger life; schools when separated from the interest of home and community; the divisions of rich and poor; learned and unlearned. (p. 82)

A democratic society will include different social groups, each with their own aims and values, but none will function in complete isolation. Different social groups such as the church, family, or members of the same occupation may overlap and have frequent interaction with one another. Dewey does not lay out an extensive theory as to how a democracy functions economically in *Democracy and Education*, but he does make it clear that a diversity of experiences will be open to everyone. By affording such experiences, the existence of a privileged and servant class will likewise be impossible, for "there must be a large variety of shared undertakings and experiences. Otherwise, the influences which educate some into masters, educate others into slaves" (p. 84).

Since a democratic society enables free interaction between social groups, every social group within a democratic society likewise functions democratically. Imagine that one of the social groups in a democracy values being isolated from the other groups. In Dewey's conception, this is because the source of isolation lies in a common intelligence that values established customs and opposes change:

The essential point is that isolation makes for rigidity and formal institutionalizing of life, for static and selfish ideals within the group. That savage tribes regard aliens and enemies as synonymous is not accidental. It springs from the fact that they have identified their experience with rigid adherence to their past customs. (p. 82)

The group's fear of change and adaptation manifests externally as hostility towards outside groups and internally as stratification within the social group so as to preserve the status quo. Within a democracy, the same logic applies; that is, a group hostile to interaction with others internally will not function democratically insofar as it depends on strict stratification. As part of common intelligence, the democratic value of increased interaction amongst participants will permeate each group and member of a democracy.

Open interaction within a democratic society does not require that different groups have a close physical proximity to one another because interaction is not dependent on physical location. Rather, interaction can occur in even the most seemingly isolated circumstances:

> The manufacturer moreover is as truly socially guided in his activities when he is laying plans in the privacy of his own counting house as when he is buying his raw materials or selling his finished goods. Thinking and feeling that have to do with action in association with others is as much a social mode of behavior as is the most overt cooperative or hostile act. (p. 12)

It follows from the social basis of the isolated manufacturer that the significant interaction between social groups occurs by each individual taking into account the consequences of their actions with regard to others. Inasmuch as interaction marks every association in a democracy, this manufacturer will consider the consequences of his actions for his employees and his employees will likewise consider the extended consequences of their actions. Unlike in an aristocracy or tyranny, no dictatorial, absolute authority acts with minimal regard to the consequences of its actions on other social groups. Those in power relate their actions to those below them and those below similarly inform the concerns of those above them, thus minimizing boundaries between the groups.

At the social and individual level open interaction manifests as an intelligence of the consequences of one's actions on other groups and individuals. At the political level open interaction between social groups generates elections, the trait normally considered to characterize democracies. The ability for each citizen to have a say in choosing the nation's leader is the large-scale manifestation of what happens on the smaller scale in democratic societies. Since democracy is primarily a mode of associated living, the large scale and small scale must function similarly: casting a vote is just as much a part of life as is earning a living. However, in Dewey's conception of a democracy, elections should be a genuine extension of the everyday interactions between individuals and groups. In cases in which elections do occur but schools, businesses, and other social groups function aristocratically, the society as a whole fails as a democracy.

The two democratic characteristics—the variety of shared interests and the free interaction between social groups—imply the ability for change. A society whose members freely encounter one another and exchange experiences will not tend to settle into a static routine. "These more numerous and more varied points of contact denote a greater diversity of stimuli to which an individual has to respond; they consequently put a premium on variation in his action" (p. 83). Both the entirety of the democratic society and its individual citizens can reorganize their conduct in response to new interactions. In a democratic society a child need not take on the same profession as his father because numerous other opportunities have opened to him by means of the people he has met, classes he has taken, and interactions in which he has taken part. These familiar opportunities for change come out of the two fundamental traits of democracy that we have identified: free interchange between social groups and increased variety of common interests.

Democratic Education

The reorganization of experience that occurs in a democracy will have as its aims these two traits: free interaction between social groups and increased variety of common interests. As part of a formalized system, the democratic education should provide experiences that lead to this sort of activity. This is primarily done in two ways: integrated subject matter and a specific student-teacher dynamic.

These two elements follow from the common interests and aims held by a democratic society. An aristocratic society has a vested interest in maintaining the separation between laborers and aristocrats. This separation both limits physical interaction between these two groups and restricts the possible courses of action in each group. A laborer cannot pursue a philosophical education nor can an aristocrat take on the profession of a builder. There thus arise separately appropriate educations for each: a cultural education for aristocrats and a utilitarian one for laborers. In an aristocracy education will "train the many for pursuits involving mere skill in production, and the few for a knowledge that is an ornament and a cultural embellishment" (p. 246). To undermine this division and separation of education would be to eliminate the aristocracy.

In contrast, a democracy aims to have minimal boundaries between social groups and allow each to share in a variety of common interests. As a mode of associated living that puts a premium on change, a democracy facilitates its members' ability to change their social status. Education facilitates this aim on an individual level:

> Obviously a society to which stratification into separate classes would be fatal, must see to it that intellectual opportunities are accessible to all on equable and easy terms. . . A society which is mobile, which is full of channels for the distribution of a change occurring anywhere, must see to it that its

members are educated to personal initiative and adaptability. (p. 84)

As noted earlier, a democracy will contain social groups such as families or businesses that have their own interests, but these are based on shared interests rather than strict social classes established through a status quo. As education causes a reorganization of experience, in a democracy this reorganization results in new instances of trying that enables the social mobility Dewey describes above.

Turning now to education as systemized in a democracy, reading Shakespeare undeniably differs from construction, but a democratic education brings these two kinds of education as close together as possible. Cultural education should include the element of utility and utilitarian education should include the element of culture. The reason for this is that since democracy attempts to eliminate the boundaries between social groups, each individual will refer his or her actions and interests to a wider range of individuals. This increased range means that one's present concerns divide less easily into being simply aristocratic or utilitarian.

What does this combination look like? An integration of cultural and utilitarian education means that culture is studied in connection with the practical affairs of managing others, solving societal problems, or other activities; and on the other side, that technical education is studied in connection with its cultural, social, and historical significance.

An education aimed at vocational work encompasses cultural, social, and historical studies. The student does not learn practical skills in isolation:

An education which acknowledges the full intellectual and social meaning of a vocation would include instruction in the historic background of present conditions; training in science to give intelligence and

> initiative in dealing with material and agencies of production; and study of economics, civics, and politics, to bring the future worker into touch with the problems of the day and the various methods proposed for its improvement. (p. 306)

In Dewey's conception, vocational education encompasses a multifaceted experience of all aspects of the vocation. A complete opposition between cultural and utilitarian approaches is absent in democratic education. Rather, in gaining intelligence about one's occupation, that is, learning its suggested meanings, history, politics, and civics are all brought into play. Dewey does acknowledge a distinction between cultural and vocational studies: some members of society will learn a vocation such as construction or manufacturing and others may follow more academic pursuits. A democratic society does not mean there is no distinction between professions, but instead prepares individuals for those professions so that they conduct their activities intelligently – realizing their full meaning. As the common intelligence between those of different social groups is extensive, this education amounts to having minimal boundaries between social groups; boundaries that an aristocratic education might otherwise enforce.

In a democratic education, Plato, Shakespeare, or Machiavelli would not be studied as cultural artifacts. Rather, students may study them as profound aids to understanding the complexities of current social life. These cultural works would be studied with reference to the current circumstances insofar as they may deepen one's understanding of complex human motivations and interactions. The study of these works may originate out of the student trying to understand the cultural context of his work and can lead to a changed course of activity by an increased understanding of the potential consequences of one's actions and the schema into which they fit. In short, since education results in the increased perception between our actions and their consequences, such an approach to 'cultural education' ensures education as Dewey understands it, in contrast to training or schooling.

The integration of so-called cultural and vocational subject matter reinforces the democratic mode of association. A system of education that unifies diverse subject matter establishes an extensive shared intelligence amongst its members. This intelligence enables individuals to clearly understand the consequences of their actions and accordingly redirect subsequent experiences so as to move between social groups. Because each student studies diverse subjects, those who ultimately specialize in science or government do not form an isolated and inaccessible social group. Since each has a clear idea as to what others are doing, professional divisions are at a minimum.

The awareness of the concerns of other professions marks the beginning of what makes this educational system democratic. Ultimately an education that combines cultural and utilitarian subjects enables each individual to more effectively contribute to the common ends of the society. It allows each person to effectively refer his or her actions to others:

> The problem of education in a democratic society is to do away with the dualism [of cultural and utilitarian education] and to construct a course of studies which makes thought a guide of free practice for all and which makes leisure a reward of accepting responsibility for service, rather than a state of exemption from it. (p. 251)

That thought guides practice eliminates the authority of a 'higher' social group over another. The activities of one who labors no longer occur in isolation from their own aims. Similarly, that the political groups have actual responsibility to act means that they cannot view their activities in isolation from those they may govern. Having cultural and utilitarian education unified is essential for minimizing social boundaries.

The second distinguishing feature of a democratic education system is a particular student-teacher dynamic. Specifically, the student and teacher dynamic reflects the democratic element of a variety of shared interests. Since the free exchange of experiences between social groups marks democracy, this same social dynamic occurs within the classroom. A form of education that set up the teacher as an unquestionable authority and source of information undermines the foundation of democracy. However, just as the governmental side of democracy does not amount to an absence of legislation, so does a democratic education not amount to an absence of the teacher. Instead, the teacher's role is different:

> This does not mean that the teacher is to stand off and look on; the alternative to furnishing ready-made subject matter and listening to the accuracy with which it is reproduced is not quiescence, but participation, sharing, in an activity. In such shared activity, the teacher is a learner, and the learner is, without knowing it, a teacher—and upon the whole, the less consciousness there is, on either side, of either giving or receiving instruction, the better. (p. 154)

This quotation embodies the fundamental principle of democratic pedagogy. In order to ensure the shared interests and social fluidity of democracy these traits must be present in the classroom. The teacher, though more knowledgeable than the student, does not represent a static authority. Similarly, the student, though developing, is not fundamentally inferior to the teacher. The student and teacher form a society that can freely exchange their experiences and shared interest in discovery. In short, they constitute part of a democratic community.

Although the social relationship between the student and teacher should permeate the teaching of every subject, the further specifics of teaching fall outside the scope of this paper. Though Dewey acknowledges that specific teaching practices will vary according the subject matter (p. 159), how the act of teaching will vary according to the materials used in different subject areas is neither a task that Dewey takes up in *Democracy and Education*, nor that we shall attempt here.[15]

Different and Better Education

Most of this paper has focused on the appropriateness of an educational system to a specific society, a democracy. After determining the distinctive traits of democratic education, we see that the differences amount to more than another example of a kind of education that one could arbitrarily choose. Democracy amounts to an educational system that in fact generates particularly high-quality education.

According to Dewey's definition of education, high-quality education increases the frequency of the two parts of education—the reorganization of experience and increased ability to direct subsequent experience. The better the education the more it ensures the possibility for such continual growth. Democracy, as defined here, establishes an extensive common intelligence that results in the ability for change that ultimately makes continual education possible.

First, as regards the reorganization of experience, the integration of subject matter in a democracy ensures its continual possibility by having minimal boundaries between social groups.

The extension in space of the number of individuals who participate in an interest so that each has to refer

---

[15] See Harvey Sarles, *Teaching as Dialogue: A Teacher's Study* (Los Angeles, CA: Trébol Press, 2013) for more about this teacher-student dynamic.

> his own action to that of others, and to consider the
> action of others to give point and direction to his own,
> is equivalent to the breaking down of those barriers of
> class, race, and national territory which kept men from
> perceiving the full import of their activity. (p. 83)

Both inside and outside of the classroom, members from a variety of social groups will be better able to continually refer their actions to others. The ability and necessity to refer one's actions to another requires that one be aware of the consequences of his or her actions. In other words, it requires the continual reorganization of one's experience and continued open interaction with those of similar interests.

The increased reorganization of experience in a democracy primarily arises from increased opportunity for activity. From the previous quotation, Dewey went on to write that "these more numerous and more varied points of contact denote a greater diversity of stimuli to which an individual has to respond; they consequently put a premium on variation in his action" (p. 83). In systematized education, the increased diversity of stimuli results from the changed social environment and also from the diversity and integration of subject matter. It follows from the integration of various subject matters that students in a democracy will have a common understanding and that they will be able to redirect subsequent experiences without having their activities confined to a single direction. Specifically, it means that they will not be trained as simply mechanics, engineers, or businessmen. In the language used previously to define 'experience,' this means increased possibilities for trying. In auto class a student may endeavor to use his knowledge of physics to solve a problem and, conversely, use his knowledge of automobiles to solve a physics problem. There is no activity that strictly belongs to auto or physics; thus new suggested meanings can constantly come into play.

Increased activity opens the possibility for a greater awareness of the connection between action and consequence to develop. The limitation on action that is present in an aristocratic education correspondingly limits the awareness of consequences. The leisure class may quote Shakespeare and read Latin, yet lack any sort of vocational skill. Conversely, manufacturers may have never read Shakespeare, yet be talented at fixing machines. Aristocratic society limits the opportunities for reorganizing experience on both sides. Since education is not subordinate to anything except more education (p. 49), such limitations indicate an educational failure: a failure that democratic education not only avoids but counteracts by expecting its members to be adaptable to change.

Democratic education also means the ability to significantly direct later experiences. It follows from the integration of subject matter that students gain an awareness of the consequences of a greater variety of actions. The same applies to the teacher in a democracy, for, by not exhibiting an unquestionable authority, the effects of his or her actions in teaching become apparent through the students' questions and responses. The student and teacher both engage in the continual reorganization of experience. Outside of the classroom, the education gained therein even more obviously affords many options for possible activity. Since democratic education largely avoids exclusive specialization, a great variety of possible occupations after formal education exists.

The sort of person produced by democratic education has more options for the direction of later experience than that from any other kind of education. As Dewey writes,

> A society which is mobile, which is full of channels for the distribution of a change occurring anywhere, must see to it that its members are educated to personal initiative and adaptability. Otherwise, they will be overwhelmed by the changes in which they are caught

and whose significance or connections they do not perceive. (p. 84)

It follows that democratically educated citizens must be the most able to intelligently direct the outcome of their actions. Whereas an aristocratic education may produce citizens that value and are able to ensure stability, this very stability restricts the variety of activities they may pursue. The opposite applies in a democracy: the integration of subject matter allows the student—who is also the citizen—to pursue a diversity of occupations.

We noted earlier that the two fundamental traits of democracy result in the ability for change. The education determined by a democracy reinforces that aim by eliminating strict divisions in subject matter and changing the social dynamic of the classroom. Combined with the necessity that education be continual growth, the ability for a democracy to change now becomes its ability to educate its citizens most effectively. The integration of cultural and utilitarian subject matter as well as the elimination of an unquestionable authority in the classroom ensures the perpetual adaptation and reorganization of experience. The influence of democracy and democratic education ultimately guarantees continual education throughout the lifetimes of its members and for society as a whole.

Reference

Dewey, J. (1916/2004). *Democracy and Education*. New York, NY: Dover Publications.

Differentiating for Democracy:
Social Processes and Civic Equality in Diverse Action Civics Classrooms

Laurel Cadwallader Stolte
Harvard Graduate School of Education

Abstract

Action civics, in which students learn to influence policy, take action on issues important to them, and reflect on their work, is a promising approach for promoting civic engagement. However, it is important to understand the unique interactions taking place in socioeconomically and ethnically diverse contexts and how they may affect the program outcomes. This analysis addresses the question: How do interactions in diverse action civics classrooms support and/or undermine the promotion of civic equality and empowerment? I explore this question through two case studies, based on observations and interviews.

In one class, individual skills development was prioritized and *authoritative* norms were established. These norms, which included facilitating teacher-led discussion and providing limited choices, reflected the social processes typically valued in schools and the teacher's own individualistic conception of citizenship. Students displayed little interest in collective action.

In the second class, the teacher hoped to instill passion for civic action and *authentic* norms, student-led discussion and consensus prevailed. Interactions in this class revealed a tension between engaging students in authentic civic experiences and structuring more equitable, yet simulated or highly-scaffolded, encounters with democratic practices.

The teacher in the second class also dabbled with *transformative* interactions, such as intentional grouping and a focus on synthetic thinking. These interactions appeared to more effectively meet the demands of heterogeneous classes and create a more inclusive conception of democracy, but educators need support in instituting these norms that challenge both the educational and civic status quo.

Keywords: action civics, authoritative vs. authentic norms, democracy and education

"What do you wish had been different about your education?" Sonia,[16] a young Latina woman, tentatively asks her fellow 11th and 12th graders. Several students begin to shout out their thoughts, and Suzanne, the teacher, suggests that they raise hands. They object, saying it slows down the discussion. "Why don't we go around in a circle?" says Sonia. I am impressed by the range of issues students mention: the lack of minority students in honors classes, the unfairness of the grading system, the need for more interdisciplinary classes. After almost everyone has shared, Suzanne prods Sonia, "Do you want to ask if more people have things to say?" One side of the circle, consisting of mostly White girls, begins to heatedly discuss the problems with homework; one makes a passionate case that the lack of sleep caused by too much homework causes high dropout rates.

This discussion continues for the next fifteen minutes. Sitting near me, Jean-Luc, a Haitian immigrant, has his eyes closed. Next to him, Lucas, an African-American, whispers loudly to David, "I think they're getting a little carried away. I don't even know what we're talking about."

Finally, Suzanne interjects, "Let's get some hands on the other side."

---

[16] All names of people and places are pseudonyms.

"You can't stop this discussion. That's democracy," counters Victoria, the articulate young White woman whom I later find out is the niece of a state congressman. "Our whole class should just be a discussion. That's civics. This class should be a model."

A few days later, I reflect with Suzanne on the class. Seemingly out of nowhere, she asks, "Did I tell you about this, about Jean-Luc and the chairs?" She describes how, at the beginning of the semester, a guest speaker came to class and did an activity where chairs are divided up unequally between students (for instance, one student gets three chairs to herself, and six students share one chair) to simulate the unequal distribution of resources and prompt conversations about inequality and justice. She tells me:

> We haven't really talked about it since, and Jean-Luc came up to talk to me [after the class I observed] …The class discussion had been all about 'We shouldn't have any homework…there's too much homework' and he said, 'You know, Ms. S, I think we should have homework, you know.' He had his head down the whole day, and he goes, 'I was really listening…but you know what I'm thinking…I just keep going back to when that guy was in our class, and I just think I'm going to end up being one of the crowded people.' And I [Suzanne] I didn't know what to say, and I said, 'Well, we have to figure out how to make that not happen.'

Victoria's claim that "democracy" is seemingly open, yet dominated by elites, is a fair assessment of the current state of the United States political system, in which participation is also "often loud, sometimes clear, but rarely equal" (Verba, Schlozman, & Brady, 1995, p. 533). Fortunately, Suzanne is not alone in her attempts to "figure out how to make [disempowerment of poor, minority youth] not happen." Around the country, action civics organizations such as Mikva Challenge, UCCP, and Generation Citizen work to promote youth civic empowerment, often in impoverished, segregated urban areas.

However, the above anecdote illustrates the complexities of this task, especially in socioeconomically and racially diverse contexts; Suzanne struggles to maintain an open classroom climate, long recognized as a hallmark of effective civic education, while simultaneously attempting to coach a student in developing facilitation skills, soliciting the ideas of less vocal (and predominantly minority, poor, and, in this class, male) students, and creating consensus from diverse perspectives that will allow the class to take action. In spite of years of experience working with action-based civic education and diverse student populations, Suzanne's uncertainty about how to practice action civics in her classroom signals the need for a closer research-based look at how social processes in diverse action civics classrooms impact civic equality and empowerment among students.

In this paper, I present case studies of classes participating in an action civics program at two multiracial and economically diverse suburban high schools. These cases are guided by my research question: How do the interactions in diverse action civics classrooms support and/or undermine the promotion of civic empowerment and equality? By examining the experiences of teachers, mentors, and students in these classrooms, I hope to generate hypotheses about the social processes that might contribute to civic equality in diverse classrooms and provide guidance for other educators hoping to make the most of the unique, challenging, and understudied context for civic development that heterogeneous schools provide.

Theoretical Framework

The Civic Empowerment Gap

Traditionally, public schools in the United States have been seen as key institutions for sustaining or promoting democracy. Early leaders such as Thomas Jefferson, Daniel Webster, and Horace Mann focused on the design of education systems that prepared students for "the social duties and prerogatives that await them" (Mann, 1891, p. 4). However, most educational discourse since the Cold War era has focused on preparation for vocational roles and economic competitiveness, reflecting a shift away from the civic purposes of schooling (Reuben, 2005; Graham, 2005; Grubb & Lazerson, 2004). The lack of attention to civic development is particularly troubling given what Levinson (2010) has labeled the "civic empowerment gap," the race- and class-based discrepancy in civic motivation, knowledge, skills, and participation. For example, Black and Latino students are less likely to feel they can make a difference in solving community problems than White students (Carnegie Corporation of New York & CIRCLE, 2003), and the wealthiest Americans are up to six times more likely to serve on the board of a nonprofit, contact elected officials, or protest than the poorest (Levinson, 2010). Moreover, research suggests that poor and minority students have fewer opportunities to engage in classroom civic learning opportunities such as debates and service learning, which have been shown to increase students' civic engagement (Kahne & Middaugh, 2008; Wilkenfeld, 2008). These differences endanger not only the ability of individuals to participate in decisions affecting their own lives, but also the quality and legitimacy of democracy itself. All students deserve "the opportunity to make the United States a more just and equitable place on their own terms" (Levinson, 2012, p. 12) through the acquisition of skills, behaviors, and attitudes needed for success within local communities and in the broader society as well as the reshaping of power relationships to allow for the equitable consideration of diverse perspectives.

Best Practices for Civic Equality

According to Marri (2005), classroom-based multicultural education, which includes problem-posing pedagogy, community building, and curriculum that incorporates both mainstream and critical perspectives, is a promising framework for promoting the democratic participation of diverse students. Levinson (2012) highlights action civics, which incorporates many of these principles, as an especially effective practice for the promotion of civic equality. In this approach, teachers or facilitators guide students in choosing and researching an issue important to them, learning about strategies for influencing policies and public opinion, taking action, and reflecting on their work (Pope, Stolte, & Cohen, 2011). These programs are centered on curricula that reflect many identified best practices in civic education, such as instruction in government, discussion of current events, application of learning to address real-world issues, and simulations (Carnegie Corporation of New York and CIRCLE, 2003). While individual teachers and local organizations have long engaged students in action civics projects, large-scale implementation of and research on action civics methodology (as well as the term "action civics") are relatively recent. Standardized testing requirements and the intensive human resources required for implementing the methodology continues to limit its widespread use (Levinson, 2012). Nevertheless, organizations such as Mikva Challenge and Generation Citizen now involve thousands of students in action civics projects each semester. Moreover, research finds that the incorporation of practices such as issues discussion and action projects into civic education increases students' civic knowledge and behavior among all ethnic groups (Feldman, Pasek, Romer, & Jamieson, 2007).

The Importance of social Processes

Although resources like action civics curricula are important targets of intervention, Tseng and Seidman (2007) argue that they are "insufficient to change student achievement; rather, social processes such as instruction and role relationships must be altered in order to trigger significant educational change" (p. 219). They define social processes as interactions (such as norms and participation patterns) between people or groups that are molded by people's roles in a setting and reinforced over time. Acquisition of knowledge, skills, and motivation depends upon these interactions that take place in one's immediate environment, as well as the interactions between various settings that an individual experiences (Brofenbrenner & Morris, 1998). Understanding these social processes is necessary to understand and change outcomes, and is especially critical when considering disparities such as the civic empowerment gap, as interactions may differ between teachers and students within a classroom. For instance, likely due to a lack of cultural understanding, teachers tend to report less positive relationships with students who are of a different ethnicity from them (Hamre & Pianta, 2001; Meehan, Hughes, & Cavell, 2003), and what is beneficial for one group of students may involve a tradeoff for others within the same class. For instance, a teacher who devotes time to pushing the thinking of a given student may be able to invest less time interacting with other students.

While much of the research in the field of civic education has focused on explicit curricular dimensions, several scholars have recognized the importance of social processes in civic development. According to Flanagan, Cumsille, Gill, and Gallay (2007), students' level of civic commitment is correlated with the degree to which they feel their relationships with teachers are respectful, fair, and tolerant. Rubin (2007) details how students' experiences of congruence or disjuncture with democratic principles in their own lives relate to the development of their civic identities. For example, many students in an affluent high school demonstrate complacency because they generalize their positive interactions with authority to less privileged members of society, while some students at a poor school display discouragement due to the gap they recognize between democratic ideals and their experiences. Levinson (2012) asserts that, intentionally or not, all schools model and provide opportunities to practice norms, relationships, and behaviors that affect students' civic empowerment. In many low-income, minority schools, these practices take the form of constant "civic microaggressions" (p. 176), such as strictly regulating student movement, that emphasize control over learning and widen the civic empowerment gap. She emphasizes the need for intentional, transparent, reflective, and authentic practices that build upon student strengths and develop capacities for leadership and collective action.

Diverse Schools as a Context for Promoting Civic Equality

One critical characteristic of social processes is that they are not traits of individuals, but of a setting (Tseng & Seidman, 2007). Different contexts are likely to engender distinct patterns of interactions, with consequences for academic and civic outcomes. Rubin and Hayes (2010) demonstrate how context, as well as the social processes within varied settings, play an important role in the outcomes of action civics programs, and argue that successful programs must be attentive to the distinct needs of communities. For instance, students in more privileged, congruent settings must be pushed to look outside of their own experiences, while students in settings of disjuncture must have academically challenging and emotionally supportive opportunities to be heard.

While the concern for the civic empowerment of youth in urban, poor, de facto segregated schools and communities is justified (Levinson, 2012), focusing exclusively on those settings will not close the civic empowerment gap. An increasing number of students, including at least a quarter of Black and Latino students, attend multiracial schools, in which more than ten percent of students come from each of three or more racial groups (Orfield, 2009). Moreover, Orfield defines the increasing diversification of the suburbs as the "race relations challenge of this generation" (p. 17). The perspectives of poor and minority students in these contexts are likely to differ from both urban youth and from more affluent and/or White schoolmates, and must be considered in attempts to create greater civic equality.

Furthermore, diverse schools are full of "possibilities and perils" (Orfield, 2009, p. 15) that matter for civic engagement. Socioeconomic, racial, and political diversity all serve as proxies for a diversity of perspective, which must be taken into account in a healthy democracy. Orfield argues that integrated schools are some of the best settings to learn valuable skills such as working together across lines of difference and understanding other perspectives, and Rubin (2007) finds that students in a racially and socioeconomically diverse school have particularly active, aware civic identities. However, even within diverse schools, tracking often separates students along race and class lines (Orfield, 2009). Moreover, Campbell (2005) demonstrates that students feel teachers are less likely to promote discussion of social and political issues when in a racially diverse class, and Putnam (2007) finds that members of diverse communities tend to be less civically engaged. These large-scale quantitative studies suggest that diverse contexts may present challenges in promoting civic engagement. However, they provide little understanding of how specific social processes relate to the development of civic and political attitudes, skills, knowledge, and behaviors for diverse individuals in heterogeneous settings. For instance, collaborative, equal-status settings are important for many social and educational outcomes (Pettigrew & Tropp, 2006), and the power dynamics present in diverse schools and communities can create unique challenges that must be negotiated in order to empower less privileged youth and adults. For instance, Carlock (2011) describes how a group of parents learning English as a Second Language collectively organized in order to challenge school restructuring plans promoted by wealthy, primarily White and English-speaking, parents. Diverse classes are likely to consist of students who regularly experience both congruence and disjuncture; these perspectives may give them greater insight into issues such as discrimination and possible solutions as they learn from peers (Rubin, 2007), but also challenges teachers to effectively meet the varied needs of students and manage a more complicated social milieu.

Little research examines multiracial, economically diverse schools, and educators have scant knowledge of best practices in these environments (Orfield, 2009). While action civics is a promising approach for promoting civic and political equality, it is important to understand the unique social processes taking place among students and teachers in these settings and how they may affect the outcomes of action civics programs. This analysis will contribute to the understanding of these mechanisms by addressing the question: How do social processes in diverse action civics classrooms support and/or undermine the promotion of civic equality and empowerment?

Methods

Case Selection

Generation Citizen is a nonprofit, based in New York, Boston, and Providence, that seeks to empower youth to become engaged, effective citizens through participation in an action-based civics curriculum. The organization's relationships with socioeconomically and racially diverse schools and other organizations provided an ideal context to address my research question, and to use my results in improving the practice of both a young nonprofit and a network of other action civics organizations. By volunteering with Generation Citizen for over two years, I built relationships with participants and gained the knowledge necessary for contextualizing my findings and ensuring that they represent multiple perspectives.

With the support of Generation Citizen staff, I identified the teachers whose classrooms serve as the cases for my study. Both schools have at least 10 percent of students from four major ethnic groups, and both classes are reflective of the school population as a whole. While many forms of diversity appear to affect social interactions and civic outcomes (Putnam, 2007; Campbell, 2005; Campbell, 2006), I have selected schools based on diversity of race and class because data on these dimensions is readily available and they are particularly strong markers of general diversity in perspective and experience (Campbell, 2005) as well as civic engagement (Levinson, 2012). Nevertheless, I have observed that political, linguistic, and gender composition also impacted social processes in the classes, as noted in the findings.

I chose to analyze two different classrooms because teachers play an important role in establishing classroom social processes, and observing multiple approaches allowed me to gain a broader understanding of the range of social processes in diverse action civics classrooms. Moreover, factors such as the age of students, the distinct variations in social class, and the degree of teacher curricular autonomy, all of which are discussed in the context section, differed between settings and likely affected classroom interactions. While I did not select research sites based on these factors, I have detailed them to help readers determine to what extent they might be an influence on social processes in these and other settings.

While two cases cannot in any way represent diverse action civics classrooms generally, I seek to provide a rich description of each context in order to enable the reader to judge if the findings make sense and may be transferable to their context. This transferability does not allow for automatic generalization to other settings, but permits a deeper understanding of how findings may be applicable to a new situation (Merriam, 1998); I anticipate that educators attempting to implement action civics in a variety of settings will be able to "extract a universal from a particular" (p. 210) that is relevant to their practice.

Data Collection and Analysis

The use of multiple methods is especially critical when studying social processes, as they take place within a group but are mediated by individuals (Tseng & Seidman, 2007). For this reason, I triangulated data from multiple observations and interviews, allowing me to enhance internal validity and gain a well-rounded perspective on the social processes taking place over time in a classroom and their relationship to action civics principles.

I observed each class three times and took detailed field notes that I shared with teachers, often provoking informal discussions. These conversations provided opportunities for multiple interpretations of the data, one means of assuring internal validity (Merriam, 1998). Both teachers noted that this opportunity for reflection also led to improvements in practice.

Within each classroom, the teacher and I used a diverse-case selection strategy (Gerring, 2007) to select three students who differed in observed classroom engagement, race, and gender; these variables are likely to signal diverse experiences of the social processes in a classroom (Pianta & Allen, 2008). I conducted semi-structured interviews with these students, their teacher, and volunteer mentors. Interviews focused on the participants' experience of social processes in the action civics classrooms, as well as how these interactions related to students' development of civic attitudes, skills, and behaviors. All interviews were recorded, transcribed, and de-identified.

To code data, I used a grounded theory approach, reading through transcripts and fieldnotes and creating codes that summarized each utterance or incident. I then compared within and across interviews and observations and grouped similar codes together (Charmaz, 2006), identifying categories of interactions in each classroom and their relationship to patterns in demonstrated skills, attitudes, and habits among students.

Context

I met both Suzanne and Beth, the teachers in the two case study classrooms, as I helped Generation Citizen facilitate a professional development workshop before the start of the 2010-11 school year. Most schools that Generation Citizen serves are located in urban centers, but both sites in this study are located just outside a large northeastern city. Thus, while Generation Citizen's participants are overwhelmingly low-income and Black and Latino overall, Durham (Beth's school) and Waterford (Suzanne's school) are more diverse. Both exemplify the multiracial schools Orfield (2009) describes, and contend with the challenges and benefits of socioeconomic difference.

Waterford is about one-third African American and one-third White. Asian and Hispanic students each comprise just over ten percent of the population. (Massachusetts Department of Education, 2012). Its median income is close to that of the state as a whole, but with substantially more economic inequality than average (U.S. Census Bureau, 2011). Just over a quarter of students' first language is not English. As the only non-charter public high school in a university town with a strong economy, the school is well resourced. While many classes at the school are highly tracked, Suzanne's new elective Civics in Action class, which she developed, attracted a wide variety of junior and senior students, ranging from the student body president and vice president to students at risk of not graduating. As measured by partisanship, the community is ideologically homogeneous, with more than 80 percent of the population voting for the Democratic candidate in recent presidential and senatorial elections (Bloch et al., 2010).

About 30 percent of Durham's students are White, and just over a fifth African American, a fifth Asian, and a fifth Hispanic (Massachusetts Department of Education, 2012). It is poorer and less socioeconomically diverse than Waterford, with many working-class families and public sector employees. Around two-thirds of students at the high school are low-income, and the town's Gini coefficient indicates slightly less income inequality than average (U.S. Census Bureau, 2011). While many families in Durham have lived there for several generations, its accessibility and affordability have made it attractive to some young professionals and a large number of immigrants. Almost half of students at Durham do not speak English as their first language. Beth taught U.S. History I, a required class for all 9th graders, and Generation Citizen was part of a department-wide initiative to develop 21st century skills through special programming. While her classes were tracked into college prep and honors levels, some students were placed into the honors track due to scheduling needs, not perceived merit, and Beth asserted (and my observations confirmed) that "the kids are all mixed, there's not one dominant ethnic group or religion or socioeconomic group." Durham is more ideologically diverse than Waterford, while still consistently Democratic. While two-thirds of voters selected Obama in the 2008 presidential elections, just over half voted for the Democratic candidate in the most recent senatorial election (Bloch et al., 2010).

Both Beth and Suzanne were experienced teachers and had experimented with other approaches that promote civic engagement in the past, such as service learning. Compared to other classes I observed, both Suzanne and Beth played an especially active role in planning lessons and often adapted the curriculum to meet the needs of their students. One feature of the Generation Citizen program that distinguishes it from other action civics organizations is that college student mentors partner with classroom teachers to teach the curriculum. The role of college mentors varies from class to class, but in Suzanne's and Beth's classes both the teacher and mentors led instruction, conferred with students, and sought out resources.

Beth's classes worked on two issues: a new school policy prohibiting the consumption of junk food, and a city ordinance that required the bagging of trash in special bags in an effort to encourage recycling. Many students were initially opposed to the school policy, crafted in response to federal guidelines. However, in small groups, students created videos, posters, and other media about healthy eating and lobbied for healthier food in the cafeteria. Students also initially opposed the recycling ordinance, and developed plans for holding a new referendum on the issue. (There was an attempt to repeal the law several years before, but it failed due to insufficient voter turnout.) However, as they researched the issue, the class decided to support the ordinance instead and developed an awareness campaign about the importance of recycling.[17]

Suzanne's class decided to focus on educational issues, and students divided in groups to take action on three issues:

---

[17] Several students expressed disagreement with project goals at various times in the semester. While some students did change their minds, Beth guided this shift. As discussed below, this is evidence of both the authoritative role she played in the classroom and of the emphasis on skills development over authenticity.

the election of a student voting member to the school board, the use of student surveys in teacher evaluation, and the creation of a financial literacy class. These issues were particularly timely, as all were being considered at the state or local level at the time. Students wrote letters to state officials and spoke with local officials sharing their perspectives. A state financial literacy bill was passed soon after students began work on the project, and details on the other projects were still being finalized when the class ended.

Findings

In the classes I studied, social processes around grouping students, participating in discussions, and making decisions emerged as important interactions that reflected distinct approaches to empowering diverse students. In Durham, the development of discrete skills took precedence and the teacher maintained power over students, providing little opportunity for them to engage in authentic civic action. In interviews, students expressed little propensity for recognizing their civic capacities or engaging in collective action or leadership. In Waterford, the teacher and mentors valued authenticity, and the meaningful context provided a range of students with opportunities to actually practice civic skills. However, the authentic civic experiences in which Waterford students engaged often replicated, rather than disrupted, power dynamics present in the school and larger society, with White and middle-class students displaying greater participation and leadership.

Through both these experiences, students developed distinct habits and attitudes that failed to narrow, and may have exacerbated, the civic empowerment gap. The interactions in each context reinforced existing power differentials. Thus, while my analysis confirms the importance of the authenticity Levinson (2012) asserts is needed to promote civic equality, it also indicates that educators must take into account the unique challenges that arise in diverse contexts and create new norms that explicitly address existing power relationships.

Case 1: Durham

"Authoritative" classroom social processes.

"How do I connect it to the curriculum?": Skills as the key to civic empowerment

Beth's approach to empowering her students was through the explicit teaching of and practice with skills such as writing, marking up reading texts, and public speaking; in fact, she describes these discrete skills as "civic engagement, really...you're going to need those for life, no matter where you go or what you do." Her methods reflected a push in her department to integrate 21st century skills into history coursework through project-based learning (PBL). Moreover, her own conception of citizenship primarily emphasized individual work and participation in organized groups, rather than collective action; she describes that her own civic involvement "came...from more the community service angle." The action component of the Generation Citizen program was a complement to, rather than a centerpiece of, the curriculum, and she saw it as "sort of overwhelming at first, just thinking how do I connect it to the curriculum, how do I fit it in?" As a result, the curriculum, rather than student interests or the specific demands of the action projects, appeared to drive instruction.

Beth carefully planned lessons to ensure that all students had opportunities to practice skills. For instance, to develop persuasive speaking skills, she divided students into groups of four. Each student took a turn playing one of four roles: speaker (extemporaneously explaining their opinion on a given topic), encourager (identifying what the speaker did well), improver (sharing an area for improvement), and notetaker (taking notes and deciding if message was clear). In an interview later that day, one student saw this skill as transferable to other contexts (though not necessarily civic action), stating, "I learned when you speak to look people in the eyes, to have proper language, and everything. That's good, because when you get a professional job you might have to use that." Beth also highlighted the use of two-column notes and other literacy activities in helping students to think critically about issues, and noted they were especially important in a diverse class "with such a range of English, with such a range of abilities, so many different backgrounds." Diversity was seen as a challenge to be confronted through the use of differentiation strategies, but not an integral part of civic education.

"They're usually good if they're not forced to work with someone they don't like": Grouping students

One way of focusing students on developing skills was through norms that minimized conflict and reduced complexity. Beth did this through grouping students, controlling classroom dialogue, and providing limited options to students.

Beth placed desks in her classroom in groups of four, and, while many students sat with their friends, she assigned seats to some students. She explained:

> There are a couple of students that kind of need to be separated...because there's some very different types of personalities and groups in that class. So I've kind of had to always try to watch and make sure certain groups don't work together. Not bad, but just a little tension there, and they're usually good if they're not forced to work with someone they don't like.

The students I interviewed described how they tended to work individually or talk with others who speak the same language. Corina said, "Me, I just keep to myself. I don't really talk to people in the class…I don't care. The only person I talk to is the kid who sits next to me." Ann, a Chinese student, explained, "I have two Asian girls in my group and me, and all of us three just talk our Mandarin to each other." Beth conveyed her expectation that students primarily work on individual skill development by assigning seats to disruptive students but not forcing the development of relationships among students, and students responded to this expectation by working individually or with students they saw as similar to themselves, especially students who spoke the same native language.[18]

"If you ask questions, they usually don't respond": Controlling discussion

The "hub-and-spoke" discussion pattern Beth established, in which conversation "radiat[es] out from and then quickly back to the teacher" (Levinson, 2012, p. 193), also served to minimize conflict and reduce complex, but possibly tangential, conversation. In the exchange below, Beth cut short a discussion that some could find offensive, but in doing so failed to engage students in discussing legitimate questions students had about the nutrition policy and the direction of their action project.

> Beth: Michelle Obama is working against childhood obesity. It would be good to find out what she's doing.
> Student 1: Why is it the kids? Adults are fat, too.

---

[18] Providing opportunities for native language use is an important characteristic of inclusive classrooms and democracies. However, there is no evidence that language was intentionally used here as a tool to facilitate learning and action.

> Beth: The reason they do in the schools is there's an increase in childhood obesity.
> Student 2: They're just going to get fat when they get out of school.
> Student 1: It's not a bad thing, you choose to be fat.
> Beth (moving on to the next group): What did you find out?

In another instance, Beth opened up a discussion before introducing a local newspaper editorial that challenged the class's dominant stance against the recycling ordinance. However, the discussion did not allow students an opportunity to share their ideas or anticipate what supporters might say.

> Beth: How many know what "going green" means?
> Student: Saving energy
> Beth: Does anyone use reusable bags? (Same student raises hand)
> Beth: Maybe "going green" isn't what's best for Durham…We're going to read this and mark it up to see if we can get more information.

While this practice is extremely common, to the point of being almost invisible to participants, it limits students' opportunities to develop and understand their own ideas and those of classmates (Levinson, 2012). Moreover, while my data do not suggest causality, there was a low level of interest in discussion among students. Beth worried that at times her class can be "all about work and focus, that can be a challenge when trying to have a discussion," and Philip tied the lack of participation in discussion to lack of interest in their action project more generally, stating that "People don't care…cause if you ask questions, they usually don't respond to them." Through her facilitation of class discussion, Beth communicated to students that while short, on-topic comments were welcomed, class discussions were not a forum for exploring new ideas.

"At what point does 51 percent decide everything?": Providing limited options

A third norm in Beth's class was providing limited options to students, by encouraging students to classify ideas into set categories and framing decision-making as selecting from a small number of choices. Students voted for their focus issue, choosing between options identified in class and chosen by the teacher and mentors. Later, as students worked on developing public speaking skills, students were asked to explain why one speaker on a video was "bad" and another was "good," rather than explaining how both speakers demonstrated both positive and negative traits. Then, to practice, mentors asked students to choose between options like "Pepsi or Coke?" going to different sides of the room to indicate their preference. Several students said, "I don't drink soda," so the mentor told those who were unsure to come up front. While students on the sides made thoughtful arguments, the number of students in the center continued to grow throughout the activity, eventually numbering more than half the class. These students were not asked to explain their thinking, and many began talking quietly to friends while the mentors focused on those on the sides. While students were expected to choose between presented options, they were not empowered to disrupt the decision-making process by taking an alternative perspective or synthesizing multiple ideas.

Beth noted that voting to decide students' action issue was problematic and did not appear to promote equality or empowerment.

> It was difficult too with the voting process, cause a lot of the topics were very close...If the class is pretty evenly divided, then what do you do then? How do we make that more democratic? And I know that's how democracy

> is sometimes…you have to accept that you're
> not always going to get what you want. But I'm
> worried with the motivation going ahead…if
> they didn't get the one they wanted, how to
> keep them going and how to keep them
> interested…At what point does 51 percent
> decide everything?

Nevertheless, the repetition of this practice in each class I observed suggests that the norm was largely invisible even to Beth. In a diverse class that was likely to have a large, perhaps even overwhelming, variety of perspectives on issues, this norm served to limit conflict and impose clarity on complex processes, which may be desirable given the focus on acquisition of discrete skills. However, when the choices presented or the decisions made did not represent the perspectives of students, engagement visibly decreased. For instance, Ann described feeling conflicted about her own love of junk food and the project's focus on healthy eating, but she grew disengaged without an opportunity to wrestle with her ambivalence about the focus issue; "I have no feeling, I'm not mad, I'm just like I don't care," she reported. Forcing students to choose between options, rather than create new ones, may be discouraging and may unwittingly sustain divisive and less inclusive political processes.

Civic equality and empowerment in Durham.

Beth established the norms described above with the intent of promoting civic and academic skill development. Providing students with the opportunity to choose their own seats and make choices about the project was designed to enhance students' efficacy, while assigning seats to disruptive students and limiting options minimized distractions. Hub-and-spoke discussions allowed students to share ideas while ensuring that conversations stayed focused on learning goals. These norms reflected a controlling yet nurturing *authoritative* classroom management style that is widely associated with the most positive student academic and behavioral outcomes (Walker, 2009).

However, students in Beth's class saw themselves as having almost no agency in making decisions in their school or community, as demonstrated by comments such as "We're only kids and students, we can't make the decisions" and "The city wants us to do it (buy trash bags), so I guess we have to do it." While they initially saw their identified issues as relevant and exciting, motivation soon waned and students saw the project as purely academic, an assignment that "was just like ok, let's get it over with."

Mentor Samantha attributed students' desire to "get it over with" to a myopic focus on discrete skill development, divorced from the demands of civic action.

> I just think it's hard sometimes when she's [Beth] trying to teach skills; she's trying to teach writing skills, note-taking skills, different things like that, but when it takes 20 minutes to take out your computer and write on your wiki page, we could be using that time to make a Facebook event and start this. Right now, the program is directed on the curriculum, and learning and doing things out of the book...it should have less to do with teaching skills, and more with doing skills.

"Doing skills," however, presented a challenge to the expectations of the school setting. While Beth intentionally gave students relatively equal opportunities to practice civic skills in the context of an action civics project, the interactions she established in her classroom were the *authoritative norms* of school, not those of politics or community action. By grouping students, conducting discussions, and limiting options in a way that reduced conflict and seemingly extraneous complexity, Beth created a setting designed to maximize the effects of classroom instruction. However, ironically, it may have actually inhibited the acquisition of civic skills. Delpit (1995) suggests that direct skills instruction is necessary for poor and minority students, but only within an authentic context. Students perceived their work on the project as inauthentic, decreasing motivation. Moreover, without a meaningful situation to reflect on, they appeared unable to transfer what they had learned to real-life civic situations. The consistently disempowered outlooks of Beth's students appear to confirm the importance of authenticity, transparency, and reflection, as Levinson (2012) argues.

Discussion

Taking 21ˢᵗ Century Civic Skills Seriously

While Beth, along with her mentors and students, played a significant role in establishing interactions in her classroom, her decisions were influenced by a school culture and wider educational climate that value individual achievement, focusing more on economic success than democratic participation (Grubb & Lazerson, 2004). In professional development sessions at Durham, conversation often focused on preparing students for district assessments, even on days devoted to action civics. Within the field of civic education, the majority of school-based programs focus on an apolitical, individualistic form of citizenship that fails to engage students in analyzing causes of social issues or acting collectively (Westheimer & Kahne, 2004); while Generation Citizen seeks to challenge this trend, teachers were simultaneously participating in other initiatives, such as service-learning trainings, that may have reinforced this conception and left them unclear about their goals for students. Moreover, since Beth's own notion of being a good teacher and citizen was that of being "personally responsible" and "participatory" (Westheimer & Kahne,

2004), she was unlikely to challenge those norms on her own. Focusing on individual skills development, rather than the action project itself, aligned with Beth's conceptions of citizenship and allowed her to align herself with her school's priorities.

The authoritative social processes she relied upon were appropriate for teaching informational content and basic skills (Walker, 2009), and were intended to create a setting that supports individual academic achievement. However, they also reflected a limited conception of the capacities students need for both academic and civic success. While the school expressed commitment to 21st century skills, it chose to focus on proficiencies, such as integrating technology into lessons, that aligned most easily with current practices and mandated assessments. Through prioritizing skills that emphasized individual achievement, important skills relevant to civic engagement in a diverse context were largely ignored, such as "learning from and working collaboratively with individuals representing diverse cultures, religions and lifestyles in a spirit of mutual respect and open dialogue in personal, work and community contexts" (Partnership for 21st Century Skills, 2009, p. 2) and "levera[ging] social and cultural differences to create new ideas and increase both innovation and quality of work" (p. 7). The diverse environment presented a promising opportunity to develop these increasingly important capacities; nevertheless, classroom social processes did not facilitate collective action. As a result, like the inhabitants of diverse communities described by Putnam (2007), Beth's students "hunker[ed] down" (p. 149), focusing only on individual achievement. However, is this decreased civic engagement an inevitable consequence of a diverse context? The case of Waterford presents a more complicated picture of the relationship between social processes and civic empowerment and equality.

Case 2: Waterford

"Authentic" classroom social processes.

"A completely different skill set": Passion (and persistence) as the key to civic empowerment

In contrast, Suzanne focused on the development of students' passions as the key to personal growth and civic empowerment, and worked to structure her classroom in a way that allowed students to explore and reflect on their interests. She explained that

> So many kids can't identify passions, or they don't know what I mean when I'm asking that…it takes a lot of coaxing and personal comfort for kids to be able to talk about what they're passionate about. I always try to put those kinds of activities in the Do Now, and then everyone share out, and I always answer the question for myself as well. Just trying to expose them, because I worry that they have this set list of things that are political action things that they've seen other kids do that they fall back on, that's why, as the teacher, I feel like I need to show them some of the world issues they haven't thought about before.

Suzanne and the mentors in her class differentiated true passion from the momentary excitement students displayed when embarking on a new project, and believed that this persistent passion was closely tied to students' sense of efficacy. Suzanne wondered "Do you need to know who you are, or have some sense of who you are, before you do something, or do you develop who you are by doing something?" while mentor James argued

We can tell them all we want that you can make a difference, but they won't believe it until they do make a difference. It's not necessarily difficult, but it takes a lot of patience. It's not difficult in the academic sense to make a difference, not like learning a really difficult equation or doing some crazy math proof. It's a completely different skill set it's like patience and perseverance, passion, just totally different.

Suzanne was particularly concerned about helping less privileged students in her diverse class identify their passions. She often met with these students, such as Jean-Luc, one-on-one outside of class, and, as director of the school's internship program, placed others with local organizations that allowed them to explore interests in more depth.

Both Suzanne and her mentors expressed frustration at how the school environment discouraged the development of passion. James felt that his attempts to discuss passions with students were met with resistance, because students believed that "school's not about being passionate," and Suzanne explained that "[t]here's always going to be something very artificial about it, because it has to end on this particular day, and on this particular time every day." However, Suzanne believed that "making it as authentic as possible" would provide students with some opportunities to pursue their passions.

"It works best in a circle": Choosing one's own place

The norms Suzanne established in her classroom mirrored those common in decision-making processes outside of school. Students were allowed to choose their own seats, frequently engaged in open discussion, and used consensus as a decision-making strategy. Suzanne placed students' desks in a circle, and then allowed students to choose their own seats. As illustrated in the opening anecdote, students tended to sit in racial and gender groups, with the most vocal segment of the circle consisting mostly of White females, and quieter groups consisting of females of color and males. Placing students in the circle was a conscious attempt to promote equality; Suzanne explained that

> Lately I've been noticing that certain kids who had not been speaking are speaking, and it works best in a circle, because they can see each other, and the kids in the back aren't in the back anymore. And I feel like I need to move around where I sit in the circle, because that will make a difference in where the top of the circle is.

When I asked about the self-grouping of students, Suzanne explained "I have such a hard time assigning seats...I think it's mean at this point or something, cause they're like 11th and 12th graders, and I'm already controlling so much in the class."

Suzanne sought to promote more equal participation in her classroom, and communicated that expectation through the arrangement of desks into a circle. However, she was hesitant to curtail students' freedom or overly structure the conversation by assigning seats. This pattern of wavering between creating more structured, yet equitable, opportunities for participation and facilitating more authentic, yet unequal experiences was also evident in students' discussion and decision-making, as discussed below.

"If you scream, your voice got across": Facilitating open discussion

To a large extent, Suzanne's class exemplified the open classroom climate that has consistently been associated with a range of civic knowledge, skills, and behaviors (Campbell, 2005; Levinson, 2012). Students discussed controversial current events and social issues, and Suzanne regularly pressed students to consider other perspectives. She reminded students of the need to adhere to classroom norms promoting mutual respect. However, while classroom discussion was open and authentic, it was rarely equitable. As described above, White girls tended to dominate the discussion. Moreover, both Suzanne and the students I interviewed suggested that while many saw the discussion as democratic, few saw it as desirable. Suzanne complained that "[the students] keep saying, let's run this class like a democracy, and what that means to them is everyone shouting things when they want." Marc, who is African American, elaborated on Suzanne's assessment of the classroom climate and described its effect on the class's thinking

> Basically if you scream, your voice got across. You had to be loud, cause we had a lot of loud people in our class. But Ms. Scott would join in at times, after a lot of people would talk, and let quiet persons speak. She would stop the loud person from trying to butt in so that student could get their opinion across, but I thought if you were able to speak up and project your voice, your opinion would be taken more into account in the discussion.

Marc and Liz, who is White, both found it hard to enter into the conversation, but felt that, in the words of Liz, "at one point everyone got to say what they had to say." However, Andrew, a White male who self-identified as the only political conservative in the class, noted that while students had opportunities to speak, minority perspectives were rarely taken seriously.

I did share my opinions, they weren't taken as well as I thought they would…When I give my opinion, everyone is like Oh my god, you terrible person…Definitely everyone who screamed got their points across, but mostly people who were in the majority…I'm not saying that everyone in the majority was loud, but people who were in the minority, which I guess I'm going to have to put myself into, didn't really get their point across.

Some students, such as Jean-Luc, responded to this pattern by remaining silent, while others, like Andrew, participated but grew increasingly cynical and frustrated. While these reactions are authentic in that they reflect many citizens' responses to political discussion today, they are also troubling. Moreover, because participation patterns corresponded to racial, gender, and ideological divides in the classroom, the norm of "everyone shouting things" reinforced the civic empowerment gap. In the larger political arena, research shows that a focus on political conflict in media leads to increased cynicism among young people (Cappella, 2002), and that aversion to conflict leads to decreases in some types of political participation, especially among the economically and educationally disadvantaged (Ulbig & Frank, 1999).

"We all had ideas, and we just had to put them together": Imagining consensus

Suzanne's concern with providing students with authentic civic experiences led her to worry about controlling decision-making processes too much and to embrace a deliberative model of classroom democracy. Most decisions about the action project appeared to emerge organically from class or small-group discussion, rather than through teacher decree or teacher-structured activities, such as voting or set procedures for action planning. Liz explained that

> We went around and did things that were like, what people wanted to work on, and a lot of them had to do with education so we narrowed it down to that…in terms of decision-making in the group, we all had ideas, and we just had to put them together. Say we needed to get into contact with someone, it was just a matter of who was going to do it, and I think we all took on certain responsibilities.

However, the use of deliberative structures for decision-making masked disagreements that existed in the class (such as the opinions of Andrew and Jean-Luc described above) and made the role that existing power relationships played in decision-making appear to be natural or inevitable (Mansbridge, 1984). Andrew, who couldn't identify a decision he helped make, said "I would say more of the decision-making went to a couple of the seniors, Victoria, who's class president, and her vice-president, Zelda. I guess those two made sizable decisions, I guess that's probably good because they were in student government and they had that natural leadership skill automatically I guess." James described the class's process of choosing a focus issue as "a fake democratic system where [the students] kind of vote on the issue and they kind of chose education but we also definitely pushed them towards choosing education in kind of undemocratic ways." For instance, Liz attributed her role in contacting the school committee to Suzanne's direct intervention: "We were going to try to contact somebody from the school committee board, Ms. Scott looked at our group and she just asked me if I would be willing to do it and I said yes." This intervention was an important moment for Liz; it helped her overcome her self-described shyness, and her subsequent interactions with the school committee taught her that "we have an important voice…that actually they cared and wanted us to speak out, that they were willing to take what we had to say into consideration, that they were willing to help us and work with us, that was exciting." Nevertheless, Suzanne's ambivalence about being too "controlling" led her to intervene sporadically and individually rather than at a class level. This likely resulted in missed opportunities for the engagement of other students - in particular poor, minority, and male students – and in missed opportunities for modeling and practicing more equitable decision-making processes. By upholding deliberative norms as an ideal and largely, but not completely, renouncing her powerful decision-making role, Suzanne renders the power relationships in her class invisible, rather than confronting them. Explicitly naming and addressing imbalances in power relationships likely would not only promote more diversity in student participation, but also make students more attentive to these issues and capable of addressing them in other contexts.

Civic equality and empowerment in Waterford.

Suzanne intentionally established *authentic* classroom social processes in an attempt to help her students develop passion for civic engagement. She explained that her own civic engagement began when she was a student at a Catholic high school, and "really concerned about issues of justice…the way I internalized the teachings were about justice for everyone." She remembered arguing with teachers who had less progressive social views than she did and that those disagreements led her to organize a social action week at her school. Later, she became involved in women's rights and international justice movements, and continues to work with asylum seekers. Her own "justice-oriented" (Westheimer & Kahne, 2004) conception of citizenship led her to engage her students in attempting systemic change in the education system and to be (perhaps overly) concerned about the power dynamics between students and teacher. Moreover, teaching an elective class at a well-resourced school (with higher test scores than Durham) enabled her to have the flexibility needed to maintain this focus.

Compared to Beth's class, students demonstrated more engagement in class activities and exhibited, through their class project, many of the specific skills (e.g., public speaking and letter writing) that Beth had hoped to develop in her students. Moreover, some students reported that they were now capable of transferring these attitudes and skills to new contexts. When I asked Liz what she had gained from participating in action civics, she appeared able to synthesize several experiences.

> I would just say the whole step-by-step process of just starting off very small, like making a plan of what you need to do, getting in touch with people, and getting information, and going from there. It's really just a small step-by-step process when you're trying to make a change. So I think that's the best thing I got out of this process, learning how the process works and what to do.

Her experience speaking with a school committee member was particularly impactful, teaching her to "just be able to say the things you have to say and actually know someone will listen."

However, the social processes in the class appeared to reinforce existing power dynamics - many, but not all, of which reflected power differentials in the wider society. Not explicitly challenging these norms and relationships allowed students to maintain disempowering attitudes. Andrew and Marc, for instance, both saw leadership potential as fixed; as quoted above, Andrew attributed the role Victoria and Zelda played in decision-making to their "natural leadership skill," and Marc, when asked how he would define democracy, replied "I think it means that everybody has an opportunity for their voice to be heard, everybody can run for office, and – I'm not really educated enough to answer that." Marc saw himself as a potential civic participant, but not a leader. He was personally interested in the issue of minorities' access to AP and honors classes and saw it as "one thing I'd be willing to devote a lot of time to" in the future, but did not see himself taking a "main job" with a program focused on that issue. Andrew, whose opinions most obviously differed from his classmates, expressed civic attitudes surprisingly similar to the "discouraged" identity Rubin (2007) found primarily among low-income and minority students, in spite of his seemingly privileged position as a White male. His comments, such as those shared above, suggest that a feeling of disjuncture can exist not only between democratic ideals and lived experiences of structural inequality, but also between ideals and social interactions within the classroom. While Andrew minimized the effects of these interactions on his identity, claiming that he was "just not into politics," his outspoken views on political issues throughout class discussions and our interview suggest otherwise. James, the mentor, recognized that many students did not feel their perspectives were valued.

> One of the big problems is that they just don't have the confidence to speak up, that they can be real members of society that can make decisions...Which is probably caused by the fact that they're going through their lives, and being told what to do at all times, and not having any power or any responsibility...I think it's dangerous to create a society like that, people who are always looking away from decision-makers, from decision-making processes.

In spite of participating in an intentional, reflective, and authentic civic experience focused on collective action, some students in Suzanne's class failed to develop leadership skills or see themselves as competent, valuable civic actors. This

148

points to a tension, which may be unique to diverse classrooms, between engaging students in authentic civic experiences (which often reflect the inequitable existing power structures present in the school and broader civic life) and structuring more equitable, yet simulated or highly scaffolded, encounters with democratic practices.

Another possibility: "Transformative" classroom social processes.

Suzanne often wrestled with this tension, vacillating between *authentic* social processes such as open discussions and seemingly spontaneous interventions designed to promote equality and enhance reflection, such as asking a particular student to take on a particular role in a discussion or project. However, Suzanne's interview indicated a desire for more systematic attention to the challenges of empowering all students in a diverse context.

> [The students] don't have a deep enough understanding I think of the challenge of pluralism and diversity, and I think I just need to do more with that. They always say that diversity, and having tons of different viewpoints is the best part about it, and then they also say it's so annoying that we have two parties. And I'm like, so what would happen if we had one party? So I feel like there's something missing, and I'm not sure how to get them to it.

While she did not practice them consistently, Suzanne shared ideas for what I call *transformative* social processes, which simultaneously build upon and challenge the authentic yet inequitable practices common in democratic decision-making today. These practices are authentic in that they could be used in settings outside the classroom; however, they intentionally restructure interactions in a more equitable way that solicits diverse perspectives and incorporates them into decision-making processes. For instance, Suzanne suggested

> I was thinking like maybe I can do ladder of feedback protocols, or work on different protocols for speaking and discussions, but at the same time I think I don't want to control things like that too much, but I can pitch it as a skill about how to deepen a conversation.

By creating a structured process that provides all participants time to share the strengths and concerns they see in a proposal in a small group, the ladder of feedback and other protocols can help all group members constructively participate in decision-making and deepen their understandings of an issue (Making Learning Visible, n.d.). While, as Suzanne notes, a protocol is a means of controlling discussion and decision-making processes, it does so in a way that encourages all participants to share ideas and listen to each other, promoting more equitable participation.

Suzanne also was skilled at modeling synthetic thinking that integrated multiple perspectives for students. Andrew noted

> [Suzanne] definitely was a very understanding person, she could take two sides and say well they do have reasons to say this, but other people also have reasons to say this, and they also have the freedom to disagree. She could take more than one idea, put them together, and present them to the class, and we could learn from that. So, yeah, she's definitely a great person to learn under.

However, Suzanne was unsure how to help her students practice this skill, especially in a large, diverse class.

> I totally want to synthesize, and that's just a challenge in the classroom, and a challenge in the country, I guess, to get to a common understanding...I feel like the reflection is where the synthesis can happen, cause you go back and you look...It just feels like that's almost its own separate class, like how do we work together, and how do we talk to each other...I think I was worried about holding on to the synthesis in a way, in doing those kinds of conversations. Yeah, I think I could have done more around civil discourse and community building, and relationship building, and I didn't.

Promoting synthetic thinking that invites conflicting perspectives but works toward a common understanding is an important skill for diverse classrooms and communities. However, it is difficult to put into practice; participants must master the distinct social processes of both democracy based on conflicting goals and democracy based on common interests (Mansbridge, 1984), and learn when to use each. Groups that must live and work together (such as classrooms) often understandably prefer to avoid, rather than provoke, conflict (Ulbig & Funk, 1999). However, without explicit attention to respectfully expressing and integrating conflicting perspectives, the voices of less privileged or powerful group members will not play a role in decision-making (Mansbridge, 1984).

Discussion

Supporting the Establishment of Transformative Social Processes

If action civics practitioners are serious about closing the civic empowerment gap, they cannot blindly adopt the interactions used in our inequitable democracy and apply them to classrooms. Rather, they must thoughtfully consider how interactions might be restructured in more equitable ways, creating *transformative* social processes. Teachers such as Suzanne do dabble in these practices; for instance, they may intentionally group students in ways that promote the sharing of diverse perspectives, use protocols to make conversations more equitable, or design assignments that push students to incorporate others' perspectives into their work. However, these practices are not widely used in schools, which tend to rely on *authoritative* social processes, or in the wider society, which is more open but also more inequitable. Without guidance and support, teachers are likely to only implement transformative practices reactively and sporadically, as Suzanne does, and to regularly revert to the status quo. As Levinson (2012) argues, this is unlikely to support student learning; consistent social processes, rather than occasional interventions, are needed to support development (Tseng & Seidman, 2007; Bronfenbrenner & Morris, 1998). By providing clear expectations and support to teachers in establishing transformative classroom social processes, action civics organizations can help to explicitly create microcosmic democracies within classrooms that better uphold values of equality. In doing this, students not only prepare to participate in unjust systems and interactions, but to gradually transform them.

Levinson (2012) argues that schools must provide civic learning experiences that teach students "how to soar in a world you've never seen – you don't know anything about" (p.

185). However, my findings suggest that while action civics programs that give students opportunities to engage in authentic civic interactions can open a window to this world, they do little to close the civic empowerment gap in diverse contexts. Establishing transformative social processes, such as the use of protocols for discussion, may help to close this gap; however, they require entering a world that few students or teachers have seen – a world that challenges the notion that diverse contexts necessitate an "inherent trade-off" (Campbell, 2006, p. 182; Putnam, 2007) in which collaborative action inevitably decreases and a world that requires a more comprehensive integration of 21st century skills, especially those focused on collaborative work and collective action, into the curriculum. In this world, new opportunities for interaction are likely to create an enhanced sense of efficacy and increased participation for students who have traditionally felt alienation in both classroom and community social processes.

However, teachers are unlikely to soar into this strange new world without support. More research is needed to identify what types of social processes are truly transformative, promoting more inclusive conceptions of democracy within diverse contexts, and feasible within the constraints of school environments. Ideally, this research should be conducted in partnership with action civics organizations and practitioners, who must move beyond a focus on curriculum development and consider how social processes affect outcomes in a variety of contexts. These examinations need to be paired with longitudinal studies that look at the effects of action civics programs on students' behaviors after program completion. The social processes I have described as transformative include practices which have been shown to promote the transfer of knowledge and skills more generally, such as the identification and use of learning strategies and reflective self-assessment (Bransford, Brown, & Cocking, 2000), but we need a better understanding of whether and how using these practices within the classroom can help students to become engaged in more inclusive democratic practices outside the classroom. Finally, researchers need to understand how teachers learn to establish these social processes. While not conclusive, this study indicates that teachers' own conceptions of and experiences with citizenship are likely to interact with contextual factors to determine what types of interactions are established in a classroom.

One hundred years from now, what kind of nation will a student like Victoria be describing when she claims "That's democracy"? The choices civic educators make today, not only about curriculum but also about classroom interactions, will help determine how that question is answered in our diversifying country.

References

Bransford, J., Brown, A. L., & Cocking, R. R. (2000). *How people learn: Brain, mind, experience, and school.* Washington, D.C.: National Academy Press.

Bronfenbrenner, U. & Morris, P. (1998). The ecology of developmental processes. *The Handbook of Child Psychology, 1,* 993-1029.

Bloch, M., Cox, A., Ericson, M., Hossain, F., & Tse, A. (2010, January 19). Results and analysis. *The New York Times.* Retrieved from http://www.nytimes.com/interactive/2010/01/19/us/politics/massachusetts-election-map.html.

Carnegie Corporation of New York & CIRCLE. (2003). *The civic mission of schools.* New York: Carnegie Corporation of New York & CIRCLE.

Campbell, D. E. (2005). *Voice in the classroom: How an open classroom environment facilitates adolescents' civic development* (CIRCLE Working Paper 28). Retrieved from http://citeseerx.ist.psu.edu/viewdoc/download? doi=10.1.1.189.682&rep=rep1&type=pdf

Campbell, D.E. (2006). *Why we vote: How schools and communities shape our civic life.* Princeton, NJ: Princeton University Press.

Cappella, J. N. (2002). Cynicism and social trust in the new media environment. *Journal of Communication, 52*(1), 229–241.

Carlock, R. (2011). *"La union hace la fuerza": Community organizing for democratic school governance: An ethnographic study in an immigrant community* (Qualifying paper, Harvard Graduate School of Education).

Charmaz, K. (2006). *Constructing grounded theory: A practical guide through qualitative analysis.* Thousand Oaks, CA: Sage Publications.

Delpit, L. (1995). *Other people's children: Cultural conflict in the classroom.* New York, NY: New Press.

Feldman, L., Pasek, J., Romer, D., & Jamieson, K.H. (2007). Identifying best practices in civic education: Lessons from the Student Voices program. *American Journal of Education, 114* (1), 75-100.

Flanagan, C. A., Cumsille, P., Gill, S., & Gallay, L. S. (2007). School and community climates and civic commitments: Patterns for ethnic minority and majority students. *Journal of Educational Psychology, 99*(2), 421–431. doi:10.1037/0022-0663.99.2.421

Gerring, J. (2007). *Case study research: Principles and practices.* New York, NY: Cambridge University Press.

Graham, P. (2005). *Schooling America: How public schools met the nation's changing needs.* New York: Oxford University Press.

Grubb, W., & Lazerson, M. (2004). *The economic gospel.* Cambridge, MA: Harvard University Press.

Hamre, B. K., & Pianta, R. C. (2001). Early teacher-child relationships and the trajectory of children's school outcomes through eighth grade. *Child Development,* 72(2), 625-638.

Kahne, J., & Middaugh, E. (2008). *Democracy for some: The civic opportunity gap in high school* (CIRCLE Working Paper 59). Retrieved from http://www.civicyouth.org/circle-working-paper-59-democracy-for-some-the-civic-opportunity-gap-in-high-school/.

Lawrence-Lightfoot, S. & Hoffman Davis, J. (1997). *The art and science of portraiture.* San Francisco: Jossey-Bass.

Levinson, M. (2010). The civic empowerment gap. In L. Sherrod, C. Flanagan & J. Torney-Purta (Eds.), *Handbook on research and policy on civic engagement in youth* (p. 331-362). San Francisco: Wiley.

Levinson, M. (2012). *No citizen left behind.* Cambridge, Mass: Harvard University Press.

Lieberson, S. (1991). Small n's and big conclusions: An examination of the reasoning in comparative studies based on a small number of cases. *Social Forces, 70* (2), 307-320.

Making Learning Visible (n.d.). *Ladder of feedback.* Retrieved from http://www.makinglearningvisibleresources.org/ladder-of-feedback-see-supporting-learning-in-groups-in-the-classroom.html

Mann, H. (1891). *Life and works of Horace Mann: Volume 4.* Boston: Lee and Shepard.

Mansbridge, J. (1984). Unitary and adversary: The two forms of democracy. *In Context, 7,* 10-13.

Marri, A. (2005). Building a framework for classroom-based multicultural democratic education: Learning from three skilled teachers. *The Teachers College Record, 107*(5), 1036–1059.

Massachusetts Department of Education. (2012). *School/District Profiles* [Data File]. Retrieved from http://profiles.doe.mass.edu.

Meehan, B. T., Hughes, J. N., & Cavell, T. A. (2003). Teacher–student relationships as compensatory resources for aggressive children. *Child Development, 74*(4), 1145–1157.

Merriam, S. (1998). *Qualitative research and case study applications in education.* San Francisco: Jossey-Bass.

Orfield, G. (2009). *Reviving the goal of an integrated society: A 21st century challenge.* Los Angeles, CA: The Civil Rights Project at UCLA.

Partnership for 21st Century Skills. (2009). *P21 framework definitions.*

Retrieved from http://www.p21.org/tools-and-resources/educators.

Pianta, R. & Allen, J.P. (2008). Building capacity for positive youth development in secondary school classrooms: Changing teachers' interactions with students. In M. Shinn & Yoshikawa, H. (Eds.), *Toward Positive Youth Development: Transforming Schools and Community Programs* (p. 21-39). New York: Oxford University Press.

Pettigrew, T. F., & Tropp, L. R. (2006). A meta-analytic test of intergroup contact theory. *Journal of Personality and Social Psychology*, *90*(5), 751–783. doi:10.1037/0022-3514.90.5.751

Pope, A., Stolte, L., & Cohen, A. (2011). Closing the civic engagement gap: The potential of action civics. *Social Education 75* (5), 265-268.

Putnam, R. D. (2007). E pluribus unum: Diversity and community in the twenty-first century. The 2006 Johan Skytte Prize Lecture. *Scandinavian Political Studies*, *30*(2), 137–174.

Reuben, J. (2005). Patriotic purposes: Public schools and the education of citizens. In S. Fuhrman & M. Lazerson (Eds.), *The public schools* (p. 1-24). Oxford: Oxford University Press.

Rubin, B. (2007). "There's still not justice": Youth civic identity development amid distinct school and community contexts. *The Teachers College Record*, *109*(2), 449–481.

Rubin, B. & Hayes, B. (2010). " No backpacks" versus" Drugs and murder": The promise and complexity of youth civic action research. *Harvard Educational Review*, *80*(3), 352–379.

Tseng, V., & Seidman, E. (2007). A systems framework for understanding social settings. *American Journal of Community Psychology, 39*(3-4), 217–228. doi:10.1007/s10464-007-9101-8

Ulbig, S. G. & Funk, C.L. (1999). Conflict avoidance and political participation. *Political Behavior, 21*(3), 265-282.

United States Census Bureau. (2011). *American Fact Finder.* Retrieved from http://factfinder2.census.gov/faces/nav/jsf/pages/index.xhtml.

Verba, S., Schlozman, K.L., & Brady, H. (1995). *Voice and equality: Civic voluntarism in American politics.* Cambridge, MA: Harvard University Press.

Westheimer, J. & Kahne, J. (2004). Educating the "good" citizen: Political choices and pedagogical goals. *PS: Political Science & Politics, 37*(2), 241-248.

Walker, J. (2009). Authoritative classroom management: How control and nurturance work together. *Theory Into Practice, 48*(2), 122–129. doi:10.1080/00405840902776392

Wilkenfeld, B. (2008, Sept.). *An ecological systems approach to the civic education and engagement of adolescents.* Paper presented at the Third International Association for the Evaluation of Educational Achievement Research Conference, Taipei, Taiwan.

Rebuilding Democracy, Rethinking Education

Giridhari Lal Pandit[1]
Centre for Ecological Economics and Natural Resources,
Institute for Social and Economic Change, Bangalore, India;
Alexander von Humboldt-Foundation, University of
Heidelberg, Germany

Abstract

The second half of the 20th century witnessed new
democracies emerge where former colonies fought for
freedom and human rights. It also saw the UNO (United
Nations Organization) and the UNSC (United Nations
Security Council) emerge as institutions of humanitarian
service and international peace. Echoing, as our world is, with
public protests against rising inequality, massive human rights
violations, state-sponsored terrorism, forced migrations,
heinous crimes against women and children, corruption, and
the totalitarianism of surveillance technology, the question
arises whether history is now repeating itself, with most
democracies worrying about economic prosperity instead of
freedom. Embedded, as we all are, in the highways of
globalization and hyperconnectivity, only the style and
discontents of protest are qualitatively different in the Age of
Digital Information.

---

[1] Dedicated to the twentieth century's uprooted and unsung children,
women as well as men, in the East and in the West, who have suffered most
from the fundamentalist terrorism, torture and violence, and above all from
the loss of Oe*kos* – and all this and more, with silence in their midst, with
their arms and eyes as wide open as the starry skies above us that never fail
in their gaze, so powerfully holding the beautiful Earth in their wonderful
embrace. The author thanks Karl Rogers and Viktoria Byczkiewicz for their
valuable comments.

It is imperative, at least at three levels of analysis, to answer the following questions: (a) Is not terrorism merely a cancerous symptom of a deeper malady lurking elsewhere in our world? (b) How can hyper-technological surveillance of citizens in a democracy, more so by the US that claims to lead the world's democracies, be at all legitimate? Yet (c) is there a way ahead for humanity, in search of *tradeoffs* between the frontiers of freedom and the capitalist technological totalitarianism limitlessly aimed at enhancing prosperity? In which *terms* should we debate the issues of rebuilding democracy and those of rethinking (i) technology and education (ii) privacy and the security-driven surveillance and (iii) human rights in developmental dimension and the UNO itself?

Keywords: human rights; developmental environment (HRDE); forms of exclusion; Technological totalitarianism; rebuilding democracy; informed consent; equality in education; United Nations Millennium Development Goals (UNMDGs); indivisibility of freedom; environmental nesting; neighborhood non-relations (NNRs)

Resilient Democracy: Freedom for One and All

"Build education systems that incorporate the advice of outstanding full-time classroom teachers when formulating education policy" (Alberts, 2013, p. 249)

In a welfare state, and under the policies promoted by the UN, argues Hardin (1968, 1998), there is a real dilemma in the global ecological-economical context how to deal with "the family, the religion, the race, or the class...that adopts over breeding as a policy to secure its own aggrandizement? To couple the concept of freedom to breed with the belief that everyone born has an equal right to the commons is to lock the world into a tragic course of action" (Hardin, 1968, p. 1246).

In the context of world's 'democracies,' some of them more successful and some of them less successful, some of them more *transparent* but some of them less so, there is a similar dilemma how to deal with the members of the UN, including the fundamentalist rogue states and their terrorist organizations that engage in heinous crimes against humanity in their own neighborhoods and in distant lands, not only engineering genocide but robbing the masses of innocent women, men and children of their individual lives, freedom and dignity, with the whole world watching (Pandit, 2005, 2006, 2010).

In taking a look at the world's democracies, one finds that massive human rights violations have become a regular phenomenon. The election scenes alone tell a lot about the capitalist vote banks (political donations, as the media prefer to call them) with little or no transparency, many democracies allowing either political parties or candidates to receive anonymous donations. It is rare when elections do not witness violence, inviting massive policing and patrolling by an army that must guard the voting booths. Worst of all, consider the decreasing voter turnout, a large percentage of voters either being disenfranchised or showing informed reluctance to casting their votes, out of sheer distrust and disgust, as they wonder why corruption and abuse of power are so widespread. This scenario takes us back to the realities of the past centuries, prompting the question what it is exactly that humanity has left behind: Can the way the world is changing be regarded as progressive or regressive?

Why do the world's democracies fail to compete where progress is most urgently needed to help humanity solve some of the greatest common challenges it faces? During the past century, if there has been some kind of 'competitive progress' among them, it is mostly to be found in science and technology funding for military purposes, in an expanding nexus between governments, industry, markets, and the corporate world.

Consider how these democracies have been engaged in an unending competition for continued heavy investment in the acquisition and development of new destructive weapons for military use. Think of their mad race for the acquisition of weapons of mass destruction, the nuclear arsenals, the nuclear capable ballistic missile technologies and the conventional arms for military use. All governments cite the perception of threat, real or illusory, declaring themselves duty-bound to prioritize annual budgets according to estimates of which new destructive weapons are needed to defend narrowly conceived regional and global interests. In spite of its being host to a remarkably fragile and complex bio-diverse world as well as to culture and civilization, the planet Earth is now completely covered with weapons of mass destruction.

But what has that to do with freedom, education and resilient civil society, the three major engines of democracy? Democracy's resilience comes neither from elections nor from investments in irresponsible arms buildup. It comes from equality in education that can foster democracy and its institutions. On the other hand, any commitment to an accelerated arms race among different countries contradicts the basic values of democracy and education. The diversion of large resources in this manner deprives billions of people, mostly the poor, not only of a simple, decent and peaceful living but of their fundamental rights and freedoms; more so in those countries that are permanently locked into neighborhood non-relations (NNRs). This situation destroys the resilience of civil society, dangerously impacting the health of democracy and educational institutional building.

As the 20th century ended, the world's economies, both centrally planned and capitalist market-oriented, began a fierce competition in the name of economic and social progress; more precisely toward urbanization, economic growth, enhanced prosperity, and globalization. How far have the world's democracies come in terms of building resilience into their institutions and creating civil societies? Take a look at the greatest frontiers of individual freedom and dignity, women's empowerment and children's welfare, fundamental human rights and the right to privacy. Why is the competition with respect to democratic values conspicuous by its absence? Slipping into one crisis after another, as they do, why have individual countries failed to make moral progress in respect of those very values by which their constitutions, governments and institutions swear in the name of democracy? Why has their commitment to promoting the development of human rights at home and abroad been merely nominal and symbolic, paying lip service to the UN human rights campaigns? Where human rights are concerned, most democracies clearly show an absence of resilience, with their institutions failing to participate in true debate and civil societies losing faith in them. This includes the educational institutions, universities and schools, the very cradles of democracy. Where else are younger generations expected to learn their first lessons *how* to inculcate democratic values and to foster these values in order to build the institutions with which humankind can make progress while resilient civil societies sustain themselves?

It is no surprise that the agonies of capitalism Marx saw in the 19th century are coming back and today's surveillance-driven world increasingly looks like one that was fragmented by the Cold War. Consider how today's racing technologies fragment our world with an unprecedented rapidity and repetition. We seem to be so proud of our ability to put new technologies on the market without ever caring to ask why and how they arrive at such lightning speed when most people wake up daily to find that they have no access even to the older, outdated technologies (Pandit, 2007, 2009). Why does technology have to divide humanity and breed inequality? Consider our frightening ability to use and abuse modern technologies, topped by hyperconnectivity-driven totalitarian surveillance of citizens across the globe. Why do those of us who can afford to buy new technologies at the same speed by which they arrive on the market invariably fail to question technology's totalitarian power for limitless surveillance? Can technological totalitarianism be justified as legitimate just in the name of security? Without our blind faith in technology, as a tool of manipulation and governance, could surveillance have gone so viral and totalitarian among the world's democracies?

More importantly, are our modern technologies meant to be some kind of magical tools in our hands to win social status and public trust so long as they can be empowering and impoverishing at one and the same time? Where our individual human rights are concerned, new technologies can be arguably so empowering that it would seem unnecessary to ask whether we, as consumers, understand their *raison d'être,* appreciating their enormous power for connectivity. On the other hand, however, they can be so *impoverishing* insofar as they serve as depersonalizing and dehumanizing tools of manipulation and governance that exercise magical power over us, capable of persuading us that the person-to-person interaction is not only waste of time but a thing of the past (Krugman, 2013). Notice how adverse the consequences of the impoverishing feats of the new technologies in question can be for education and for resilience of civil society if we simply recognize how frighteningly global technology trends breed inequality by turning against workers, instead, as was thought in previous decades, of raising the demand for highly educated workers while reducing the demand for less-educated workers:

> Today…a much darker picture of the effects of technology on labor is emerging. In this picture, highly educated workers are as likely as less-educated workers to find themselves displaced and devalued, and pushing for more education may create as many problems as it solves. (Krugman, 2013, p. A27)

As technology races ahead of the worker, the victims of technological governance and manipulation will, paradoxically as it were, always include the same workers who are "currently considered highly skilled, and who invested a lot of time and money in acquiring those skills," but whose skills may be devalued at any moment by further technological advance. "Education, then," argues Krugman (2013), "is no longer the answer to rising inequality, if it ever was (which I doubt)" (p. A27). If mechanization and technology as tools of manipulation are as dehumanizing, devaluing and hurtful to the worker today as they were during and after the Industrial Revolution, and if these tools tend to benefit some economically by raising their living standards, at the high price of hurting others, then how can we live with the *forms of exclusion* they breed?

Where then, exactly, are the world's democracies and international institutions supported by breeding such forms of exclusion? More importantly, what about education as an institution to serve and promote democracy (Rogers, 2008; Zyngier, 2012)? Democracy, argues Zyngier (2012),

> must be constantly cultivated, conceptualized and re-worked, with less dependence on the formal political process and cycle of elections, and on critical engagement in developing the conditions for emancipation, enhanced power relations, and epistemological discovery that may lead to some of the virtues that are commonly extolled when discussing democracy (freedom, liberty, rights, common virtues, etc.). (p. 3)

In this very context, notice how Giroux (2000) aptly laments a shift from responsibility for creating a democracy of citizens to producing a democracy of consumers while pointing out that public education

> becomes a venue for making a profit, delivering a product, or constructing consuming subjects,

education reneges on its responsibilities for creating a democracy of citizens by shifting its focus to producing a democracy of consumers. (p. 173)

Excessively focused on money, power and the capitalist vote banks, where has the world that we have built landed us? Where all that we wanted to foster is concerned – technology as a tool in aid of education (rather than manipulation), business-supply chains, communication, education, and democratic governance – we have landed in a paradox. As individuals and as societies, we all live hypocritical lives, swearing by what we intend to aim at but doing everything to the contrary (Pandit, 2001a; Rogers, 2008, pp. 1-5). Boasting as we so arrogantly do that we know what democracy is or means, hardly a day passes when we do not fail to live by its basic principles. Are the world's democracies then mere shadows more or less sharing among themselves a conceptual resemblance of democracy? Why do failing democracies divide people in the same tired fashion when in actuality there are no democracies? The same question can be conceptualized differently in terms of our failure, first, to keep up our commitment to development and human rights and, second, to question capitalist technological totalitarianism that further fragments a world already badly fractured by structural violence and forms of exclusion, not least by one of its worst offshoots – terrorism (Pandit, 2001a, 2007).

How we perceive, and what we understand by, democracy depends largely on whether we are interested in democracy, together with education, as a project with the goal of empowerment, equality, freedom, and resilience, to enhance people's participation as autonomous individuals, so that they may enjoy equality and freedom of choice. It also depends on whether we are interested in cyclical elections and capitalist vote banks that bring the contesting political parties to power or out of power. True democracy, deeply reflected in its institutions, is essentially about civil society's resilience and empowerment, about good and just systems of education and participation. In a democracy, laws and institutions shaping people's lives ought not to be taken as something that can be made and remade in the contexts of rights-violations, in the contexts of impoverishment, as is the case at present in most countries, notably those of South Asia (Suraiya, 2008). On the contrary, laws ought to be made in the contexts of rights-fulfillment, in the contexts of empowerment of men, women and children. Thus, we must never fail to ask what kind of education makes democracy resilient. What kind of resilient democracy is it that education can be held responsible for? What kind of education can produce the kind of democracy that we, as beings born free with human rights, might deserve or aim at? And what kind of education can contribute to a human rights developmental environment (HRDE)?

In an interesting conceptualization that is particularly instructive in the context of the world's degenerating democracies (Rogers, 2008, pp. 1-128), Zyngier (2012) examines "perspectives and perceptions of democracy of pre-and-in-service teachers as well as teacher-education academics in Australia in order to develop a robust and critical democratic education" (p. 1), distinguishing between 'thinner' and 'thicker' democracy. A *thicker* democracy is "reflective, critical, participatory, tolerant and non-hierarchical" (Zyngier, 2012, p. 17). On the contrary, a *thinner* democracy is authoritarian, "based on uncritical knowledge, standards and competencies as the measure of the 'good citizen'" (Zyngier, 2012, p. 17). Following Reid (2000), we can say with Howard and Patten (2006) that a *thick* democracy focuses on "how citizens understand themselves as members of a public with an obligation to promote the public good" and "the competencies required of civic citizenship that encompass informed and active citizens participating in political debate and action on equal terms." There is no doubt that education needs to assume a "deep democratic engagement" (Reid, 2005, p. 311). Thick democracy rejects the "top-down imposition of policies designed by 'teams of experts' in favor of the active involvement of the least powerful" (Reid, 2000; Zyngier, 2012). To generalize Zyngier's (2012) conclusion (p. 18), what the world's democracies need most is an educational framework of teaching not for *thin* democracy that leads to disengaged citizens (Dejaeghere & Tudball, 2007) but for *thick* democracy, that is, a thickening of thin democracy, if we care for a more participatory, empowered, and engaged citizenry and more inclusive participation in, and therefore safeguarding of, a strong democracy (Rogers, 2008, p. 115).

In what follows, I shall argue from the indivisibility of human freedom how we might, individually and collectively, (i) *foster* a human rights developmental environment (HRDE) to embed democratic and educational values; (ii) *rebuild* democracy and resilient civil society in terms of various *tradeoffs* between the frontiers of freedom and capitalist technological totalitarianism limitlessly aimed at ever-enhancing prosperity with economic growth; (iii) *overcome* contradictions within the policies of the UN and its member countries that have failed to safeguard free access to human rights; and (iv) *discover* strong correlations between *human rights* in developmental and educational dimensions *and* the imperative of *rethinking* the UN at various levels, notably in the globally *critical* area of neighborhood non-relations (NNRs).

Human Rights, Participation and Transparency

The truth is that those with the most power over who can speak and who can be heard in the Internet age aren't judges or prosecutors or even the President. They're officials at Internet and telecom companies like Google, Facebook, Twitter, Verizon and AT&T. Call them Deciders…and while Internet companies must obey the law, their decisions about whether to cooperate with government surveillance requests will determine the future of free speech as much as any prosecutor or judge. Today's unprecedented centralization of information means that whoever controls the databases holds the real power to decide who can speak and what we can say. (Rosen, 2013, p. 24)

In a seemingly fast-changing, globalized world, conflicting interpretations of democracy suggest that either it is going bankrupt or the interpretations themselves are changing anarchistically as technology advances as a tool of political power and manipulation. As technology advances and civil societies lose resilience, are we to take the world's democracies as being in perpetual flux, inversely? If democracy is about individual freedom, human dignity, and a resilient civil society, how radically can the world's democracies diverge from one another? Can they arguably be expected to converge on projects of building resilience into civil society, more so in a highly globalized yet fragmented world faced with regional and global crises? To find an answer, it is imperative to have more and more publicly funded institutes across the globe dedicated to the study of democracy, exploring ever better democratic alternatives to the present brands of 'liberal' democracy.[2] It is imperative to determine where exactly the world's democracies are most challenged. The single biggest challenge comes from

---

[2] A rigorous and comprehensive discussion on liberal democracy is to be found in Rogers (2008, pp. 12-25). No doubt, there are so many different brands of 'liberal' democracy, none of them capable of being a perfect or true version. In most cases, it is a form of government "in which representative democracy operates under the principles of liberalism," characterized by fair and free elections, a separation of powers into different wings of government, the judiciary and the parliament above all, the rule of law in everyday life as part of an open society, and the equal protection of human rights, civil rights, civil liberties, and political freedoms for all persons.

the *forms of exclusion* they themselves breed in the process of state-building, election after election. A second challenge has to do with their paradoxical dependence on the totalitarian power of self-interested capitalist market rationality which pushes everyone to acquire enhanced economic prosperity by any means, generating a chain of structural violence within the society. A third challenge relates to the lack of transparency in the role the capitalist vote banks are invariably playing in electoral democracy, elections being taken as the only way of ushering the contesting political parties into the power-sharing equations. As a fourth challenge, one might wonder why it is invariably the case that those who are above suspicion of corruption and dishonesty are not attracted to politics, while those who are prone to be corrupt are? Must democracy be marred by corruption even before it begins to function?

A fifth challenge relates to how every thinking individual is wondering whether Uncle Sam is watching them in every electronic step taken, in every digital move made (Rajghatta, 2013a). Consider how the world has woken up to news "that the U.S. government's surveillance of people is much broader, wider, and deeper than initially thought and extends beyond America – into the whole world" (Rajghatta, 2013a, p. 22). At least for the last six years, the secretive U.S. National Security Agency (NSA) has been able to pluck data, including emails, videos, pictures, social networking details, and connection logs from the main servers of the major American technology giants Microsoft, Google, Yahoo, Apple, AOL, Facebook, and Skype, making the world's Internet infrastructure. The NSA's collection of metadata from Verizon is reported to be the tip of the iceberg in the Obama administration's spying overreach (Rajghatta, 2013a, p. 22; Rajghatta, 2013b, p. 24). The NSA spies on millions of Americans' phone records and on the Internet activity of hundreds of millions of foreigners across the globe. Like the U.S., other states involved in this kind of top-secret surveillance program defend the abuse of power by claiming how it strikes "the right balance between keeping its citizens safe from terrorist attack and protecting their privacy" (*The Economist*, 2013, 15th-21st June, p. 12). The latest development relates to the U.S. Secretary of State, John Kerry, acknowledging that the NSA may have "gone too far" in its secretive Internet surveillance programs, reaching far too inappropriately and eavesdropping on a large number of the world's leaders in Asia and Europe (Rajghatta, 2013b, p. 24). Unfolding the fragility of a world so alarmingly and massively fragmented and filled with scandalous abuses of technology and political power, we learn how one set of states is set against other states, while all the states are set against their civil societies. There is no word, not even a whisper, from the international institutions. However, the American technology giants are reported to be preparing to support legislation authored by U.S. lawmakers to end the NSA's bulk collection of phone records (Rajghatta, 2013b, p. 24).

The Human Rights Watch has rightly expressed apprehension that most countries in the world are misusing the new surveillance capabilities to target critics, journalists, and human rights activists. Governments and bureaucrats use its tools for political reasons instead of security purposes. What is worse is that they use it in a covert way, violating human rights. India's recently rolled out Central Monitoring System (CMS) is intended to provide "centralized access to the country's telecommunications network and facilitate direct monitoring of phone calls, text messages, and the Internet use by government agencies, bypassing service providers" (Sinha, 2013a, p. 14). In order to prevent surveillance from going viral in total disregard for human rights, it is imperative for any state that does not want to function like a dictator to guarantee transparency regarding (i) who will be authorized to collect data; (ii) what data will be collected; (iii) how these will be used; and (iv) how the right to privacy will be protected (Sinha, 2013a).

Certainly, the ringing of the alarm bells of a totalitarian takeover of individual freedom and individual privacy can be heard, no matter which democratic form of government you vote for, every four or five years. The use and abuse of hyper-technological surveillance capabilities raises some fundamental legal and ethical questions. Most important, what happens to *informed consent* in the present digital age of globalization? How is the right to *informed consent* to be safeguarded? How transparent can an authorization of surveillance be in the absence of *informed consent*? And, how informed can informed consent itself be in absence of *informed access* at various levels and in variable contexts (Pandit, 2009)? In the case of the NSA's massive surveillance of people, the basic distinction between who is a suspected criminal or terrorist and who is not becomes altogether obliterated.

It is difficult to capture in simple words the myth and reality of today's crises-ridden world as headed by the UN. No ethical rules bind our world together, not even on the burning issues of global warming and climate change challenge. In this scenario, what is it then which brings all countries together annually at the UN, irrespective of whether you are permanently locked into neighborhood non-relations (NNRs), no matter whether you swear by communism or by religious fundamentalism? Is it the self-interested capitalist market rationale of making profits, becoming prosperous and famous by any means (Gupta, 2013)?

This raises the question where exactly we might look for those factors that the world's democracies may be said to share. There is one thing that they have in common; the rights-awareness campaigns that are aimed at telling their citizens, struggling for survival or for dignified life, how to exercise their right to peacefully fight for their basic human rights by approaching the local or regional bureaucracies and mechanisms of governance. Before they do so, citizens are supposed to know that they have a right to peacefully fight for their basic human rights, for their freedom and dignity. In order to exercise their right to put up a legal fight, many lucky citizens do find their way into the law courts or Human Rights Commissions (HRCs). But most others, who are poor, deprived and voiceless, have no luck with the bureaucratic channels or HRC-mechanisms that must be skillfully navigated. They leave everything to God, to the temples of the heart where they go regularly to pray. This shows that in absence of resilient civil societies and sound educational systems, people, in particular the poorer sections, have to put up an individual fight for dignity and freedom.

Human Rights:
How the World Fails to Safeguard Free Access

All men, women, and children are born with fundamental or basic human rights. Yet, like the moral and ecological concepts of the autonomy interests of whole ecosystems in nature and of individual men and women within society and culture, basic human rights have a long developmental history. Best documented in the "Universal Declaration of Human Rights" (UDHR) proclaimed by the UN General Assembly on December 10, 1948, some of them have found expression in the very assumptions and insights underlying the Preamble and the Proclamation parts of the UDHR. Proclaimed "as a common standard of achievement for all peoples and nations," the UDHR (Article 1) states that "all human beings are born free and equal in dignity and rights. They are endowed with reason and conscience and should act towards one another in a spirit of brotherhood." The UDHR can be regarded as a decisive step forward in improving our common understanding of how the state and individuals should act towards one another given that the assertion and reassertion by the individual of his/her autonomy interests, dignity, and rationality, and the sociocultural, economic, and political pressures make their relationships ever more fragile and complex. Think of the tensions between the state and society that result in human suffering on a very large scale – cruelty and crimes against women and children in male-dominated societies being just one example. The UDHR carries the insight that these tensions, like all our inventions, can be controlled and tamed to keep them within reasonable limits. Our search for knowledge of human rights and our relentless effort to safeguard and promote them in our highly troubled world may be arduous. The prospects of safeguarding them will, however, depend upon whether we can single out for purposes of research and development a set of basic autonomy interests and welfare interests of all men, women, and children. It is imperative to study the whole causal dynamics of recurring violations of human rights on a very large scale, particularly against women and children. It is these violations themselves, no less than the UDHR, which have played a key role in unfolding the developmental history of human rights in its full complexity and diversity (Pandit, 1982, 1995).

The present dismal scenario of human rights takes us back to *The Subjection of Women* (1869) authored by John Stuart Mill (1806-1873), the British philosopher, together with his wife, Harriet Taylor Mill. Focusing on women's rights, in violation of their equality before law, they argued against the *forms of exclusion* arising from the rights violations. In today's world, the state and its lawmakers, instead of guaranteeing individuals and communities their right of free access to fundamental rights, allow these rights to be violated in one way or another to make room for the bureaucratic mechanisms of 'governance' such as the Human Rights Commissions (HRCs). In their turn, as we noted earlier, the mechanisms of 'governance by the state' are more and more set in the context of rights violations than in the context of their fulfillment (Suraiya, 2008). Thus, it must make laws that narrate how the aggrieved individuals and communities, as well as ethnic minorities, can exercise their right to fight for their basic human rights, spending huge sums of money and investing lots of time in filing petitions, should they think that their access to their basic rights is blocked, threatened, or violated.

Public policies and mechanisms of the state, worldwide, continue to focus on the ways and means that lawmakers may from time to time make available to individuals and communities, in case they feel aggrieved and want to fight for their human rights of which they are being deprived either by governments themselves or by terrorists. In most advanced and wealthy countries, such as the EU-member countries like Germany, aggrieved individuals can seek redress only through their attorneys, filing petitions in the courts and paying large sums of money which they must borrow, particularly if they are foreigners. Happily, the responsible representatives of the governments do occasionally recognize the need for making this world – the world driven by the profit-making global market – accessible to those people who have been left behind by the very forces of globalization and market rationality. But elsewhere, in many parts of the world which are still suffering under dictatorships, the state is preoccupied with strategies of fortifying its own mechanisms and less bothered over the freedom and dignity of its citizens.

This takes us back to the division of India in August of 1947, which set into motion an unending chain of human suffering in South Asia, particularly in Kashmir. The local people who have actually suffered as a result of these intrigues have either become forced migrants or refugees or died at the hands of Muslim terrorists trained and inspired by Pakistan (Pandit, 1998, pp. 135-137, 2006, 2010, 2013b). Consider how during 1989 and 1990, the minority community of Kashmiri Pandits (over 500,000 women, men, and children) was terrorized and forced to abadon their homes in the Kashmir Valley (Pandit, 2005, 2006, 2008a, 2010, 2013b). Using state-sponsored terrorism, Pakistan made a massive attempt to uproot the peace-loving Kashmiri Pandits, the original inhabitants of Kashmir Valley. Neither the state of Jammu and

Kashmir nor the federal government of India took care to prevent an attempted genocide in which many innocent members of the Pandit community lost their lives. Those who could not bear the trauma died prematurely elsewhere in tropical India, while many others died of snake bites in the refugee tents raised outside the Kashmir Valley. The question of the human condition of their rights has yet to receive the attention it deserves. They have still not been able to return and rebuild their homes that were destroyed by the Pakistani terrorists. Note that their properties and houses were destroyed subsequent to their forced exodus, ensuring that neither they nor their children would find returning easy.

The state government maintains a firm silence on this question. The government of India finds its hands full of other issues. Who is then going to pay attention to the human condition of the Pandits' rights? Indian lawmakers most probably would say that the community, given its inalienable right to fight for its rights, should file a petition before the HRC if it feels that its rights have been violated. The lawmakers have yet to wake up to the fact that the Pandits are not even included on India's list of recognized minority communities (Pandit, 2008a). Should they first prove that their right to life, to property, to freedom of speech, to cultural activities, to the Seer Lala Ded's Kashmir Valley (Koul, 1967),[3] as their homeland, have been violated and continue to be violated in everybody's presence? The fact that since 1990 they have lived everywhere in the world except in their homeland, Kashmir, is not to be counted at all.

---

[3]The 14th century Kashmiri poet and mystic Lalla Ded (1320-1389), also known by her formal name Lalleshwari, is a key symbol of Kashmir's multifaceted culture. Through the beauty and wisdom of her verses (*Lalla Vakhi* or "wise compositions of Lalla Ded"), she has dominated and inspired the life-world of every Kashmiri household, irrespective of their religion (Dutt, 1986; Kak, 1999; Koul, 1967).

Human Rights Developmental Environment (HRDE)

Yet, we must ask what are the challenges and tasks ahead for humanity, particularly for democracies of India'a size, if all men, women and children are to have the right to "the enjoyment of life and liberty, with the means of acquiring and possessing property, and pursuing and obtaining happiness and safety" (Malouf, 2011). This is apparently a question addressed to the research communities and policymakers concerned with development on the one hand and human rights on the other, as if these were two separate agendas altogether. The truth is that the two agendas are inseparable (Pandit, 2001b). At an International Conference held in Aachen, Germany in November 1999, I was the first to point out the urgency of an environment in which human rights were unified with development (Pandit, 2001b). A later study of the current state of human rights and development debate initiated by the UNMDGs (2000), advocating this unification of aims, explores the reasons why the two agendas – human rights and development – resemble ships passing in the night, even though they are headed for very similar destinations (Philip, 2005).

It is quite clear that flooding a population of India's size with human rights campaigns is not really different from flooding a country, where millions of impoverished people live, with the conventional economic prescriptions such as the optimal utilization of resources to make more goods and services available when it should be well known that for a variety of reasons the target population cannot access them. That is to say, the enabling developmental environments must be created first, where people's entitlements, and the capabilities these entitlements generate, are far more important than the conventional economic prescriptions (Meier, 1990).[4] Huge public expenditure on human rights commissions and rights awareness campaigns is not going to change the kind of deprivation under which massive violations of human rights of women and children, reported and unreported, are occurring every 20 minutes in South Asian countries (Feingold, 2013, p. 6), as in other parts of the world. In a vicious circle, it is only going to legitimize it. Similarly, unless the gap between the social services and government spending on economic development and the needs of target populations is closed, we will only be eliminating poor people, not poverty. Thus, the most important question concerns the access-giving human right developmental environments in which ordinary citizens do not feel threatened in any way by insecurity of life and property, nor deprived for lack of access to education, goods, or social services.

But what is it that we can regard as a human rights developmental environment? What kind of an enabling or empowering environment, educational, legal, social, and ecological-economical, qualifies? To begin with, think of conditions that enable an individual to access his or her human rights freely, without any hindrance or obstacle. Where security of life, freedom, and dignity are concerned, if living conditions are threatening, putting these at the mercy of the state, its bureaucracy and its law-and-order machinery does not qualify as a human rights developmental environment. The promotion

---

[4]According to Meier (1990),"Entitlement refers to the set of alternative commodity bundles that a person can command in a society using the totality of rights and opportunities that he or she has" (p. 30). Amartya Sen's work on the Bengal famine of 1943 is relevant in this context, since it shows that the famine occurred in a year when the food crop was good. And yet millions of people starved because they were unable to access (or purchase) food, for a variety of reasons, including the government's failure to gauge the situation.

of human rights is possible only in a scenario of resilience, not in the *environs of terrorism*. Think of the forms of exclusion that are easily bred in absence of an environment favoring the development of human rights. Think of poor people living under deprivation, without adequate food, proper drinking water, electricity, health care, or primary education. Think of a community that has been uprooted and torn apart by the failure of the retreating state to curb the terrorist violence against it. Think of *environs of terrorism* in which women and children feel neither free nor safe to move around even during daytime. Think of heinous crimes regularly being committed against them in South Asian countries, thanks to environs of terrorism. Examples are manifold. Without creating a resilient environment, neither the state, nor the civil society by which it is supported, can lay claim to the protection of individual human rights. In the absence of a human rights developmental environment, the creation of human rights commissions (HRCs) and the launching of human rights awareness campaigns by the state and the media hardly make any difference. On the contrary, they tend to generate an illusion in public perception as if all were well with the health of the state and society as a whole.

If the most serious challenge facing India, as all of South Asia, is the paradox of promoting human rights in the absence of such an environment, then what is the way ahead for India to making drastic improvements over its 134th position on the Human Development Index of 2011? Sixty-six years after independence, we cannot say that all Indians have won freedom from abject poverty, ignorance, and squalor. So what is the way ahead to economic and intellectual freedom, or to moral progress, for millions of people excluded from development? For example, large tribal populations of India have not only been excluded from development but deprived of their land. They do not even have access to safe drinking water. The same is the case with millions of slum dwellers living under subhuman conditions on the peripheries of India's

7,935 towns. Finally, then, how are *environs of terrorism* transformed into enabling environments, so that women and children can enjoy a semblance of human dignity, without being easy prey who are terrorized into submission and exploitation every few minutes?

For governments and their mechanisms, there cannot be any excuse to allow the known environs of terrorism to thrive unhindered, breeding the worst forms of terrorism. Even those governments in the poorest of the poor countries, there cannot be any excuse to leave issues of security, safety, and the empowerment of women and children to police, or to judiciary, or to human rights commissions, or to the newly cropped up NGOs, as if these were the mechanisms for the daily victims of heinous crimes to exercise their 'right' to fight for their human rights. Yet, the statistics of regularity with which women and children are being subjected to the brutalities of sexual abuse and rape on a large scale in South Asian countries indicate how the environs of terrorism breed heinous crimes against humanity, with governments and their mechanisms seemingly helplessly watching.

If rethinking how human rights must be safeguarded at any cost has become imperative, should not civil society wake up to collectively fight existing policies and practices? Should it not think of ways and means of "educating" politicians, preventing them from fooling the public through awareness campaigns that aim at making women, subsequent to being robbed of their dignity and freedom, aware of their right to fight for their human rights through the just-alluded to mechanisms? Or should we leave everything to the mechanisms of the government, presuming that the police, judiciary, HRCs and NGOs would lose their jobs and reputations if there were no heinous crimes being committed against children and women on a regular basis? Would these mechanisms be lying idle if there were no children and women exercising their 'right' to fight for their basic human rights?

A Closer Look at the Environs of Terrorism

Terrorism brings to mind horrifying images of heinous crimes being committed against whole communities and populations of innocent men, women, and children. It is ironic that in their current policies on terrorism, world leaders tend to be divided if asked when and how terrorism began in the 20th century. How can we forget that many European countries were familiar with it long before September 11, 2001? Think of the Red Brigades, Baader-Meinhoff, the Basque Freedom Army, and the IRA. Think too of the two World Wars, both of which were accompanied by prevailing terror in many places in Europe. In Asia, particularly in the Indian subcontinent, terrorism did not begin on September 11, 2001. It began much earlier (Bamzai, 1973; Pandit, 2005, 2006, 2008a, 2010), when Pakistan (an Islamic state newly born on August 14, 1947) invaded Jammu and Kashmir, a land-locked Kingdom, on October 22, 1947 (Bamzai, 1973, p. 738). In order to annex it by force, Pakistan sent in a whole army of tribal raiders (Qabayalis in local Kashmiri jargon), the faithful precursors of contemporary "Taliban" (meaning Islamic students), to loot and plunder, rape women, and kill innocent men in order to terrorize a whole population, and the Royal Army, into submission. The then-King of Jammu and Kashmir, Maharaja Hari Singh, had the option of freely deciding whether to continue to remain independent in the wake of India's independence. He did not want the Kingdom to become a part of Pakistan. Yet Pakistan decided to teach him a lesson, taking Jammu and Kashmir by force of violent terrorism. How Pakistani designs of occupying Jammu and Kashmir succeeded, while the U.S., the U.K., and the UN watched, illustrates one of the ugliest games of international politics ever played out by the big powers. The barbarism of Pakistani terrorism did not stop at that. It did not stop even after Maharaja Hari Singh and the then-popular Kashmiri leader, Sheikh Abdullah, calling for India's military help to throw the Pakistani Qabayalis supported by the nascent Pakistani regular army back into Pakistan, sought Kashmir's integration with free India.[5]

The present scenario raises the question as to what should be the role of civil society in the context of regional and global challenges facing humanity, particularly in developing countries like India. What should be its role in the sub-continental context of combating the *environs of terrorism?* What are the fighting frontiers of human dignity and individual freedom where every member of civil society must feel actively involved with a sense of high moral and personal commitment? These questions assume importance, because governments will come and go but there will always be civil society confronted with resilience tests. As the recent records show, the attitude of civil society in India, as well as of the media, to social injustice and the violation of human rights,

---

[5] The way the Western world responded as India agreed to help Jammu and Kashmir during its last minute integration with India in 1947-1948 made the situation more difficult for India and Kashmiris. As soon as the Indian Army began pushing back all the Pakistani terrorists from the occupied territory of Jammu and Kashmir, the UN Security Council (UNSC), led by its dominant powers, notably the U.S. and the U.K., ordered a ceasefire between India and Pakistan. India stupidly accepted, resulting in Pakistan's continued occupation of a part of the Indian state of Jammu and Kashmir. As we now stand at the beginning of the 21st century, the global road map of terrorism still starts and ends in Pakistan. At the latest Manmohan Singh-Barack Obama summit in Washington, the Indian Prime Minister articulated what obstacles India faced because of Pakistan being the epicenter of terrorism. Three things are quite noteworthy in this scenario. First, regionally and globally, the challenge of combating the *environs of terrorism* without shifting the problems to future generations remains largely unaddressed. Instead, there is a felt absence of the collective will of the nations of the world to identify the roots of the challenge. Second, during the past 66 years, India has failed to combat the environs of terrorism in and around Jammu and Kashmir and elsewhere in the country. And third, the demands for a Supreme Court level of inquiry into the mass killings by terrorists, resulting in mass exodus from the state of Jammu and Kashmir in 1989-1990, have been conveniently ignored (Pandit, 2010).

particularly heinous crimes against women and children, has been far too poor, indicating not just a lack of resilience but serious foundational gaps in the entire education system. Yet there is no reason to give up all hope of civil society's strong involvement in coping with the challenges of the global village and in guiding humanity at the crossroads, relentlessly fighting at the forefront of equality in education, individual freedom, and human dignity. At this great frontier, as I have argued elsewhere (Pandit, 2009, 2013b), the way ahead lies in first addressing the issue of recognizing the rape and abuse of children as a heinous crime against humanity, in violation of fundamental human rights, and punishable with the severest punishment conceivable under law. Second, if we carefully build ourselves into a resilient civil society embedded in a resilient human rights developmental environment, can we hope that the world we leave for future generations will be a world free from both the *environs of terrorism* and heinous crimes against women and children?

Since we live in a global village, it is not surprising if the human condition in one country affects the human condition in other parts of the globe.[6]

---

[6] Think of the 2007-2010 Global Financial Crisis. And think of the tragedy of the brutal gang rape of a 23-year-old medical student in New Delhi on December 16, 2012, resulting in her death, a tragedy which has received global attention thanks to *media advocacy* (Pandit, 2007, 2013b). *Media advocacy* "becomes imperative where our goal is (i) to influence changes in policy to promote educational, social, political, and environmental development; (ii) to focus public debate on policymakers and corporate executives whose decisions structure an environment in which policies affecting the quality of life of people are framed; and (iii) to enable whole communities that feel *excluded* or *threatened* to participate in impacting policy change in desirable directions. The most fundamental ethical task of *media advocacy* is then the innovative and strategic use of media to bring the stakeholder perspective to bear upon problem perception, policy framework and decision-making as issues of deep concern to civil society and mankind. Therefore, the motto of the media advocate should be: *participate and reconnect in order to improve the human condition"* (Pandit, 2007, pp. 172-173).

Regardless of geographical boundaries, there are good reasons why each generation must do rethinking and soul-searching. Each and every member of civil society must keep asking unconventional, deep questions: First, how can education in social justice help to prevent and curtail the environs of terrorism?

Second, how are we as a civil society going to make a humble contribution to the improvement of the human condition of children, women and the voiceless poor, and of the uprooted communities, wherever they may be, taking care that we do not pass on our present problems to future generations? Third, how do the technologies that both bind and divide us create deeper economic chasms? If civil society cannot influence local politics or public policy in different walks of social and political life, it can at least resort to media advocacy. Above all, a civil society must under all circumstances support equality in education that can bring resilience into it, enabling it relentlessly to fight at the frontiers of human dignity and individual freedom (Pandit, 2009).

In this context, it is imperative to rethink the institutions and mechanisms of the state, particularly *education* as a project of equality, social justice, and empowerment, taking care of ecology, ethics, and delivery mechanisms. In particular, the very ecology built into and around the institutional framework should reflect a sound approach to a human rights developmental environment. Significant improvements in the ecology of institutions can mean significant steps towards an institutionalization of resilient human rights developmental environments toward enabling human wellbeing and dignity (Philip, 2005). The setting up of national HRCs, as India and some other countries did a few years ago, may be helpful only insofar as these can convey official recognition to the *absence* of a resilient human rights developmental environment in a particular society, institutionalizing human rights violations.[7] They do not themselves represent a solution to the problem of rebuilding resilient democracy embedded in a resilient educated civil society.

Educational and Moral Challenges

"In thinking about what one gains as a university student, we speak of knowledge and skills and sometimes values: why is it that we do not so often speak of wisdom?" (Markwell, 2007, p. 178)

It may sound an exaggeration to say that even education, a public good, can be abused. But the worst atrocities in modern memory, including those perpetuated in Nazi Germany, were carried out by highly educated people. Whatever we may mean by education, we should never forget the ecological self in all of us, especially children, when it

---

[7] India's *ad hoc* approach of the last 66 years has eroded the distinction between external and internal security threats and made its citizens, even the entire communities in Punjab, Kashmir, and the northeastern states vulnerable to terrorist violence, more so in areas of neighborhood non-relations. During the summer months of May and June 1999, the Indian air force and infantry were engaged in a warlike situation in Kargil in Jammu and Kashmir to fight Pakistani intruders who had occupied positions on mountainous terrain inside Indian territory. With history repeating itself, this was not so surprising in the context of Pakistan's proxy war in Kashmir that began in the late 1980s. The two neighbors have seen wars before – in 1947, 1965, and 1971. As noted above, in 1947, Pakistan invaded Kashmir, forcibly occupying parts of Jammu and Kashmir. During the last 66 years there has never been a period of time when there have not been wars, or war-like situations, between India and Pakistan. Even today one can hear firing by enemy troops along the Line of Control (LOC). To quote India's National Security Advisory Board Chairman, Shyam Saran: "We should welcome a civilian democratic government in Pakistan, and would like to see its hands strengthened vis-à-vis the military. However, we need to deal with the reality on the ground, which is continuance of cross-border terrorism and provocative action on the LOC. Engagement must seek to address this reality" (Saran, 2013, p. 19).

comes to designing school buildings, a campus and curriculum.[8] More generally, one might ask whether education systems across the globe do not rest on false foundations. Yes, they do, as is clear from the way universities function without a healthy dynamic. To do away with this dysfunction, a real bottom-up approach is needed so that faculty take decisions instead of arriving at "resolutions" for approval by top bureaucrats. The rituals of the rector's nod should be done away with.

Educational development, including research on the impact of new information technologies on cultural value systems and human rights developmental environments, is an area of great potential for rethinking and innovation. After 66 years of freedom from British rule, India's progress in the field of higher education and research has been only nominal. In the context of the larger issues of rebuilding democracy and rethinking education, particularly in South and West Asia and sub-Saharan Africa, with approximately three-million girls being married by the age of 15 and 3.4 million young women giving birth by the age of 17, the biggest challenge is the corruption-free investment in girls' education, guaranteeing all children equal access to education. Equal access to education would not only mean equality in education for children but also a big step towards reducing the high rate of child and maternal mortality in the long run. In India there are over a million girls still out of school, although the Right to Education Act 2009, making it obligatory to enroll children in the 6-14 age group in elementary schools, was notified by the Government of India in 2010. Again, India has a very high rate of child and maternal mortality.

---

[8] Inspired by "tapovanas," the ecologically based forest schools of ancient India, the poet-seer Nobel Laureate Rabindranath Tagore founded Visva-Bharati University in rural Bengal (now West Bengal) in 1921, where world-renowned scholars were invited to teach fine arts, music, humanities, and social sciences in open spaces under beautiful trees. Have we learned anything from this?

According to a recent survey by the National Sample Survey Organization, compared to the 1991-2000 period when the attendance rates in higher education in India (college and university level) for the 20-24 age group was 19% for boys and 8% for girls in rural areas and 33% for boys and 24% for girls in urban areas, 2001-2010 saw attendance rates for the 20-24 age group growing: 71% for boys and 11% for girls in rural areas and 40% for boys and 45% for girls in urban areas. On the other hand, for the school-going 5-14 age group, 2001-2010 saw 87% of boys and 84% of girls attending school in rural areas and 91% of all boys and girls in urban areas. Sadly, these figures are contradicted by a high dropout rate at all these levels. Girls and children in the above age groups are often found fearing for their safety both inside and outside of *poorly designed schools*, and there is a high frequency of abuse by criminals roaming free in the *environs of terrorism*. Additional reasons such as rural poverty and child marriage cannot be ruled out. Just think of India's current 24 million child brides, the highest absolute number, which is 40% of the world's 60% million child marriages (Sinha, 2013b, p. 9). The first-ever UN resolution against the early and forced marriage of children, supported by more than 107 countries but rejected by India, aims at including children who are forced into marriage in the post-2015 international developmental UNMDGs agenda. Notice that child marriage, a menacing evil in society, "does not constitute a single rights violation – rather, every instance of child marriage triggers a continuum of violations that continues throughout a girl's life" (Sinha, 2013b, p. 9).

In India, it is the responsibility of the states to develop innovative strategic policies to eliminate child labor and child marriage and to guarantee free and compulsory education for children up to the age of 14. The political class and the bureaucracy in different states have yet to address the issues of child marriage, rural poverty, agricultural stagnation, unemployment, minimum wages, food security, health care, and equal access to meaningful education to millions of children seen begging on the roads.[9] The most important point to note is that "child labour is not only a consequence of poverty, but also one of its causes. Its removal is likely to increase the well-being of the poor" (Weiner, 1991, p. 187). Exposed to violence and abuse, vulnerable to crime, addiction and trafficking, children in the streets and slums of Calcutta and other Indian cities are struggling for basic human needs. No doubt, the states provide primary education. But do they invest in the properly ecologically designed school buildings and in systems of healthy and accountable educational institutions to create responsible, healthy, and happy citizens? The answer is in the negative.

In the field of primary and higher secondary education, any innovation in India would have to take into account possible linkages between (i) the skills, knowledge, beliefs, values, and attitudes acquired in the early years of schooling and productivity in relatively low-skilled occupations (Meier, 1990); (ii) female education and fertility rates as also between education and public health; (iii) education and participatory behavior where technological innovation and interest in politics and civic affairs are concerned; and (iv) primary education, mass literacy and political behavior (Meier, 1990, p. 185). In any case, it can be argued that the universalization of primary education is the first step to developing a resilient human rights developmental environment in which individuals can access their human rights in the pursuit of their aims and objectives in life.

Important questions arise about the possibility of structural changes in the economy such as the introduction of

---

[9] In order to stop the violation of the child labor Prohibition and Regulation Act of 1986, the Supreme Court bench ruled in 1996 to ban the employment of children in hazardous industries. But even this is regarded as inadequate, since bans rarely work in India. On the contrary, every ban is seen as opening up a new avenue of corruption.

technologies that require education or an increase in demand for labor as a result of rapid economic growth (Meier, 1990, p. 187). Recent discussions show agreement among teachers, pupils, parents, and employers that the goal of education "should be to foster such qualities as initiative, problem-solving ability, the ability to work with others, and the ability to understand and influence society" (Raven, 1994, p. 1). Any innovation in the management of education in India would have to find ways and means of investing in human rights developmental environments as the best strategy suited to achieving this very goal. But this also entails necessary changes in the disciplinary matrix, that is, the institutional framework of bureaucratic-hierarchical control. The price for change in the disciplinary matrix for managing education must be paid in terms of the cultural choices that the society and the state ought to make. A culture of participation in the management process must replace the culture of bureaucratic-hierarchical control where the problem of coming to terms with values is concerned. In a nutshell, the society and the state themselves must change their traditional, or habitual, approach to the problem of uplifting children from deprivation and adults from illiteracy. The larger question is what kind of change in attitude to our ancient traditions and values will either precede or follow the rethinking that has become imperative. Primary education is a problem area where there is a vast scope for rethinking and innovation to improve the ecology and productivity of education, with power and resources shifting from state capitals and centralized bureaucracies to local communities or villages in far-flung areas.

Development and Regulation of New Technologies

"It is imperative to foster and develop sciences and technologies that facilitate democratic participation, as well as broaden the public understanding of the nature and purposes of science and technology..." (Rogers, 2008, p. 4)

In the context of technological advances that trigger radical change in society or nature, and in the narrower context of urbanization which is believed to have sparked urban prosperity, how apt is Joseph Schumpeter's (1942) description of "creative destruction"? In a sense, it may be partially correct to claim that modern technological advances have transformed incomes and social indicators of well-being in last two centuries since the Industrial Revolution, while having constantly uprooted existing forms of work, occupations, and social and industrial organization. But an oversimplification such as this can be highly misleading, because "creative destruction" comes at irreversible ecological costs. Unless we identify well-being and prosperity with wealth creation, or limitless economic prosperity, I cannot think of an ecologically neutral criterion with which we may judge radical changes brought about by technological advances *as* ushering in prosperity for one and all. We never care to assess beforehand what freedoms new technologies will take away from ordinary citizens in the name of enhanced prosperity. Dependence on technology could even prove crippling for my health in a city that many may consider to be an engine of limitless economic growth and prosperity.

Turning our attention to media, science, technology, and public policy, how do these impact human life and activity in a globalizing world, particularly in the context of an ecologically challenged Earth? How do they change human society and culture on the one hand and the interaction between man and environment, on the other? Both media and technology create the illusion of bringing people closer, making them feel as if they were more secure than ever before. The truth being quite the opposite, they drive people further apart, creating an unprecedented sense of insecurity, and leading to equally unprecedented fragmentation within society and culture. Consider, for example, the fact that being located somewhere is no longer relevant to human activity or human communication. Think of the technological self. It occupies multiple locations. Within the local communities, what we knew and experienced until recently as the *cultural or ecological self* has become something else – a *mobile self* with multiple locations, or no location at all. As the world gets more and more technologically complicated, global displacement makes room for shifting identities of the *mobile self*. To cite Eldredge (1995), "we told Mother Nature we didn't need her anymore. More frightening, he thinks, is that humans have in recent years moved even further away from the natural processes of life by becoming globally linked – economically, politically and culturally. No other species has defied nature in this way, and Eldredge suspects there will be hell to pay" (Small, 1996, p. 88B). If the ecological and cultural self in us is lost, how can humanity reconnect itself with nature? Despite globalization, how can local communities sustain themselves if they are unable to reconnect with a resilient nature?

The attitude of putting absolute value on mechanization, automation and speed – from the use of machines, in place of human labor, to control systems and information technologies – to optimize productivity in the production of goods and delivery of services leads, in most cases of "creative destruction," to an accelerated domestication of nature (Pandit, 2013a) without any regard for nature or for traditional cultures as *safety filters* of our interaction with nature. As Rogers (2008) puts it, this may allow "human beings to live comfortably in cities, developing politics and the other arts, but, ultimately, humanity will become dominated by its dependence upon artifice, which perpetually creates and destroys, as it drives human beings to innovate an inhumane world that is beyond human control" (p. 38). Since we will always be in search of new technologies, is it possible to distinguish between them and rank them according to their power to accelerate the domestication of nature on the one hand and the dislocation of the worker on the other, both of these at heavy ecological costs? Think of technologies which we should continue to develop and use as against those which, as a matter of policy, we should not develop *without* sufficient caution and further research.

Technologies in aid of Education, Research and Human Development
These technologies, an imperative, contribute to the three most basic dimensions of human development: (i) educational attainment (from schooling onwards) and acquisition of knowledge; (ii) a long and healthy life; and (iii) a decent standard of living. They can be of immense help in promoting equality in education, across the industrialized countries as well as developing countries.

Technologies of Economic Development
These technologies are useful for (i) invigorating the economy and creating or rebuilding the infrastructure for cities and suburbs (e.g., roads, metros, public transport, railways, motorways, buildings, electricity, and means of communication); and (ii) development so that there are more jobs, increased production and quality of life, and workers can attend duty at their place of work, farmers can work at their agricultural fields, public servants can attend their offices, rural populations can do business with the urban institutions, and so on and so forth. These technologies invariably result in accelerated domestication of nature (Pandit, 2013a).

Technologies of Mass Production
Think of capitalism's dominant technologies, over and above mechanized agriculture, automated mass commodity production, transportation and global digital information networks, which involve heavy investment in machines for mass production of consumer goods, guided by the capitalism of the free market and rational consumer. They are deployed to replace man with machines in order to produce more and more not just to reach the ever-widening and ever-growing

consumer world, satisfying their growing needs, but to ensure increasing profits. In genetic engineering, for example, such technologies are deployed to produce designer babies or genetically modified crops and processed food for growing populations. The same is true of biomedical research, as in assisted reproductive technologies and reproductive health technologies (Pandit, 2009).

Technologies of Automation and Accelerated Dislocation
As a step beyond mechanization, these technologies greatly dispense with the need for human sensory and mental requirements while increasing load capacity, speed, and repeatability. They play an increasingly important role in the world economy and in daily experience, accelerating the dislocation of man, and creating a virtual world, known as the global village in popular jargon. In the global village, being located is no longer important to self-identity and human activity. That is to say, location is no longer necessary to extending man's dominion over nature. The virtual world is filled with the illusions of life and activity freed from the conventional distances and physical barriers, as if human beings, societies, and cultures are now becoming closer to one another than ever before. The biggest illusion it creates is the illusion *as if* one were not just an ecological or cultural self within a local community but a mobile self, empowered to occupy multiple identities and to trigger any action with global effects. For example, in conventional wars, location is relevant to strategic human action, so long as identifying and fighting the enemy is important. The location of the armies along the border is of crucial and strategic importance. The question arises whether location is at all so important to destroying an enemy when using nuclear weapons which can be carried and delivered at amazing speeds by deploying appropriate missile technologies. The use of nuclear warheads and missile technologies does not depend on where the fighting armies are located along the border. They can be launched from space or from any third country willing to lend its facilities for such

purposes, managing dislocation and speed simultaneously and aiming at massive destruction in the enemy country. In conventional wars, on the other hand, dislocation and speed are not so easily manageable. Nor is massive destruction easy to manage in such wars. And when destruction is massive, say in a unconventional war, it destroys both man and nature. The damages caused are global and irreversible.

Technologies of Health Care, Environment and Agricultural Production: Redefining Food, Population, Medicine and Public Health Locally and Globally

In the twentieth century the three nutrients, nitrogen, phosphorus, and potassium, enabled agriculture to increase its productivity and the world's population to grow more than sixfold (Vaccari, 2009, p. 43). Thanks to technologies of agricultural production, health care, and medical research, the world recorded the growth of human population from one-and-a-half billion in 1900 to more than six billion in 2000. But the pressure on Earth's finite resources increased so much that her ecosystems suffered a great loss of biodiversity, depletion of water resources, land degradation, exhaustion of fisheries, and an increase in pollution, climate change, and the depletion of the ozone layer.

Technologies of Waste Recycling and Restoring Balance to Ecosystem Services

For example, the inedible parts of plants and animal waste, including bones, which are phosphorus-rich, could be recycled to again become the main sources of fertilizers (Vaccari, 2009, p. 46). Again, recycling urban waste could return phosphorus (and nitrogen) to the land, instead of allowing phosphorus in our diet to go through waste treatment plants and end up in landfills and waterways (Vaccari, 2009, p. 46).

Enabling Technologies for Sustainability (ETS)

ETS refers to innovative technologies which enable policymakers, businesses, and societies to achieve their sustainability objectives. These could include technologies of abatement and emission reduction. Such technologies deal with climate change caused by global warming, itself triggered by human activities, and notably accelerated domestication of nature by creative destruction. Their development is now an imperative for humanity's own survival.

Technologies Used in Biodiagnostic Tests
A major challenge in the diagnostic field is the development of robust, portable, and low-cost technologies that will allow disease markers to be detected reliably in places as diverse as the battlefield, the developing world, community hospitals, the doctor's clinic, or at home (Giljohan & Mirkin, 2009, p. 463). The development and adoption of such technologies by various stakeholders, from researchers, industry, and regulatory bodies to doctors and patients, are not without their challenges (Giljohan & Mirkin 2009, p. 464).

Technologies of Security: From Technology as an Object of Governance to Technology as a Form of Governance
Technologies that are in use and that are being developed in the name of our fight against terrorism raise serious issues of their misuse and abuse. Technologies of security and surveillance easily lend themselves to becoming a form of governance and a form of manipulation *without* transparency and *without* informed consent. Each and every individual, each and every community, becomes a target of suspicion and surveillance. The best example is provided by the NSA's surveillance of Americans and foreigners in the name of the American 'war on terrorism.'

Enter the Era of Warring Technologies
Will not the 21st century unfold as a century of warring technologies to save humanity from its own inventions? Are we not witnessing a new race for hyper-technological capitalist economy which takes pride in developing technologies to *rescue* technologies in disrepute? Do we not live today in a highly

insecure world, with highly insecure information and telecommunication technologies? Why are these technologies being viewed with increasing suspicion and seen more and more as the newest battlefields between states rather than as powerful tools of empowerment of citizens? After the shocking revelations about the totalitarian surveillance by the NSA, does the world need new technology to prevent cyberspace from being misused as a weapon of undeclared war? Does it need new technology to save humanity from its own inventions such as the Internet? As a global policy response to the surveillance-driven violation of basic human rights, freedom of expression, and privacy of individuals, the world might opt for a civilian multilateral framework for governance and regulation of the Internet. The creation of new devices and technologies that are government surveillance resistant is conceivable. But how effective is that going to be in the face of continued government interference? Will that be enough to prevent the misuse of cyberspace and to tame Internet anarchy? Will that prevent powerful nations like the U.S. from subjecting its own citizens and citizens in other countries to totalitarian surveillance? The answer is that history will keep repeating itself: As surveillance can always go viral among nations, the world will race for new technologies that can cope with surveillance as well as bring enormous profits to industry.

In short, if we humans could change not just our bodies and brains but our souls at will, it would be routine to imagine as well as foresee how we might cope with the accelerated advances of technology and their misuse in all areas of experience. It would be routine to imagine how we might cope with the accelerated domestication of nature and creative destruction, how we might cope with a world without nature where everybody lives in cities that promise enhanced prosperity, and how we might cope with the accelerated dislocation of man where, in creative human problem-solving activity, ecology would be a thing of the past. All these would be as manageable as accelerated advances of technologies of totalitarian surveillance that promise security to one particular country at the cost of insecurity in another country. Alas, we humans can change neither our bodies and brains nor our souls at will. While addressing citizens' human rights-related security and privacy concerns, policymakers as well as research communities must instead focus on the dilemma as to how the (retreating) state should gather intelligence using cyberspace, information, and telecommunication technologies.

Tradeoffs between Prosperity and Freedom

> Each generation has an obligation to protect productive ecological and physical processes necessary to support options necessary for future human freedom and welfare. (Norton, 2003, p. 293)

What, then, has freedom in common with education? Is not education the key to freedom that demands thick democracy as a way of life – as a way of organizing economy, society, and governance? The answer is yes, if education is not taken to be only about acquiring more and more knowledge and skills that can make one a better citizen. Education is also about instruction in methods and the inculcation of values that turn the resources of knowledge into *resources of wisdom* so that the world's 'knowledge communities,' in particular the rationality of science, do not turn into yet another 'religion' (Pandit, 2008b). In this sense, there can be no freedom without education that ought to cultivate the ecological and cultural self. If there is anything common between freedom and education, one may, first of all, think of their *indivisibility* insofar as any impoverishment of individual freedom, or of education, in one country or region or group necessarily affects other countries or regions or groups, even more so in today's global village. Secondly, as a corollary, both freedom and education are best approached as humanity's projects of empowerment, which are not without their frontiers. What is

199

true of freedom and education is also true of the basic human rights, generally. If people in one part of the world are not able to enjoy freedom and basic human rights, like those or living in subhuman conditions in the world's slums, or in Tibet (Pandit, 2005), then how can people living in their neighborhood claim to be free individuals, even if they are able to enjoy 'prosperity,' 'freedom' and basic human rights strictly within the geographical boundaries of their own countries or communities? Freedom and universal human rights are *indivisible.* Yet their indivisibility is threatened by *forms of exclusion- and human rights developmental ecology (HRDE)-deprivation* that prevails in many countries across the globe.

In the typical South Asian country, there is the appearance of enjoying political freedom, arguably during the elections for representatives to Parliament. However, the majority know that they do not enjoy economic freedom even after decades of political freedom. They know that mere political freedom does not promote prosperity and other positive conditions of human well-being. They also know that it is economic freedom that can free them from government dependence, allowing them to make their own economic and political choices. Economic freedom may be a necessary condition for prosperity. But is it also necessary for building resilient democracies, by empowering the citizens? The answer is in the affirmative.

As citizens, either we are *all* free, enjoying universal human rights, or we are all *not* free at all if some are unable to enjoy basic human rights in their own countries. In our highly vulnerable and fragile world, which is deeply divided between the rural and urban populations, on the one hand, and developed and developing nations, on the other, none of us can claim to be free so long as there remains even one single individual who is not able to enjoy basic human rights and economic choices. Even if one has everything, still one is not free so long as there is a child next door who regularly goes hungry, who has no access to treated drinking water, and who has no access to education. How can we claim to be free when the recently released Global Hunger Index puts the number of the world's hungry at 842 million in 2011-2013, out of which 210 million, or one-quarter, are in India (Varma, 2013, p. 10)? Millions of children in many countries are not free because they have no access to school, marking a dark spot on humanity. Again, whether or not they are prosperous, under Chinese rule, the Tibetan people are not free. A Tibetan cannot protest against the government policies in his own homeland without inviting prison or death. The example of China as an emerging prosperous economy without democracy is quite instructive. Being prosperous economically does not necessarily mean being free morally or politically. Who can deny how difficult it may turn out to be to sustain economic prosperity without democracy and freedom?

I have argued that freedom and education are as indivisible as are human rights in general. But is prosperity or its enhancement also *indivisible*? I think that it is not indivisible insofar as it enhances and extends the quantitative aspects of economic and intellectual well-being within an ecologically challenged Earth. Whether you are rich enough to buy the goods and services you need to live an easy life or able to save enough money for tomorrow is a question of prosperity in economic dimension. There are urban and rural prosperity just as there are urban and rural poverty. The richest percentage of the global population are the most prosperous in the world. But on the other hand if one has access to education, can express an opinion freely, and criticize the government or its bureaucratic mechanisms without fear of losing one's freedom or other human rights, then it is possible to enhance the quality of life and uphold a sense of dignity – even if going hungry every now and then, even if the need for the latest technologies on a self-interested market remain at arm's length, even if one never has a chance to live an affluent lifestyle in a modern city. Freedom and education as the enhancers of life quality have their frontiers where one learns to recognize first that there are limits to freedom in which education alone can enlighten us, and second that as a moral good freedom needs to be relentlessly safeguarded. But prosperity as an economic good, in contrast to freedom as a moral good, may know no limits (Rogers, 2008, pp. 17-24). Perhaps we should pose this whole question to world's billionaires.

In this sense, the capitalist market rationality and corporate culture, more so the enhanced prosperity they promise, are *asymmetrical* with freedom (Rogers, 2008, p. 20). Capitalism may have brought enhanced prosperity to billions of needy people in the world's cities by leaving out billions of other people in rural areas and urban slums. Must capitalism, therefore, reinvent itself in order to address the pressing problems of growing income and wealth inequality which capitalism itself breeds? Think of a 'sadhu' in prayer, realizing his ecological self in the deepest forests of Himalayas. Think of the ascetic who renounces the amenities of life in favor of a life dedicated to prayer, meditation, and contemplation of the highest spiritual goal, feeling happy and free in his own right. And think of children coming from the poorest of families, passionately seeking their freedom in poorly designed schools and colleges across rural and urban areas in South Asia, making education a primary life goal. And, equally instructive, think of prosperous parents in the developed countries, such as in Europe, who cannot guarantee quality of life to their own children (Pandit, 2007).

The UN Millennium Development Goals (UNMDGs)

To complete my argument from the *indivisibility of freedom*, it is necessary to turn to the UN Millennium Development Goals (UNMDGs), with a view to further conceptualizing fundamental issues concerning human rights.[10] Soon the UN will be 70 years old. A celebration of its 70th year of existence should be a matter of joy everywhere in the world. Its great achievements in helping to build an atmosphere for resilient democracies in conflict zones, in human development, and in the promotion of human rights in the relatively darker parts of the world should not blind us to the fact that its increasingly powerful military role in peace-keeping is indicative of its weakness rather than its strength. In the world's troubled regions that warrant its intervention, are there no other options open to the UN Security Council? I argue that it might be possible for the UN to restore to itself its prime responsibility of defining, reviewing, and monitoring good neighborly relations among the member states, since it is resilient bilateralism more than anything else that is the key to regional and global stability. Thus, I suggest that the key to the UN's success, both morally and legally, lies in adopting a principle of exclusion in order to fight those *forms of exclusion* that flourish in our world, notably the perpetuated hostile neighborhood non-relations (NNRs) among the member states.

It is high time that the UN prioritizes the agenda of a universal declaration on NNRs, if only to give teeth to its other declarations adopted earlier, such as the one on human rights (UDHR, 1948). The reason why this is crucial to its very foundations and future success is that the guiding principle of UN intervention for bringing about any kind of improvement

---

[10] Respect for the sovereignty, territorial integrity, and political independence of every state is a fundamental principle of the UN Charter, in which Article 25 declares that member states "agree to accept and carry out the decisions of the Security Council" in accordance with the Charter (UN, 1983/2011, p. 15). Two types of UN intervention are UN military Observer missions and UN peace-keeping forces. In either case, the necessary contingents are made available by the member states. But should peacekeeping be the prime responsibility of member states themselves under the UN authority?

in a worsening world situation should not be how fast it is able to deploy "its peace-enforcing forces" but how fast and decisive it is in expelling a member state from the UN for failure to maintain healthy neighborly relations. I propose to call it the guiding principle of exclusion to fight the specific *forms of exclusion* that arise in areas of NNRs among the UN member states. Such *forms of exclusion* are known to have caused immense suffering to people in the affected regions. Let us not forget that good neighborly relations among the members of the UN are most crucial not just to world peace but to the UNMDGs and to the indivisibility of human freedom. There is every reason to prioritize it as an agenda at the level of the UN itself.

The asymmetry of prosperity and freedom I argue for here extends to quality of life (Pandit, 2007, 2001a). Indivisibility of freedom, therefore, raises a number of fundamental issues. First, what tradeoffs can there be between freedom, which is indivisible, and enhanced prosperity based on economic growth which is not indivisible, at least in the same sense? Second, what political, educational, and moral challenge does this asymmetry pose to humanity? Third, it was in 2000 that the UN set the UNMDGs to (1) eradicate extreme poverty and hunger; (2) achieve universal primary education; (3) promote gender equality and empower women; (4) reduce child mortality; (5) improve maternal health; (6) combat HIV/AIDS, malaria and other diseases; (7) ensure environmental sustainability; and (8) promote global partnership for development. As an initiative by the UN that for the first time, recognizes how inseparably human rights and human freedom are connected with human development and quality of life, do not the UNMDGs[11] seriously fall short of our expectations, with the deadline fast approaching in 2015?

---

[11] See www.un.org/millenniumgoals/ for further elaboration on the UN Millennium Development Goals.

As will become clear in what follows, what is worse is that the UNMDGs represent a hopeless task without first turning the NNRs into good neighborly relations among the member states of the UN.

Fourth, at what stage of their impact on individual men, women and children, or on an entire society, can we declare recognizable *forms of exclusion* as morally evil or undesirable, inviting creative human intervention on the pattern of the UNMDGs or Universal Declaration of Human Rights (UDHR)? What can the world or the UN do about these forms of exclusion? What can the UN do in order to bring into harmonious relationship with one another the conditions of our knowledge – the state of the art of our discourse on human rights – and the conditions of individual freedom and creativeness under varying political circumstances that prevail in and between different states enjoying membership in the world body?

Picking up a clue from this last question itself, we can look for the *forms of exclusion* in those areas of our daily experience where the two kinds of conditions alluded to do not correlate with each other rationally or harmoniously under the given circumstances, be it in NNRs, in religion and society, in international relations, in science and technology or in academic disciplines. In other words, for a society and a state that is serious about improving the quality of life of its own people, it would be rational to strive after such harmony and irrational not to do so. When it does so, the conditions of knowledge and the conditions of individual freedom would tend to correlate with each other rationally and harmoniously. As a consequence, there will be less and less of the violation of human rights by the individual state itself. And under the opposite circumstances, the two kinds of conditions would appear to exclude each other. It is this kind of situation – where collective failure to use knowledge to safeguard and promote individual freedom and creativity takes place – that I would regard as paradigmatic of morally and legally undesirable *forms of exclusion*. Below, it is my aim to show that a properly worked out higher-order principle of exclusion is at present the best strategy for the UN and world's democracies to fight the undesirable *forms of exclusion* such as exist among the NNRs.

Neighborhood Non-Relations (NNRs)

If we do not undertake creative steps to turn NNRs into neighborly relations, democracy in South Asia will remain in peril and civil society will remain without resilience. These creative steps include investment in education, fostering human rights development environments (HRDE), and ensuring freedom and access to human rights. As a key concept, NNRs refer to forms of exclusion between any two nations locked into a warlike conflict of interests. The indicators of NNRs among the nations of a particular region may be briefly characterized as follows: (1) frequent indulgence in propaganda wars against each other in the international arena; (2) contradictory and widely differing perceptions of their territorial or ideological disputes, if any; (3) surveillance over each other's developmental activities and military defense strategies; (4) negative policies that discourage or prohibit the people-to-people cultural and civilizational interactions; and (5) a race for weapons of destruction such as nuclear-capable ballistic missiles.

Asia, particularly South Asia, provides a very good example of NNRs. Most countries live here in fear of one another, with the NNRs regularly casting their shadows on ordinary citizens, on whole civil societies, preventing them not only from enjoying their basic human rights but from professional mobility and intellectual interactions across vast neighborhoods, without which it is not possible to build lasting bridges of mutual understanding or to help humanity cope best with the global challenges.

Let the 21st century be dedicated to the transformation of NNRs into good neighborly relations among the regional/sub-continental neighbors where people-to-people cultural and civilizational relations are conspicuous by their absence, either because of their failure to resolve disputes over territory or because of extreme differences of political, religious, and ideological nature coming in between them, or because of unilateral policies of using state-sponsored terrorism as a tool to settle the disputes. A paradigmatic case is Pakistan, with the state policy of seeking self-determination for Muslims living in India, which still has the largest Muslim population after Indonesia. With Pakistan pressuring India for self-determination for its growing Muslim populations, the question arises how many more Pakistans should be carved out of secular India to persuade Pakistan to shut down the terrorist machine it has built against India over more than half a century.

In its 68 years of evolution, the UN has made several efforts to improve the human condition. And it has had considerable success. Think of the improvements in sharing and communicating our understanding and knowledge of human rights across the different parts of the world. As signatories of the UDHR, the member states have become beneficiaries insofar as their citizens are concerned, and at the level of the UN or the member states themselves they cannot escape the scrutiny of the monitoring agencies, the so-called HRCs. Yet there regularly arise *forms of exclusion* between the member states which can be regarded as violations of human rights in that these are directly reflected in the development and the quality of life of their respective populations. Where any two member states, engaged in a perpetual state of hostile NNRs, are not willing to explore priorities for inclusive forms of development that could engage the creative attention and imagination of the people across the two counties, what can the UN, or its agencies, do? Where state policy and political leadership knowingly hamper those forms of development that presuppose not just adequate resources to pursue them but also good neighborly relations among the states, what are the options? After all, it is the human rights of people themselves that suffer most under hostile NNRs between any two states. Has the UN ever paid sufficient attention to the question of how to safeguard human rights in such situations of exclusion?

Sadly and strangely enough, the UNMDGs do not even mention this problem. It might be said in reply that every year the UN plays host to its members that include warring representatives from hostile neighborhoods, with the explicit intention of providing them a forum for debate. But does this lead the UN or the countries in question anywhere? Is not a better role for the UN thinkable if it is to save its time and funds for more urgent humanitarian tasks? For example, it is certainly a more urgent task to identify and to declare hostile NNRs as a major threat to world peace, on the one hand, and as a major cause of global human rights violations, on the other. Think of the right to better education, better standards of living and development, and better quality of life. They demand a resilient HRDE for their fulfillment.

Those neighborhoods that show a strong or a chronic tendency to perpetuating hostility between member states at the cost of the quality of life of the people themselves are the best candidates for exclusion at appropriate levels of UN membership. How can their membership in the UN go hand-in-hand with their perpetuation of hostile NNRs without serious contradiction? Evidently, the latter are damaging to the very cause for which the UN came into being. It is high time that the UN debate hostile NNRs across the world in depth. And it should lose no more time in according highest priority to a universal declaration on them as posing the greatest danger to humanity and to the UN, UDHR and UNMDGs. In failing to do so, the UN only invites its own abuse by the member states in question. It is needless to emphasize here that even in the case of hostile NNRs inherited from the past, the respective governments are normally expected to work speedily to reduce hostility and to come down with a heavy hand on any kind of concerted attempt to exacerbate NNRs. The puzzling silence of the UN on hostile NNRs amounts to connivance with those very forces that are determined to perpetuate them, for whatever reason. If the UN is to develop as expected into a strong moral and legal force of an international culture of peace and human development, then it is imperative that it prevents its own abuse and promotes exclusion as a guiding principle to fight *forms of exclusion* that mushroom as hostile NNRs between its members. Terrorism is just one symptom of such *forms of exclusion*.

Rethinking the UN

As regards the UDHR and UNMDGs, I want to draw attention not just to a serious lack of conceptual clarity on fundamental issues but to the collective moral failure of mankind, current forms of the UN intervention notwithstanding. No part of the world is without its serious violations of human rights. Perpetuated hostile NNRs among the member states in South Asia, and between Israel and its Arab neighbors, pose problems of chronic violation of the human rights of present and future generations of people living in those parts of the world. In the context of human rights, human development, and an international culture of peace, we must ask whether the member states that perpetuate hostile NNRs between and among themselves deserve to be the beneficiaries of continued UN membership. A member state that fails to see and remedy the contradiction of its status as a member state is not fit for such membership. The real limbs of the UN are its member states. By virtue of being included in its body-politic, they cannot choose to remain outside its programs, policies, declarations, and commitments such as the UDHR and the UNMDGs. In the case of perpetuated hostility with a neighbor, a member state should either voluntarily opt out of the UN or be expelled.

The threat of loss of membership is the first decisive step toward deterring irresponsible governments. At the same time, potential expulsion should have great motivational value, for it can bring about positive change in the behavior of political leaders, particularly those whose perceptions of crime against humanity vary directly in proportion to their thirst for ruthless personal power and prosperity.

The three biggest challenges before the UN and the world's democracies are first, to turn the NNRs into good neighborly relations, keeping individual human rights in view; second, to promote human rights in their developmental and educational dimensions; and third, to address the heinous crimes that statistics reveal are being committed against women and children in various nations on a regular basis. I have argued that the second challenge of promoting human development and education, best represented by the UDHR and UNMDGs, is a near-hopeless task without rationally addressing the first challenge of eliminating NNRs. If there is an urgency to adopt a fresh universal declaration on eliminating NNRs, then it is no less urgent to do the same on the third challenge by adopting a declaration that recognizes that the rape and abuse of children constitutes a heinous crime against humanity in violation of basic universal human rights.

Moreover, the UN has not yet mandated an ethical orientation to the concept of a member state. Nor is the member state concept a well-defined concept. Thus, the UN is in a peculiar position. It enjoys supremacy in defining human rights. But it can do very little about their being regularly violated, particularly in regions of chronic hostile NNRs. Before debating the options that may be open to it in such situations, the UN must confer moral value on the concept of a member state. In other words, the UNSC and UN General

Assembly must adopt a suitable declaration which requires that a member state shall be committed to good neighborly relations even in worst of circumstances. Of course, the details need to be worked out carefully. Such a declaration would go a long way to prevent UN membership from being abused by the member states themselves. Further, it would be a valuable step towards the fulfillment of the UDHR and UNMDGs. To this very day, in known hostile NNRs, the role of the UN has been interpreted to mean either its active military intervention by maintaining its presence in those regions that invite its attention or its readiness to offer its fora for the demonstration of respective standpoints by the member states concerned. This approach is entirely wrongheaded.

A universal declaration on good neighborly relations between member states and on the unacceptability of the rape and abuse of children as heinous crimes against humanity in violation of human rights is long overdue. The governments of the respective member states will come and go every four or five years. But a situation of perpetually hostile NNRs brings enormous protracted suffering, including mental suffering that these member state's peoples certainly do not deserve. The perpetuation of NNRs also subjects the UN to grave abuse by the warring neighbors who invest heavily in their propagandist debates at the UN. The UN's role as a forum for these debates only encourages member states to maintain or escalate their tensions so long as they are assured the provision of this permanent forum.

Think of any two member states engaged in a perpetuated hostility and conflict, as a result of which their respective peoples are excluded from one another in vital areas of educational, economic, cultural, scientific and human interaction. Not only this, within their own respective boundaries they are excluded from better standards of living and better quality of life. Often, in the name of hostility and conflict, politicians justify keeping themselves in power. It is

211

needless to add how the two governments must compete in arms build-up, in military expenditure, and in propaganda. Who pays the price in this type of situation? Certainly, it is their respective peoples and future generations, and not their governments. In any case, what is the best form of UN intervention in such situation? It is not allowing them to perpetually debate their differences at the UN, as Pakistan and India are doing. Nor is it an active UN presence in their respective territories, in whichever form it be, as is the current practice. I have argued that the best course of the UN intervention is to penalize the member states in question by cancelling their memberships until such time when they work for good neighborly relations, bringing relief to their peoples by reducing the hostility. Such a course of UN action can be supported not only on the grounds of its non-violent character and in terms of its new declarations on good neighborly relations but also on the grounds of the probable healthy consequences this will have for the well-being of the present and future generations.

Among the probable long-term consequences of new universal declaration for which I have argued, the following are notable: (1) It would raise the stature of the UN and enhance the quality of discussions and debates on vital issues other than the NNRs; (2) It would direct the UN's attention to developmental and educational dimensions of human rights in every state, promoting the UDHR and UNMDGs; (3) It would greatly reduce the capacity of member states to abuse the UN's fora by resorting to propaganda and misinformation about each other; (4) It would greatly reduce the capacity of the superpower(s), or any group of countries, to fish in the troubled waters across the world; and (5) Above all, it would enhance the image of the UN as the world body that cares to implement and monitor implementations of its own declarations by its member states. At present, the UN is increasingly taken for granted as a peace-enforcing body. But my proposal is intended to raise it to a new level, if only to bring its earlier declarations in harmony with its ethical and legal tasks. Let the peace-enforcing be a fundamental moral and legal responsibility of each member state under UN authority. Given good neighborly relations between the member states – in the minimalistic sense of the anticipated revised universal declaration – the UN could assume more serious duties for improving the human condition on Earth while promoting the UDHR and UNMDGs at the same time. In any case, rethinking the UN is imperative for purpose of building its resilience and for rebuilding democracy on a global scale.

To conclude this discussion, it might be asked how the present and the future generations will be equipped to (i) universally cope with the state of void into which the state of governance, conspicuous by its absence, has slipped; (ii) rebuild democracy and create resilient society; (iii) safeguard free access to human rights, under the retreat of the state (Pandit, 2000; Strange, 1998); and (4) fight at the frontier of gender inequality in education. The challenge presented by these tasks is universally felt by freedom-loving individuals in today's highly globalized world. In this world, the state and the people, living amid each other's fears and in fear of terrorism, must increasingly push themselves into situations in which they are obliged to confront each other as strangers and rivals. Consider, for example, the homeland security scenarios across the world. These are no different from public security scenarios at international airports. The latter increasingly look like concentration camps in which every passenger is treated and harassed as a 'terrorist' until they manage to reach home safely. The larger question is how frighteningly the state of void is engulfing the entire world. The situation has become worse in South Asia. In India, the most ordinary people, who try to solve the everyday problems of living independent of any help from the complicated bureaucratic mechanisms of the state, have wondered for the last several decades whether they and the future generations will ever enjoy their basic human rights to liberty, dignity, and security of life, free from the fear of terrorist strikes.

In simpler words, if there is a single universal human right that underscores the unstated assumptions or subtext of the UDHR and the ritual dynamics of the rights-awareness campaigns across the globe, it is *the one and only one* human right that entitles one and all to relentlessly fight for basic human rights, no matter how long it takes and no matter how high a price it demands. This may provide the best explanation why it has been so difficult and complicated for the members of the UN to implement the UDHR, not merely in the policy dimension but in the developmental and educational dimensions. But it raises a deeper question: Which of these human rights is then more fundamental? Is it *the one and only one* human right to fight for all other human rights that is most fundamental? Or, is it the latter that are more fundamental, so that the right to fight for all other rights is not a fundamental right? If the answer to the latter question is in the affirmative, then an individual's right to fight for all other rights is seriously undermined. If the answer is in the negative, then the UDHR leaves us with human rights which are not so fundamental.

On the other hand, any program of empowerment, education, and quality of life is bound to remain flawed, fragmented, and incomplete if the issue of the breach of gender equality in education is not seriously addressed. In rethinking education, in particular in the context of developing countries, the single biggest challenge is that the whole meaning and purpose of education, at every level, is lost within and between the bureaucratic structures and organizations of the educational institutions themselves. Second, these institutions fail to inspire a sense of personal security, confidence, and problem-solving initiative among the younger generation, particularly among children. Third, they fail to inculcate a culture of wisdom and values of social justice. Finally, any program of empowerment of the masses of rural and urban poor children, promising to lift them out of poverty and illiteracy, is easily breached by the environs of terrorism. Chronic absence of a developmental environment, within as well as outside the school, where children, particularly girls, can feel safe and secure creates alarming patterns of school dropout, seriously impacting higher education in the colleges and universities. How alarming the situation is can be gauged from the resulting gender gaps in education at all levels.

These conditions raise the most basic questions as to how prepared as a whole the world is to foster a universally democratic climate. When individual countries as members of the UN still do not offer safe conditions for women and school-going children, when they fail to work effectively under the jurisdiction of their governments to transform environs of terrorism into environments conducive to development, and when they fail to transform the chronic evils of neighborhood non-relations that prevail across different continents into those of good neighborly relations, these are not conditions conducive to building a democratic world. Many of the world's nations have thus far failed to deliver on agendas of empowerment through education, as promised, in terms of the UN Millennium Development Goals. The goals of suitably educating all of the world's inhabitants must be fulfilled in order to move forward in building a democratic world.

References

Alberts, B. (2013, April 19). Prioritizing science education. *Science, 340*, 249.

Bamzai, P. N. K. (1962/1973). *A history of Kashmir.* Delhi, India: Metropolitan Book Centre.

Buckley, R. (2006, April 13). Industry: Speak up to stop its pressure on academia. [Correspondence]. *Nature, 440*, 868.

Clemenz, G. (2007, August). *Our knowledge of markets for knowledge.* Symposium conducted at the meeting of the International Wittgenstein Symposium, Kichberg, Austria.

Clos, J. (2012/2013). The world urban forum edition of the state of the world's cities report. [Foreword]. Prosperity of Cities, United Nations Human Settlements Programme (UN-HABITAT). Retrieved from www.unhabitat.org

Dejaeghere, J., & Tudball, L. (2007). Looking back, looking forward: Critical citizenship as a way ahead for civics and citizenship education in Australia. *Citizenship Teaching and Learning, 3*(2), 40-57.

Dutt, J. C. (1986). *Rajtarangini of Jonaraja.* (Kashi Nath Pandita, Trans.). Delhi, India: Gian Pubishing House.

The Economist (2013 15th-21st June), p. 12.

Eldredge, N. (1995). *Dominion.* New York, NY: Henry Holt and Company.

Feingold, S. (2013, August 25). One rape every 20 minutes in country. *Sunday Times of India*, p. 6.

Germund, W. (2013a, January 4). Tages Thema: Protest und Populismus. *Berliner Zeitung*, p. 2.

Germund, W. (2013b, January 5/6). Politik: Indien streitet über die Todesstrafe. *Berliner Zeitung.* p. 7.

Giljohan, D. A., & Mirkin, C. A. (2009, November 26). Drivers of biodiagnostic development. *Nature, 462,* 461-464.

Gill, K. S. (2013, June 3). Righting the basic wrongs. *The Times of India*, p. 14.

Giroux, H. A. (2000). *Stealing innocence: Youth, corporate power and the politics of culture*. Basingstoke, U.K.: Palgrave.

Gupta, D. (2013, May 25). Corruption of the American dream. *The Times of India*, p. 14.

Hardin, G. (1968, December 13). The tragedy of the commons. *Science, 162*, 1243-1248.

Hardin, G. (1998, May 1). Extensions of the tragedy of the commons. *Science, 280*, 682-683.
Retrieved from www.sciencemag.org

Howard, C., & Patten, S. (2006). Valuing civics: Political commitment and the new citizenship education in Australia. *Canadian Journal of Education, 29*, 454-475.

Kak Odin, J. (1999). *To the other shore: Lalla's life and poetry*. New Delhi, India: Vitasta Publications.

Koul, S. C. (1967/1946). *Srinagar and its environs*. Srinagar, India: Utpal Publications.

Krugman P. (2013, June 13). Sympathy for the Luddite. *New York Times*.
Retrieved from
http://www.nytimes.com/2013/06/14/opinion/krugman-sympathy-for-the-luddites.html

Malouf, D. (2011). *The happy Life: The search for contentment in the modern world*. London: Chatto & Windus.

Markwell, D. (2007). *A large and liberal education: Higher education for the 21st century.* Melbourne, Australia: Australian Scholarly Press.

Meier, G. M. (1990). *Leading issues in economic development.* Delhi, India: Oxford University Press.

Mitra, D. (1977). *Pandrethan, Avantipur and Martand.* New Delhi, India: Archaeological Survey of India.

Nagarajan, R. (2008, August 31). Will changing land laws ensure peace? *The Sunday Times of India,* New Delhi.

Norton, B. G. (2003). *Searching for sustainability: Interdisciplinary essays in the philosophy of conservation biology.* New York, NY: Cambridge University Press.

Pandit, G. L. (1982). Human rights: A delimitation of political ideology. *Akashvani 47th Year: A Human Rights Special Issue, 7,* 5-7.

Pandit, G. L. (1995). Von der Oekologie des Bewusstseins zum Umweltrealismus: Die Wiederentdeckung menschlicher und nicht-menschlicher Interessenssphaeren. *Wiener Vorlesungen, 41.* Vienna, Austria: Picus Verlag.

Pandit, G. L. (1998, Jan-March). [Review of the book *The clash of civilizations and the remaking of world order,* by S. P. Huntington, 1997.] Viking: Penguin India. *World Affairs, 2,* 135-137.

Pandit, G. L. (2000, January-March). [Review of the book *The retreat of the state: The diffusion of power in the world economy,* by S. Strange, 1998]. *World Affairs: The Journal of International Issues* 4: 113-115.

Pandit, G. L. (2001a). Participate and reconnect: The problem of improving the human condition. *Systemica, 13*, 337-341.

Pandit, G. L. (2001b). Tradition and innovation in Asian culture: India. Raul Fornet-Betancourt (Hrsg.) *Kulturen zwischen Tradition und Innovation: Stehen wir am Ende der traditionellen Kulturen?* IKO: Verlag fuer Interkulturelle Kommunikation: Frankfurt, Germany, 48-64. Dokumentation des III. Internationalen Kongress für Interkulturelle Philosophie: Aachen, 22.-25. November 1999.

Pandit, G. L. (2005, Jan-March). World's refugees. *World Affairs, 9*, 148-156.

Pandit, G. L., (2006, July-Sept). Exclusion and uprootment in Kashmir. *World Affairs, 10*, 152-171.

Pandit, G. L. (2007, August). Ethical tasks of media advocacy in the 21st century. Philosophie der Informationsgesellschaft / Philosophy of the Information Society, Beiträge des 30. Internationalen Wittgenstein Symposium (5 - 11 August 2007), Volume XV. In H. Hrachovec, A. Pichler, & J. Wang (Eds.), pp. 169-173. Kichberg am Wechsel. Austrian Ludwig Wittgenstein Society. Retrieved from http://wab.uib.no/agora-alws/

Pandit, G. L. (2008a, February). Unrecognized minorities. *Combat Communalism Forum, 14*, 1-3.

Pandit, G. L. (2008b, July). Universities with a room for wisdom inquiry. *Friends of Wisdom Newsletter, 3*, 4-9.

Pandit, G. L. (2009). Ethics in the public domain: Biomedical research and beyond. In A. Srivastava and I. Roy (Eds.),

Bio-Nano-Geo Sciences: The Future Challenge, Humboldt-Kolleg-Palampur (India). New Delhi/Chennai/Mumbai, India: Anne Books. 187-208. See also www.science-cooperation.org/www.science-circle.org

Pandit, G. L. (2010, Jan-March). State of collective crimes. *World Affairs,14*, 164-176.

Pandit, G. L. (2013a). Ecosystem resilience: A long journey to nature policy. In S. Nautiyal, K. S. Rao, H. Kaechele, K. V. Raju, & R. Schaldach (Eds.), Knowledge Systems of Societies for Adaptation and Mitigation of Impacts of Climate Change (Environmental Science and Engineering). Berlin/Heidelberg, Germany: Springer Verlag, 57-86.

Pandit, G. L. (2013b, March). Against the state of collective crimes: The way ahead to the improvement of the human condition. Manuscript in preparation.

Panun Kashmir Movement (2004). *Kashmir Documentation: Pandits in exile*. New Delhi, India: Utpal Publications, p. 494.

Philip, A. (2005). Ships passing in the night: The current state of the human rights and development debate seen through the lens of the millennium development goals. *Human Rights Quarterly, 27*(3), 755-827.

Pinter, H. (2005, Dec. 7). Harold Pinter Nobel lecture: Art, truth and politics. Retrieved from nobelprize.org

Rajghatta, C. (2013a, June 8). Out in the open: U.S. e-surveillance goes beyond America. *Times of India*, p. 22.

Rajghatta, C. (2013b, November 1). NSA went too far spying: Kerry. *The Times of India*, p. 24.

Raven, J. (1994). *Managing education for effective schooling*. New York, NY & Ontario, Canada: Trillium Press.

Reid, A. (2002). Public education and democracy: A changing relationship in a globalizing world. *Journal of Educational Policy 17*, 571-585.

Reid, A. (2005). Rethinking the democratic purposes of public schooling in a globalizing world. In M. W. Apple, J. Kenway, & M. Singh (Eds.), *Globalizing education: Policies, pedagogies & politics*. New York, NY: Peter Lang.

Rogers, K. (2008). *Participatory democracy, science and technology: An exploration in the philosophy of science*. Basingstoke, UK, and New York, NY: Palgrave Macmillan.

Rosen, J. (2013, 24 June). The deciders. *Time*, *24*.

Saran, S. (2013, October 13). *Sunday Times of India*, p. 19.

Schumpeter, J. (1942/1962). *Capitalism, socialism, and democracy*. New York, NY: Harper.

Sinha, K. (2013a, June 8). Is India snooping on its citizens like the US? *Times of India*.

Sinha, K. (2013b, Oct.14). India rejects UN resolution against child marriage. *Times of India*.

Small, M. F. (1996, March). Paleontological predictions. [Review of the book *Dominion*, by Niles Eldredge]. *Scientific American*, *274*(3), 112-114.

Suraiya, J. (2008, August 11). God, you're useless. *The Times of India*. New Delhi.

Strange, S. (1998). *The retreat of the state: The diffusion of power in the world economy*, Cambridge, UK: Cambridge University Press.

United Nations, *Basic Facts About the UN*. (1983/2011). New York, NY: UN Publications.

Varma, S. (2013, October 15). India home to a quarter of the world's hungry. *Times of India*, p. 10.

Vaccari, D. (2009, June). Phosphorus: A looming crisis. *Scientific American*, 42-47.

Weiner, M. (1991). *The child and the state in India*. Princeton, NJ: Princeton University Press.

Zyngier, D. (2012). Rethinking the thinking on democracy in education: What are educators thinking (and doing) about democracy? *Education*, *2*, 1-21. doi:10.3390/educ2010001

Deweyan Democracy, Cosmopolitanism, and Music Education in South Africa

Alethea de Villiers
Nelson Mandela Metropolitan University, Port Elizabeth,
South Africa

Abstract

John Dewey saw the role of society as developing characteristics in children so that they conformed to group norms. He viewed the school as an environment that purposefully influenced the mental and moral dispositions of learners. Though Dewey's philosophies precede the human rights documents of the twentieth century, these documents resonate with his philosophies and have led to education for democratic citizenship in schools comprising multicultural content across the curriculum, active teaching and learning strategies, human rights education, and learning about and experiencing democracy. Since the adoption of the new Constitution in South Africa it became policy to educate for democratic citizenship. I provide a concise background of the situation prior to South Africa's becoming a democracy and reflect on and analyze educational practices within the community of music education students whom I teach and prepare for their future role as teachers in a democratic society. The framework for music education draws on the broader Deweyan definition of creating democratic communities and on subsequent related work on cosmopolitanism by Osler and Starkey.

Keywords: democracy, John Dewey, cosmopolitanism, music education

In his seminal work, *Democracy and Education,* first published in 1916, John Dewey states that the importance of education lies in its role of giving children opportunities to adapt to learn about the society in which they live. A society's continued existence is dependent on its members learning about group practices. Modern societies are sophisticated, which results in a gap between the abilities of their young, uninitiated members, and adults. For this reason the young need education in order to participate as vested members. Education is an activity through which children are raised to become vigorous stewards of its resources and ideals. This will ensure the continued survival of the society. Education is the vehicle that shapes, forms and molds the individual for a purpose through example, and from Dewey's perspective this purpose is educating for democratic citizenship. Within a social environment, the young learn that their actions affect others. Members of the group, as social beings, have an intrinsic need to be part of the group and fear ostracization. This inherent need of the young to belong leads them to conform to group norms. The school creates an environment that serves to influence the mental and moral dispositions of the learners so that they conform to the expectations of the norms of society (Dewey, 1940, pp. 6-8; Dewey, 2009, pp. 9-13).

Dewey and Citizenship in a Democracy

Dewey's views are still relevant to education today. He considered its heterogeneous nature as one of the most important characteristics of society. Although the society of his time was not as heterogeneous as that of today, Dewey nevertheless recognized that what on the surface could appear to be a fairly homogeneous society on closer inspection would reveal pluralities. Dewey observed that within a society there exist many smaller diverse groups, each with its own rules and traditions. These groups may be political, religious, familial, or otherwise binding its members. Each of these groups is characterized by members having common interests and interacting and cooperating with each other. A further characteristic of groups is that they socialize individuals to become fully fledged members of the group. Dewey acknowledged that each group within a society functions as a unique and independent entity that sometimes intersects at points of common interest such as in the school community. Dewey compared society to schools. He viewed schooling and the teaching and learning engaged in by both the learners and teachers as a social process. The populations of schools belong to diverse groups who coexist and interact with each other daily within the school. School can be seen to be a microcosm of society with the potential to educate for democratic citizenship. Supporters of multicultural education share this view (Banks, 1989, pp. 13-14; Dewey, 1940, p. 8; Dewey, 2009, p. 46).

Dewey therefore questioned the validity and appropriateness of education if it did not consider the pluralities represented in the broader society (Dewey 2009, pp. 46-47). Another important aspect of Dewey's definition of democracy is that it is more than a form of government: democracy is essentially a way of associated living. He therefore stressed the fundamental importance of educating for democratic citizenship to develop the appropriate dispositions for people to interact with each other in pluralistic or multicultural societies. These dispositions include appreciating cultural diversity, promoting tolerance and making a positive contribution to a democratic society. Developing these dispositions is crucial for citizenship education today.

Dewey's definition of citizenship in a democracy is linked to the philosophy of the Enlightenment and most specifically cosmopolitanism. Cosmopolitanism is an extension of liberalism, which is the moral philosophy underpinning liberal democracy with "upholding the dignity and inherent rights of individuals that can be considered to be universal human rights" (Beiner, 1995, p. 2, as cited in Osler & Starkey, 2005, p. 20).

Dewey furthermore states that an undesirable society is one in which there are barriers to free intercourse and the communication of experience. An ideal society is one in which provisions are made for participation in its good for all its members on equal terms. There should also be an assurance that institutions can adjust through interaction. Such a society then needs a system of education which gives its members a personal interest in social relationships and control and the habits of mind which can lead to social changes without leading to chaos (Dewey, 2009, p. 55). Dewey had in mind a universal type of citizenship that was not linked to the nation-state. Osler and Starkey (2005) reiterated Dewey's viewpoint that citizenship should be cosmopolitan, transcend the barriers of nationhood, and rather focus on people's humanity (p. 19; Dewey, 2009, p. 52). In many countries the state took over the role of educating its citizens from the church and made education compulsory. In these countries the goal of education then became linked to the goals of the state. As a result, education became a tool of the state to shape its citizens for their designated roles in society. In many instances this education was nationalistic as the state sought to educate for the role of patriotic citizen. The role of teachers was also redefined so that they in a sense became agents of the nation-state and were expected to show loyalty and promote patriotism. The state deemphasized its people's humanity and supplanted cosmopolitanism with nationalism (Dewey, 2009, pp. 52-53; Osler & Starkey, 2005, p.19). Consequently, the Deweyan ideal of cosmopolitan humanitarianism was lost (Dewey, 2009, p. 53).

The specific context for this paper is a South African university music education program presented from a Deweyan perspective. Dewey was writing in the U.S. which, from its inception, was intended to be a democratic nation.

However, it was only over a period of time that various groups, including freed slaves and African Americans, were able to become full members of the democracy.

In contrast, before 1995 South Africa was a polarized society, with all spheres of life including education segregated according to race. While segregation had a negative impact on all non-White groups, including Coloureds and Indians,[19] I will focus on the impact of apartheid on the Black population. Blacks were denied South African citizenship, had no political rights, and could not own land. The *Bantu Education Act* of 1953 resulted in education for the Black population, which had been offered by missionaries but was then taken over by the apartheid state. State control led to an inferior school curriculum to match the state's envisaged future life roles for them as blue collar workers. Considerably less money was spent on the education of the Black child. Additionally, there existed an official policy of Christian National Education which enshrined White Afrikaner dominance. The role of teachers became that of agents for the apartheid state as teachers were compelled to teach the inferior school curriculum and promote Christian National Education. The segregation extended to higher education when liberal English universities that were racially integrated came under fire. Legislation resulted in the creation of racially exclusive universities (Davenport, 1988, pp. 361-381). South African society was undesirable because there were barriers to free intercourse among the different racial groups and education was used as a vehicle of indoctrination to realize and perpetuate gross inequalities.

---

[19] In South Africa the term Indian refers to someone who is from India or whose ancestors originally came from India. The term "Coloured" refers to people who have both ancestors who are White and ancestors who are indigenous to Africa. Though pejorative in the U.S. and other parts of the developed world, racial terminology is still used in South Africa today for purposes of redress and equity and as such is retained in this paper.

The period 1956-1978 was characterized by the enactment of various laws to strengthen apartheid alongside resistance to the apartheid state (Davenport, 1988, pp. 382-437). The early 1980s to the early 1990s was a time of civil unrest and simultaneously a period when the presiding government sought ways to transform South African society (Blumfield, 2008). From the late 1980s the government began to address the inequalities in education. The National Policy Initiative (NEPI) Report of 1992 made various statements, including that curriculum policy in South Africa be based on an analysis of existing circumstances and combined with the goals of social development. According to this report, education and training would need to be integrated and address the job market and inequalities in education (Malan, 1997, p. 3). In 1992, certain changes occurred in education. These included the abolishment of education financing, the change of the status of schools, reflection on a different model for education and the implementation of multicultural education (de Villiers, 2000, p. 11; van Wyk, 1992, as cited in Le Roux, 1997, p. 4). Various types of schooling systems came into being in South Africa in the early 1990s. These schooling systems were private, state-subsidized, and state-funded schools. Due to these changes former Whites-only schools became more accessible to other population groups. The historically Indian and Coloured schools also became more racially and culturally integrated, while former Blacks-only schools remained homogeneous. With the adoption of a new Constitution the racially separate education departments were abolished and new legislation introduced. This led to a single education system with one education policy and one national curriculum that promoted democratic citizenship.

The new Constitution was the turning point in South African history as we as a society began our journey as a democracy based on human rights. The South African Constitution defines citizenship as a common South African citizenship and states that all individuals have the rights, privileges and benefits of citizenship and that they are subject to the duties and responsibilities of citizenship. Additionally, the Constitution identifies the national anthem and the national flag and promotes multilingualism. In the Preamble there is a phrase that reads that we are "united in our diversity" (Constitution of South Africa, Act 108 of 1996). While citizenship is not defined in cosmopolitan terms, the definition of South African citizenship promotes diversity of language yet not culture, although in South Africa, language is most often synonymous with culture.

Citizenship is further defined in school curriculum documents. Earlier versions of the post-1994 school curriculum explicitly stated that its overarching aim was to develop learners' ability to play a constructive role in a democratic, non-racist and equitable society (Department of Education, October 1997, p. 4). This definition has been modified in subsequent revisions of the school curriculum and references to citizenship include the infusion of the principles and practices of human rights, inclusivity, and environmental and social justice. Diversity should also be valued within the classroom across all the learning areas and subjects (Department of Education, 2011, pp. 14-15).

To support the school curriculum that is infused with the values of the Constitution, the National Department of Education embarked on various initiatives to support the Constitution and education policy. One of these initiatives was the Values Manifesto of 2001. The Manifesto recognizes ten fundamental values derived from the Constitution and serves to embrace the spirit of a democratic, non-racial and non-sexist South Africa. These values are democracy, social justice and equity, equality, non-racism and non-sexism, Ubuntu (human dignity), an open society, accountability (responsibility), the rule of law, respect, and reconciliation. Institutions were expected to use this Manifesto to develop values statements and a values action plan. The Values Manifesto lists a number of educational strategies to realize the values.[20]

In South Africa we have experienced the adoption of the Constitution based on a bill of rights and goals for education that are both humanitarian and cosmopolitan in their focus. Cosmopolitanism is evident in the concept of Ubuntu and infusion of values across the curriculum. The African philosophy of Ubuntu is closely linked to cosmopolitanism and humanitarianism. According to the Values Manifesto, Ubuntu includes mutual understanding of others. Mokgoro (1997) stated that Ubuntu is synonymous with humanity. A person can only be a person through others. In accordance with our democracy the Values Manifesto makes explicit that Ubuntu refers to appreciating, valuing, and respecting diversity.

The intention of education policy according to the Values Manifesto is that South African schools be democratic communities of practice where democratic principles are experienced in both formal and informal curricula so that learners develop the disposition for living democratically. This proposed approach is very similar to Dewey's ideal of the school as a community in which democracy is practiced as a way of life. Nevertheless, as a direct result of our past we have a situation in which the young are uninitiated and the adults who are supposed to guide them also have not been initiated in democratic practices.

In many Western democracies over the last century the characteristics and dispositions that have been developed through citizenship education have derived from an assimilationist, nationalist and patriotic approach that loses

---

[20] The Values Manifesto can be found at
http://www.info.gov.za/view/DownloadFileAction?id=70295

sight of the diversity of identities that exist within modern societies. Despite this nationalistic approach to democratic citizenship in the twentieth and twenty-first centuries, citizenship education in schools, having grown out of a need to sustain democracy in modern times (Print, 2008, as cited in Arthur et al., 2008, p. 96) has been greatly influenced by the education articles contained in the Universal Declaration of Human Rights (UDHR) and the Convention on the Rights of the Child (CRC).

Both these documents inform human rights and have an impact on the constitutions of democracies and by implication the education policies in democracies (De Villiers, 2004, p. 36). This is also true for South Africa which contains the Bill of Rights in chapter two of the Constitution. The Universal Declaration of Human Rights (UDHR) was adopted by the General Assembly of the United Nations in 1948 and can be regarded as the beginning of the establishment of universal human rights. Its articles define rights and fundamental freedoms for all of humanity. Article 26 of the UDHR states the following:

1. Everyone has the right to education. Education shall be free, at least in the elementary and fundamental stages. Elementary education shall be compulsory. Technical and professional education shall be made generally available and higher education shall be accessible to all on the basis of merit.
2. Education shall be directed to the full development of the human personality and to the strengthening of respect for human rights and fundamental freedoms. It shall promote understanding, tolerance and friendship among all nations, racial or religious groups, and shall further the activities of the United Nations for the maintenance of peace.

3. Parents have a prior right to choose the kind of education that shall be given to their children.[21]

The inclusion of the right to education was the beginning of a larger attempt by the United Nations to promote social, economic and cultural rights together with civil and political rights. The indivisibility of these rights is guaranteed by the 1989 Convention on the Rights of the Child (CRC). The CRC became law on 2 September 1990 and is legally binding on all states that ratify it.[22] The Convention on the Rights of the Child and specifically Article 29 resonate with the Deweyan perspective of citizenship, with an emphasis on common humanity and interpersonal interaction. Article 29 states the following:

Education for the child shall be directed to:

(a) The development of the child's personality, talents and mental and physical abilities to their fullest potential;

(b) The development of respect for human rights and fundamental freedoms, and for the principles enshrined in the Charter of the United Nations;

(c) The development of respect for the child's parents, his or her own cultural identity, language and values, for the national values of the country in which the child is living, the country from which he or she may originate, and for the civilizations different from his or her own;

(d) The preparation of the child for responsible life in a free society, in the spirit of understanding, peace,

---

[21] The Universal Declaration of Human Rights can be read on the United Nations' website at http://www.un.org/en/documents/udhr/

[22] The Convention on the Rights of the Child can be read at http://www.ohchr.org/EN/ProfessionalInterest/Pages/CRC.aspx

tolerance, equality of sexes, and friendship among all peoples, ethnic, national and religious groups and persons of indigenous origin; and

(e) The development of respect for the natural environment.

Citizenship Education in Democracies

Education policies in many democracies from 2002 onwards have begun to address the issue of educating for democratic citizenship in schools. This is specifically the case in the U. S., the U. K., and Australia (Hahn, 2002, p. 77; Hahn, 2008, pp. 268-270; Osler & Starkey, 2001, p. 85; Parker, Ninomiya & Cogan, 2002, p. 153; Print, 2008, pp. 96-97; 104). According to various sources, an analysis of the curricula for citizenship education reveals that the traditional republican model with a focus on patriotism, such as knowledge of laws, government structures, and voting practices is the norm (Banks, 2008, pp. 133-134; Evans, 2006; Parker et al., 2002, p. 153). This means that the values articulated in the human rights documents that promote a more universal view of humanity have been consistently ignored. Simultaneously the Deweyan philosophy of citizenship as a way of life is also ignored.

This approach is partly true for South Africa as well. However in South Africa there is an attempt to address citizenship education on two levels. One is the direct or traditional approach of patriotism, knowledge of laws and government structures, and the second approach is the infusion of social values and multiculturalism across the entire school curriculum (Department of Education, 2003; Department of Education, 2011[b]; Department of Education, 2011[c]).

Despite the dominant view held by major Western democracies, a divergent approach to citizenship education similar to Dewey's perspective, recognizing that people have multiple identities, has developed. This approach was developed mainly in Western, multicultural societies, in contradiction to the mainstream. This theory of citizenship is a more inclusive and values-based conception of citizenship that embraces the perspective of common humanity.

Banks (2008), well known for his work in the field of multiculturalism, supports this inclusive definition of citizenship and challenges the approach to citizenship that ignores cultural diversity. He echoes Dewey in contending that the cultural identity of individuals should be considered in citizenship education. Banks therefore proposes a more cosmopolitan approach to citizenship education. This cosmopolitan approach also has support in the U.K. Kerr, Smith and Twine (2008) reported that changes in curriculum policy in the U.K. from 2004 onwards have included a focus on social cohesion that speaks to a more cosmopolitan strand of citizenship education (p. 255).

A Deweyan Approach to Citizenship: Cosmopolitan Citizenship

There are close links between the philosophy of Dewey, the UDHR, the CRC and the practices of multicultural education. Multiculturalists believe that education should be based on the democratic principles of anti-racism, equality, human rights and affirmation of cultural diversity, with the main aim of education being to develop appropriate dispositions, skills, knowledge and values that will ensure positive interaction in a democratic society. Like Dewey, they also recognize cultural diversity (Banks & Banks, 1989; Gollnick & Chinn, 1994; Grant & Sleeter, 1998; Nieto, 1992).

Osler and Starkey (2005) identified citizenship as having three important complementary dimensions. These are status, feeling, and practice. The status of citizenship affords citizens protection by the state through laws and policies and provides collective benefits for citizens. In turn, citizens pay taxes and possibly serve in the military. They also have a sense of belonging to a community together with other citizens. In pluralistic societies, feelings of identity or community are often found at the local level, not at the more abstract level of the nation-state (Osler & Starkey, 2005, pp. 9-11). This connects with Dewey's recognition of diverse communities within a larger society. Citizens practice their citizenship through an awareness of human rights, participating freely in society and associating with others for political, cultural, or economic purposes (Osler & Starkey, 2005, p. 14). Osler and Starkey (2005) further redefined citizenship in terms of cosmopolitan citizenship (p. 23). Cosmopolitan citizenship is a way of being a citizen at the local, national, regional, or global level and is based on feelings of solidarity with one's fellow human beings. Cosmopolitan citizens synthesize their multiple identities and actively reflect on the various communities to which they belong and the bonds that join these communities. They see others as similar to themselves and reach a sense of citizenship based on conscious humanity rather than on state allegiance. Cosmopolitanism celebrates human diversity and is a perspective that accepts that all human beings are equal in dignity and in rights. Cosmopolitan citizenship is a way of thinking, feeling, and acting as a citizen (Osler & Starkey, 2005, p. 24). This perspective resonates with Deweyan philosophy and affirms the human rights documents of the twentieth century. The South African definition of citizenship is similar to a cosmopolitan conception of citizenship.

The Impact of the Past on Citizenship Education in South Africa: Reflections

According to policy, the approach of citizenship education in South Africa today is similar to Dewey's ideal of the school as a community that practices and lives democracy. However, the reality in South African society is very different, as practice contradicts policy. Violence is experienced by many learners on a daily basis both within their communities and in schools (Burton & Leoschut, 2013). Democracy as a way of life or the opportunity to develop appropriate dispositions for life in a democratic society is not a reality. Furthermore, one has to take into account the legacy of apartheid which has led to a considerable portion of the population not having the experience of having lived in a democracy, nor have they experienced democracy at any level in their own education, which was segregated according to race.

As South Africans we have been initiated into society either as oppressors or as the oppressed. The younger generation have lived in a country with democratic laws but not necessarily democratic institutions. Segregation is still experienced by the majority of Black school children in South Africa, as schools in the Black townships do not attract learners of other ethnicities or racial classifications due to lack of resources.

Despite our backgrounds, as educators we are expected to incorporate democratic citizenship in our teaching. My own life experience includes having attended a multiracial private school from the late 1970s to the early 1980s. I have also extensively read and conducted research in multicultural education and educating for democratic citizenship. Added to this, as a Coloured female, I have lived the reality of apartheid in South Africa. As a result of my life experiences and research I have come to realize that it is only through making deliberate decisions that one can hope to change behaviors, attitudes, and perceptions in daily practice. Realizing the democratic ideal for society does not happen without concerted endeavor. As an educator one is in a unique position to serve as a role model to one's students and to infuse one's practice with democratic principles and values.

Citizenship Education and Music Education

Does the Deweyan, cosmopolitan definition of citizenship education have relevance for music education? It does. In the Music Methods course I intentionally socialize the students to be fully fledged members of a community of practicing music teachers. I consult education policy documents and the values that underpin the Nelson Mandela Metropolitan University (NMMU), where I teach. The University's values are similar to the values found in the South African Constitution. The values of NMMU as stated in the Prospectus (2013) include respect for diversity, excellence, Ubuntu, integrity, respect for the natural environment, and taking responsibility. NMMU's policies also aim to develop human potential across diverse groups to pursue the goal of democratic citizenship. Furthermore, according to policy, NMMU subscribes to a humanizing pedagogical approach that respects and acknowledges different types of knowledge traditions and engages students critically in participatory strategies so that they can contribute to a multicultural society. This description makes explicit the values that all students at NMMU need to experience in their teaching and learning experiences.

The NMMU is a merged institution that is made up of three tertiary institutions, namely the former University of Port Elizabeth (UPE), which dominated the merger. UPE was a conservative, Afrikaans university that supported the ideologies of the apartheid government, even insofar as it had a military unit, the UPE Commando, for male staff and students who were conscripted for active duty in the townships to oppress protests to the apartheid regime. The other institution was the former Port Elizabeth Technikon, a Whites-only institution that offered vocational qualifications, and the third institution was the Port Elizabeth branch of the multi-campus Vista University, which was an institution for Black students. The initial purpose of Vista University was to improve the qualifications of teachers. From 1982 onwards the quota system was introduced to restrict the enrollment of Blacks at former Whites-only institutions (Blumfield, 2008). In 1984, when I enrolled at the former UPE, it was the first year that persons of color could study full time at the institution.

As the new institution NMMU has staff from the previous institutions who may still support the old ideologies and as such not promote the current democratic values. Some departments, including Music, did not exist at the former Vista University. Consequently the Music Department has brought the discourses of the past forward into the new institutional context. We still promote Western Art music and only in recent years have introduced a jazz program. Indigenous African music is allocated one module at the first-year level yet is not presented by a qualified ethnomusicologist nor necessarily by staff who embrace multicultural or democratic values.

At the university, it is a requirement that academic staff develop outcomes for the modules they teach. Nevertheless, it has never been a requirement to incorporate values as part of the outcomes of the teaching modules. Instead, the only criteria have been that the module outcomes match the level at which the module is pitched. In other words, heads of academic departments do not make explicit the values of the NMMU to their staff. If staff were supporters of apartheid ideology how committed would they be to promoting democratic values? I contend that the values should therefore be made explicit for all the modules.

A Deweyan approach to Music Method Modules

The Music Methods Modules are all electives and not core modules, so they are not compulsory. Only a small percentage of students enroll in these modules. The theory and history of music content is taught in the core music curriculum.

The emphasis of the method modules and outcomes are knowledge and understanding of the school curriculum, teaching methodologies, planning, and assessment practices.

If one agrees with the viewpoint that the role of schools is to prepare the next generation for their role in a democratic society, then it is necessary to approach education from this perspective. As a result, in my curricula I include practices that prepare students for active citizenship by being competent teachers who know their subject area. Furthermore, I incorporate democratic principles into the modules so as to create a democratic community of practice according to Deweyan and cosmopolitan ideals. These democratic practices are realized through sharing knowledge, active practice, modeling and mentoring.

Not all students come to university equally prepared to study music. As a consequence of the apartheid policy in South Africa, music as a subject in secondary schools was the preserve of the former Whites-only schools. Schools designated for other racial groups were denied access to instrumental tuition and Music theory. In the early 1980s there was an attempt by the Tricameral government to introduce instrumental music into the Coloured schools. This experiment was not successful and it was not sustained after 1994. Since then, the situation has not changed, so that in Port Elizabeth, my hometown and the fifth largest metropolitan area in the country, only 11 out of a total of 85 secondary schools, including government and private schools, offer music as a subject. While two schools formerly designated for Blacks only are included in this group, they lack the resources required to effectively implement the curriculum. The Music curriculum that is followed in all of these schools is Western Art music with a very limited inclusion of the indigenous African music. In the rural areas of the Eastern Cape province which were formerly the Black homelands, Music as a subject is completely nonexistent. The language of teaching and learning is either English or Afrikaans. Music textbooks for schools are either in English or Afrikaans. There are no textbooks for music in any of the other official languages, including isiXhosa, the language spoken by the majority of the Black population in the Eastern Cape. Dictionaries with music terminology in isiXhosa are also not available. At NMMU our language policy is contrary to the official policy that promotes multilingualism. The medium of teaching and learning in the Music Department is English.

The Music Department offers both a Diploma in Music and a Bachelor degree in Music. While I lecture both groups of students, sometimes for the same module, here I describe my interactions with the Diploma students.

The profile of students enrolled for the Bachelor degree of Music is that they are usually White, English- or Afrikaans-speaking, and have attended schools that offer music in grades 10 to 12. The schools they attended would have been well equipped in terms of physical resources and qualified teachers. This in direct contrast to the majority of students enrolled for the Diploma in Music. These are usually Black students whose mother tongue is Xhosa and who have attended schools that did not offer music in grades 10 to 12. Some of these students are also from the rural Eastern Cape and would have attended poorly resourced schools.

The diploma students gained entry to the course on the basis of an audition. Once enrolled, they start at the very beginning and have to learn all the content and skills needed to successfully complete the diploma in three years. These students are at a distinct disadvantage and also fit the profile as being the most at risk of not completing their qualification or taking considerably longer to complete it. Various governmental reports including that of the Council on Higher Education refer to this situation. The relevant statistics on student throughput are also available at the universities. In our department, at risk students are expected to attend tutorials to address any deficits they may experience. These tutorials are for Music Theory and/or Harmony and Music History in the first year of study only. Tutorials in the Music Department do not continue beyond the first year of study. Despite being behind, these students have a strong desire to improve their knowledge and understanding of music, a willingness to learn, respect for others, and a sense of collegiality or spirit of Ubuntu. They also promote music in the wider community and in so doing create their own communities of practice.

As the Music Methodology lecturer I help students to develop the knowledge and skills they will need as a competent teacher. What happens in the first lecture? In the first lecture we introduce ourselves and each person says something that is unique to them. The parameters for our engagement are also set. These parameters are based on Deweyan philosophy. After the rules for engagement are set, we have a discussion about a teacher who had a positive impact on our lives. Students describe the characteristics that had the greatest impact on them. These characteristics are written on the board and discussed. The most common answers are that the teacher who made the biggest impact was always prepared for class, knew the material, and was approachable. We then go on to read and discuss literature on characteristics of good teachers and discuss the impact teachers have as role models, both positive and negative, on the lives of learners. I explain to the students that during our interactions we should strive to develop certain characteristics by making conscious decisions regarding our actions.

Due to their being behind, we spend the first term consolidating the school curriculum, working systematically through it by means of learner-active methodologies for teaching and learning. By following this approach I model the active teaching and learning strategies I wish students to engage in. A thorough understanding of the school curriculum is essential to realize their potential in their roles as both music students and future teachers who are successful academically and who are confident to implement the curriculum. By using interactive approaches to teaching and learning I aim to develop reflective practices and critical thinking. Students need to be able to explain music concepts and not merely regurgitate knowledge. At the end of the six weeks students write a theory test based on the school curriculum. We reflect collectively on any challenges that the school curriculum may present and revise those aspects of the work again. During the reflections students are given the opportunity to use their own experiences to explain concepts to their peers. We work as a group to ensure that everyone will be successful. After the test, the students are given the answer sheets and take responsibility to visit specific websites and complete theory tests online for self-improvement.

Throughout the year, students are given theory activities to complete in order to consolidate the school curriculum. While they complete these exercises I engage them with questions relating to the different concepts and methodologies so as to develop their comprehension and reasoning abilities. Critical thinking skills are also developed when they reflect on and analyze theory worksheets and make suggestions for improving the worksheets by adding higher order cognitive questions.

The teaching and learning environment that I create is nonthreatening and open, with students having their own voice. Criteria for assessment are explained and discussed beforehand. Student voice is evident in peer evaluation of lesson presentations and open discussions on any topic at the beginning of lectures. In the peer assessments, students at first tend to allocate very high marks even when they are not justified. Due to the fact that they also provide verbal feedback to identify strengths and weaknesses measured against the criteria helps to balance out the peer assessment. Over the course of the year students develop the capacity for critical evaluation and the ability to justify their mark allocation. We reach a stage where there is a very small difference of marks among the whole group, including myself.

When participating in reflective and critical thinking activities some students tend to introduce political debates and proceed to comment critically on specific events in South Africa, student politics, the perceived ethos of the Music Department, and the relevance of the courses in which they are enrolled. It should be noted that, on the whole, the students practice rational discourse by giving each other the space to express contrasting views, and show maturity in the way they express themselves when debating issues. Once the lecture commences, they cooperate with each other without undue tension as they apply themselves to teaching and learning.

The discussions and feedback provide opportunities to develop tolerance within the group. The content that students are required to teach in the Music Methods modules is the school curriculum, where the music theory component is Western Art music theory or jazz theory. The scope for developing tolerance through multicultural content does not exist in the theory methods module, but rather in other music education modules that have multicultural content.

When students go to schools for practicum I make every effort to ensure that they are placed so that they can experience a multicultural school environment where they manage teaching and learning. When they teach their peers, the students use interactive teaching and learning approaches to explain the music concepts. Following the Deweyan ideal, the approaches are intrinsically linked to the content, which is music theory. A multisensory approach is followed, including aural and visual senses. The methodology consists of explaining a concept and giving opportunities for the class to interact by means of expressing the concept in their own words, explaining to a partner, applying the concepts, writing down answers, verbally answering questions on the topic, as well visual and aural recognition of the concepts. Music concepts are taught in a spiral manner and topics are revisited in later presentations when the assessment is at higher cognitive skills. Morality, honesty, and ethics are linked to the conduct of the students while they practice their role as teachers. Honesty is measured in the student's practice of citing sources.

Due to the power relationship inherent in teaching and learning, students are penalized for not complying with the rules and by implication not realizing the Deweyan ideal. I praise students so that their positive behavior receives attention as well.

Final Reflections

Dewey viewed education as a vehicle for educating for active participation in democratic society. In this article I have described the commonalities of Dewey's philosophy of educating for citizenship and education policy in South Africa. Although Dewey wrote about educating the child, his writing has relevance for educating prospective teachers who would be educating for democratic citizenship.

In the Music Methods Modules I follow a Deweyan approach in order to develop some of the characteristics needed for democratic citizenship. For the duration of the module, the students practice responsibility, tolerance, morality, ethics, honesty, critical thinking, and rational discourse. Added to this, I attempt to develop cosmopolitanism for school-based practice so that students not only identify with each other but with a broader global community of music teachers.

As the year progresses I constantly monitor and observe how students conduct themselves. In spite of following a Deweyan approach, I have found that a minority of students from the group need to be reminded about the rules of engagement, such as not heckling their peers when they teach, or not interrupting or belittling someone when they are speaking. The same group of students also need to be reminded about punctuality, attendance, and being prepared for their lectures, and have marks deducted when they hand in assignments late or fail to do a presentation on the date allocated to them. I have found that the behavior of these students is consistent across all the modules in which they are enrolled. The majority of students show evidence of being good citizens within the parameters of the class. A small minority exceed expectations with respect to their embrace of Deweyan values and dispositions and how they create their own communities of practice with peers and at schools beyond the classroom environment.

One of the challenges of educating for citizenship in a young democratic society such as South Africa is that policy is not always put into practice. The young need to be initiated into democratic practices by adults who are not always themselves aware of democracy. There is therefore no holistic approach at the institutional level to educate for democratic citizenship. This decision is left to individuals to make. This is true even for universities that pride themselves in the democratic values they have adopted.

Given South Africa's repressive past which was counter to democracy, it is necessary that teachers at all levels are initiated into democratic practice. Furthermore, at the university level more should be done to ensure that the values that have been adopted are realized at all levels of teaching and learning. Without making an attempt to socialize for democracy, there is the possibility that we perpetuate the past in the present and into the future.

Developing dispositions such as morality, responsibility, critical and creative thinking, being able to participate in rational discourse, and respect and tolerance through education at various levels would to a large extent serve to ensure that we have democratic societies in the future. The Deweyan perspective that democracy is a way of life should therefore become part of practice.

References

Banks, J. (1989). Multicultural education: characteristics and goals. In J. Banks & C. Banks (Eds.), *Multicultural education: Issues and perspectives* (pp. 2-26). Boston, MA: Allyn and Bacon.

Banks, J. (2008). Diversity, group identity, and citizenship education in a global age. *Educational Researcher, 37*(3), 129-139.

Blumfield, B. (2008). *A timeline of South African events in education in the twentieth century: 1900-1999.* Retrieved from http://sahistoryofeducation.webs.com/SA%20timeline.pdf

Burton, P., & Leoschut, L. (2013). *School violence in South Africa: Results of the 2012 national school violence study.* Retrieved from http://www.cjcp.org.za/articlesPDF/65/Monograph 12-School-violence-in-South%20Africa

Constitution of South Africa. (1996). Pretoria, South Africa: Government Printer.

Council on Higher Education. (2013). *A proposal for undergraduate curriculum reform in South Africa: The case for a flexible curriculum structure.* Retrieved from http://www.che.ac.za

Davenport, T. R. H. (1988). *South Africa: A modern history.* South Africa: Macmillan.

de Villiers, A. C. (2004). *How effective is teacher education in South Africa in addressing the challenges of educating for democratic citizenship?* (Unpublished Doctoral Dissertation). University of Port Elizabeth.

Department of Education. (1997). *Policy document: Intermediate phase.* Pretoria: Government Printer.

Department of Education. (2003). *National curriculum statement (NCS). Further education and training phase. Grades 10-12. History.* Pretoria: Government Printer.

Department of Education. (2011a) *National curriculum statement (NCS). Curriculum and assessment policy statement (CAPS). Further education and training phase. Grades 10-12. Music.* Pretoria: Government Printer.

Department of Education (2011b) *National curriculum statement (NCS). Curriculum and assessment policy statement (CAPS). Further education and training phase. Grades 10-12. Life orientation.* Pretoria: Government Printer.

Department of Education. (2011c). *National curriculum statement (NCS). Curriculum and assessment policy statement (CAPS). Senior phase. Grade 7-9. Social sciences.* Pretoria: Government Printer.

Department of Education. (2002). *Language in Education Policy.* Retrieved from http://www.info.gov.za/otherdocs/2002/languagepolicy.pdf

Department of Education. (2001). *Values Manifesto.* Retrieved from http://www.info.gov.za/view/DownloadFileAction?id=70295

Dewey, J. (1940). *Education today.* New York, NY: Greenwood Press.

Dewey, J. (2009). *Democracy and education: An introduction to the philosophy of education.* United States: Feather Trail Press.

Evans, M. (2006). Educating for citizenship: What teachers say and what teachers do. *Canadian Journal of Education, 29*(2), 410-435.

Gollnick, D. M. and Chinn, P. C. (1994). *Multicultural education in a pluralistic society.* United States: Merrill Publishing Company.

Grant, C. A. and Sleeter, C. E. (1998). *Turning on learning: Five approaches for multicultural teaching plans for race, class, gender and disability.* Upper Saddle River, NJ: Prentice-Hall.

Hahn, C. L. (2002). Education for democratic citizenship: One nation's story. In W. C. Parker (Ed.), *Educating for democracy: Contexts, curricula, assessments. Vol. 2* (pp. 63-92). Charlotte, NC: Information Age Publishing.

Hahn, C. L. (2008). Education for citizenship and democracy in the United States. In J. Arthur, I. Davies, & C. Hahn

(Eds.), *The SAGE handbook of education for citizenship and democracy* (pp. 263-278). Los Angeles, CA: Sage.

Kerr, D., Smith, A. & Twine, C. (2008). Citizenship education in the United Kingdom. In J. Arthur, I. Davies, & C. Hahn (Eds.), *The SAGE handbook of education for citizenship and democracy* (pp. 252-262). Los Angeles, CA: Sage.

Malan, B. (1997). *Excellence through outcomes.* Pretoria: Kagiso Press.

Mokgoro, J. Y. (1997). *Ubuntu and the Law in South Africa.* Retrieved from www.ajol.info/index.php/pelj/article/download/435 67/27090

Nelson Mandela Metropolitan University. (2013). *General prospectus 2013.* Port Elizabeth, South Africa.

Nieto, S. (1992). *Affirming diversity: The socio-political context of multicultural education.* New York, NY: Longman Publications.

Osler, A., & Starkey, H. (2001). Legal perspectives on values, culture and education: Human rights, responsibilities and values in education. In D. Lawton, J. Cairns & R. Gardiner (Eds.), The world education yearbook, 2001: Values, culture and education. London, England: Kogan Page.

Osler, A., & Starkey, H. (2005). *Changing citizenship: Democracy and inclusion in education.* Maidenhead, England: Open University Press.

Parker, W. C., Ninomiya, A. & Cogan, J. J. (2002). Educating 'world citizens': Toward multinational curriculum development. In W. C. Parker (Ed.), *Education for democracy: Contexts, curricula, assessments,* Vol. 2, (pp. 151-182). Charlotte, NC: Information Age Publishing.

Print, M. (2008). Education for democratic citizenship in Australia. In J. Arthur, I. Davies, & C. Hahn (Eds.), *The SAGE handbook of education for citizenship and democracy* (pp. 95-108). Los Angeles: Sage.

United Nations. (1948). *Universal Declaration of Human Rights.* Retrieved from http://www.un.org/en/documents/udhr/

United Nations Children's Fund [UNICEF]. (1989). *Convention on the rights of the child.* Retrieved from http://www.unicef.org/crc/fulltext.htm

Democratic Education Practices in South Africa:
A Critical Reflection on a Dialogic Perspective

Alon Serper

Nelson Mandela Metropolitan University, Port Elizabeth,
South Africa

Abstract

This paper critically reflects upon my practice of contributing to the transformation of South Africa from apartheid and colonialism to a participatory democracy of and for all its citizens and residents in dignity, humanity, and equality. My practice draws on the premise that a transformation of educational practices and policies is essential to the courageous transformation of South African education based on the practices of (1) encouraging and eliciting critical reflection and self-reflection; (2) dialogical co-enquiring of equals; and (3) encouraging the acts of challenging, critiquing and testing established ideas, premises and norms among South Africans. I start with an account of "Bantu education" and a critical reflection on my own experiences with the hierarchical systems' expectations of subservience. I follow with a brief account of how the new South Africa has begun to transform its tragic history. Subsequently, I account for my own practices of eliciting critical reflection, self-reflection and dialogical co-enquiring among students and staff at my South African university by testing and critically reflecting upon an applied dialectical model of studying and conceptualizing human beings and human existence in order to meaningfully contribute to the endeavors of the new democratic South Africa. My model is embodied directly in the practice of participants to improve their self-fulfillment, wellbeing and quality of life. It is a reaction to the reduction and objectification of the study and conceptualization of human beings to disembodied linguistic propositional abstractions.

Keywords: Bantu education, critical reflexivity, dialogics, democracy and education, South African education

This paper reflectively looks at my experience learning about emerging practices toward a more democratic system of education in South Africa. Below, I reflect on my own practice and ideas as a theorist in dialectical psychology and education with an orientation towards wellbeing, personal growth and social transformation. I move from putting together a theoretical model of a dialectical method for individuals to learn to improve their experiences of personal satisfaction about the way they live their lives to that of practicing methods of encouraging dialectical thinking, dialogue, and reflection in post-apartheid South Africa. In illustrating the importance of critical and dialectical thinking, I call for ongoing reflexive self-enquiry and dialogical co-enquiring to achieve the goal of democracy in education.

Education for me is the practice of attaining analytic thinking and communication skills that enable human beings to sustain their wellbeing, autonomy and personal growth and also learn how to engage in productive relationships with other people and themselves. Democracy for me is a culture where individuals collaborate and work together to promote and protect their growth, freedom, and prosperity as both individuals and a collective of individuals. The anti-educational and anti-democratic autocratic demand for unconditional acceptance of indoctrination, oppression, objectification, dehumanization, and degradation by the state is achieved by the use of authoritarian "education" theories and policies. Contrary to this demand a dialectical approach provides us with educational and democratic traits and acts of empowering and raising critical consciousness, autonomy, individuality, and personal and community and national growth for everyone.

South Africa formally became a democracy nineteen years ago. It had moved from oppressive autocratic minority rule to a democracy of and for all South Africans through a process of negotiations of power sharing and ceding. The two adversary sides (the White minority government and the non-White majority) worked hard to avoid a violent coup and a revolution. Through examining the tensions that have arisen in the ongoing process of moving from an authoritarian to a dialectical approach to education in South Africa, I explore the relationship between my own concerns with dehumanization and oppression with how to improve human dignity and wellbeing. This is situated in the context of a country that seeks to transform the oppression and degradation of a past autocratic regime that is still strongly embedded in its national identity and consciousness. My interest in how the new South Africa is transforming and improving the life of its people has offered me one of the world's most innovative and dynamic laboratories, as was pointed out by de Wit (2013) in reference to Neville Alexander's[23] suggestions. The most prominent feature of such experimentation and inquiry is the exploration of the different aspects of the movement from official State policies of Apartheid to those of a democracy.

To this end, I shall discuss how education instills, encourages, and sustains among the people the important traits and skills of reflective and analytic self-discovery, national and community consciousness, empowerment, and an ability to participate in social enquiries and national debates and dialogue. I also discuss how hard it is, despite noble intentions and humanistic values, to reverse the effects of oppression. The ideas of Paolo Freire and John Dewey can be applied to contribute to the transformation of the country.

---

[23] Neville Alexander was the anti-apartheid scholar, teacher, lecturer, author, and activist who was imprisoned for ten years on Robben Island by the apartheid regime. Alexander was an advocate of multilingualism and Socialist ideas and policies in post-apartheid South (b. 1936- d. 2012).

Here, I briefly describe my theory of studying human beings in dignity and authenticity directly within the praxis of their accounting for their idiosyncratic learning how to transform and improve their experiences of self-satisfaction, empowerment and wellbeing and achieve a life of greater meaning, personal satisfaction, and relationships with other people and themselves, which is an applied dialectical method based on critical thinking, enquiring, reflection, and dialogue. I further describe the oppression and dehumanization that took place in South Africa and the efforts of the new democratic regime to address and transform its past. This paper represents my first attempt to apply this new theory to the context of the transformation of South Africa. This paper consists of five sections and aims to provide readers with knowledge of the following: (1) a new possibility in the field of ontology (that in this context I define as the science of being and human existence); (2) the contrast between South Africa's past apartheid regime and its present democratic regime; (3) the fields of democracy and education and teaching and learning as dialogue and critical reflection; and (4) the critical self-reflection approach and the value of a reflective self-narrating (reflexive) account.

I conclude this paper by expressing my opinion on what is presently the obstacle to the participatory democratic reconstruction of South Africa, and the world in general. I suggest that until this obstacle is rectified, critical reflection and dialogical co-enquiring will have limited success in the transformation of South Africa to a true democracy.

The paper is based on the work of Donald Schön, Paulo Freire, and John Dewey. I have used Schön's (1983, 1987, 1991, 1995) work on the epistemology of the reflective practitioner and Freire's (1973, 1996) work on dialectical education for social transformation (Serper, 1999, 2010). The epistemology of the reflective practitioner includes the post-positivist method of the practitioner critically reflecting on his or her professional practice and development. It enables the practitioner to embody him- or herself in his or her own practice and to critically reflect on his or her own experiences of problems with and the improvement of a practice. This approach empowers critical self-evaluation and analytical, reflexive, and free and dialectical thinking.

This form of pedagogy perceives dialogue as a human and humanizing activity that complements and transforms individualistic thinking in isolation. Its aim is essentially political: to empower individuals who have been previously deprived of participation in social activism. It does so through enabling them to acquire literacy and social skills that permit them to learn about their world, and to liberate and empower themselves as dignified human beings.

I have also been influenced by John Dewey's ideas about actively involving learners in their own education as individual participants within a community that is working together on improving the collective quality of life and its community relationships. The participants in such a community are encouraged to critically reflect in their classrooms on their experiences and to share their input in a bid to improve their lives and the life of the community.

An Applied Dialectical Method

The traditional social and human sciences reduce the conceptualization and study of human beings to abstract linguistic propositions through following the Popperian and Aristotelian method of validation (Serper, 1999). The Popperian method of validating scientific theories consists of validating an abstract linguistic proposition by falsifying the alternative abstract linguistic propositions and discarding them in favor of the validated ones (Popper, 1963; Schön, 1991). This means that no contradictions can exist in the construction and validation of an argument and theory. In the case of the study and conceptualization of human beings, this means that every thirty years or so researchers have eliminated and replaced previously legitimate explanations of what it is to be human in order to validate the new theory to which they are committed (Serper, 1999, 2010). For instance, the conceptualization and study of the human being as a behaving organism, as the behaviorists theorized her to be, was eliminated and substituted by the representational cognitive psychology theory that a human being is a cognizing being, rather than mere a behaving organism. This theory was eliminated and replaced by the post-positivist social constructionist assertion that a human being is a social being who interrelates with other human beings and not merely a cognizing individual who accesses and retrieves stimuli from the environment. Thus, the human subject was reduced and objectified to abstractions and contradictory propositions of the human subject as a behaving organism, a cognizing being, or a socially interrelating being. In the traditional "either-or" logic of the Popperian and Aristotelian logic of validating and constructing scientific theories in which a theory is a single proposition, these propositions cannot coexist. Consequently, the traditional propositional logic that dominates human and social sciences (as discussed by Collingwood, 1939; Gadamer, 1975; Schön, 1991; Serper, 2010) significantly limits the study and theorization of the human subject and human existence (Serper, 1999).

Conversely, dialectics is a method for qualitatively transforming an argument and the understanding of a given phenomenon under discussion in the quest for truth, knowledge, and wisdom. Qualitative transformation takes place through heuristic enquiry and creative dialogue (which includes self-dialogue or reflection) and the creative use of contradictions and questions and answers to strengthen the enquiry and argument. Greenberg et al. (1993) noted that "dialectics in its most essential form is the splitting of a single whole into its contradicting parts. The polar parts when brought into contact interact to produce transformation. Novelty then emerges from a dialectical synthesis" (p. 55). Riegel (1979) contended that a thing is the "totality of all the different, contradictory notions about it to which the thing in itself stands in contradictory relation" (p. 39) and thus "*dialectical thinking* (Vernunft) comprehends itself, the world, and each concrete object in its multitude of contradictory relations" (p. 39). Lerner (2002), whilst reviewing Riegel's work, and reminiscing about Hegel, spoke of a dialectical change "which is always in the same direction, that of a synthesis between two "conflicting" opposites (termed thesis and antithesis)" (p. 40).

Hence, instead of eliminating the contradictory propositions, as is the case in traditional propositional logic, dialectical logic uses and fuses contradictions to forge a new construction that transforms both the contradictions and itself. During dialectical thinking, there is an enquiry and dialogue during which one propositional response pushes forward and transforms the one preceding in the search for truth and a solution to a presented problem and enquiry (Collingwood, 1939; Gadamer, 1975). Different relevant propositional enquiries and responses transform each other. They are not eliminated but are rather included in the analysis and the construction and validation of the dialectical theory. Furthermore, as far as the area of ontology, or the study of human beings is concerned, according to the dialectical thinking and logic of "and" (rather than "either/or"), a human being is a whole being-in-the-world who is behaving, cognizing, and socially interacting in, with, and towards the world. Consequently, the dialectical logic is able to significantly expand the limited theorization of the human subject and human existence by the limited propositional logic (Serper, 2010).

My theory of the applied dialectical method focuses on the idea that a transformative action research[24] cycle of a critical self-reflection followed by a dialogical co-enquiring and an implementation in reality, which is once again self-evaluated and discussed, will improve the participants' quality of life and produce living and embodied accounts that could be shared and learned from and reflected and enquired into within a group dialogue. In using this idea I drew on Winter's (1989) definition of action research as a "dialectical, reflexive, questioning and collaborative form of inquiry" (p. 9) that is embodied "within the action researchers'…own sustained educative relationships in their workplace action research cycle." This is based on the use of Freire's (1973, 1996) praxis of interrelating theory and practice. Action research cycles involve (i) enquiries, enquiring and the logic of questions and answers, as opposed to the logic of formulating, testing and validating, or invalidating, abstract linguistic propositional assertions (Collingwood, 1939; Gadamer, 1975); (ii) the fusion of contradictions to create novelty (Greenberg, Rice, & Elliott, 1993; Kahle, Liu, Rose & Kim, 2000; Lerner, 2002); and (iii) the dialogical co-enquiring that complements and transforms critical reflection in isolation (Freire, 1973, 1996).

How do I lead a more meaningful existence? How do I change and transform my personal dissatisfaction into satisfaction and fulfilment? And, how do I avoid being reduced and objectified to a set of linguistic propositional assertions?

---

[24] Action research is an orientation to inquiry whereby the enquirers become the researchers of their own practice in order to systematically work on improving what they are doing in the midst of action, rather than long afterwards. The term "action research" was first coined by Lewin (1946), who advocated the use of a spiral of steps, each of which is composed of a circle (or cycle) of planning, action, and fact-finding about the result of the action in order to evaluate and improve the practice. I describe action research, in light of Schön and Freire's work and my own theorized method that I describe in this paper, in Serper (2010), and papers that I have prepared and submitted for publication in *Action Research* and *Educational Action Research*.

Gadamer (1975) contended that dialectics is an art of testing which in turn is an art of questioning since questioning implies laying open and, contrary to the solidity of opinions, making the object and all its possibilities fluid (pp. 330-333). He followed Collingwood's (1939) suggestions that "you cannot find out what a man means by simply studying his spoken or written statements" as "in order to find out his meaning you must also know what the question was (a question in his own mind, and presumed to him to be yours) to which the thing he said or written was meant as an answer" (p. 31) and the argument "that truth…was something that belonged not to any single proposition, not even, as the coherence-theorists maintained, to a complex of propositions taken together; but to a complex consisting of questions and answers" (Collingwood, 1939, p. 36).

Using this dialectic, the participants answer the above questions by reflecting (or dialoguing with oneself) on their lives. They critically and phenomenologically orient to, enquire into and reflect, on their own, on a particular experience in their lives in which they had failed to live what they value and define for themselves as a satisfying, meaningful, and fulfilling life (Landsman, 2002; Moustakas, 1994; Serper, 2010; Van Manen, 1990). Phenomenology describes how a person orients to a lived, living, embodied, and situated experience in the world over time, space, and action (Moustakas, 1981, 1990, 1994; Van Manen, 1990). It is grounded within continental (European; mostly German and French) ideas and aims at gaining a deeper understanding of the nature or meaning of individuals' experiences of everyday phenomena. It joins with existentialism to make up the humanistic movement in continental philosophy. When using phenomenology, the individual delves inside the experience in its immediate, purest, rawest, most authentic, spontaneous, and pre-analyzed form and reflects on it and its implications for himself and his being while living and developing in the world. Landsman (2002) provided a practical phenomenological analysis of his personal experiences of being an Orthodox Jew and Israeli psychologist of southern American origin working with Palestinian mental health professionals in Gaza and Nablus in 1994 and 1995. In an attempt to transform my own counterproductive and unpleasant ontological experiences into constructive and pleasant ones, I have used phenomenology in conjunction with dialectics to evaluate my experiences through working out ways of improving them so as to lead a more satisfying and meaningful life (Serper, 2010).

Dialectics fuses contradictions, or the thesis with the antithesis, to create the desired qualitative transformation. The idea is that the overwhelming shock of observing and reliving the antithesis, which is the opposite of what individuals see as a satisfying life and behavior, induces individuals to work out ways of changing their behavior. After re-experiencing a tension upon this realization, the participants examine the meanings and roots of their experiences of personal dissatisfaction. They then work out a series of action plans to rectify this tension and in turn to reconstruct a more meaningful and satisfying life for themselves.

Dialectics transforms reflection into dialogue with other people and empowers further self-reflection. This process follows Freire's (1973, 1996) suggestion that reflection is limited and that dialogue with other people complements and transforms one's reflections. After participants work out their suggested action plans to rectify tensions and revert contradictions into what they seek and value, dialogue enables them to further develop their idiosyncratic action plans and improve their wellbeing and quality of life vis-à-vis the communities of which they are a part. They form a community that works together to improve the lives of its individual members. They take turns in expressing their views and learn to collaborate with other people through dialogue and thereby transform their own reflections.

In the next section, I describe the way the apartheid regime and its formal education system oppressed the majority of the inhabitants of South Africa whilst indoctrinating the minority to portray itself as the "master race." I show why free and critical thinking and dialogue are crucial to the success of the new South Africa, and illustrate an example of the antithesis in what I call anti-education and the thesis in what I call education to explain how dialectics and dialogue can transform an autocratic regime into a democracy.

Apartheid and Education

My aim in this section is to describe the anti-education South Africans were subjected to under the apartheid regime that continues to influence the life of every South African even today. All South Africans above a certain age, including teachers and academics who are training the new generation of higher education students, were subjected to this form of dehumanizing pedagogy and systematic indoctrination and oppression. The results of dehumanizing practices of centuries of colonization and decades of apartheid remain embedded in the minds and cultures of the South African people. It will take much longer than the two decades of democracy, as of this writing, for the effects of this indoctrination to be shed and transformed to the liberal democratic education that South Africa needs. It may be several generations before liberation from the oppressive and painful inculcations can be achieved.

The European arrivals in South Africa fled the horrific wars and religious persecutions of the 17th century before the Age of Enlightenment (Tabata, 1959). They intended to prosper in the new land, where they encountered native African tribes with "strange" customs and beliefs that the Europeans considered primitive. These European immigrants adopted the principles of Calvinism, began calling themselves

"Afrikaners,"[25] and aimed to prosper economically and socially in their new home. In the early decades of the 19th century, the British colonized South Africa. Education during British colonization and the pro-British regime in the period between independence and apartheid was a system of segregated and unequal education. The State was in charge of the education of White children, while the education of non-White children was the responsibility of missionaries. While the schooling of Whites was free, compulsory, and expanding, the education of Blacks was not free, profoundly neglected, and confined to the objectives and interests of the missionaries. South Africa won its independence from the British Empire in 1910 after the Anglo-Boer Wars. In 1948, the Afrikaner national party won the elections and took over from the pro-British party. During Apartheid, the State closed the missionary schools, took over the education of the non-whites and imposed the ideology of the new regime on its educational policies and structures. The informal racial discrimination and segregation of the past had become an official policy of the ruling regime.

Throughout the apartheid era, South African education was conducted along the ideological lines of the Afrikaner nationalist "Christian National Education," which was based on the Calvinist doctrine of predestination that was itself based on the Old Testament idea of the "chosen people" and preached that there are a selected few destined by God to salvation. The rest, considered by God (prior to their birth) unfit to earn salvation, are consigned to eternal damnation.

---

[25] The Afrikaners are a South African ethnic group who are descended from 17th century Dutch, German, and French settlers to South Africa. The Afrikaners slowly developed their own language and culture when they came into contact with Africans and Asians. The word "Afrikaners" means "Africans" in both Dutch and Afrikaans. About three million people out of South Africa's total population of 42 million identify themselves as Afrikaners. Their language, Afrikaans, is essentially a creole of a simplified Dutch mixed with words from French, Portuguese, native South African languages and Asian languages and other languages the Afrikaners came across. It is now one of the eleven official languages of South Africa.

Furthermore, the Calvinist doctrine was also based on the notion that strict and uncompromising discipline must be exercised by the Church in all aspects of life to control the individual. The doctrines of the Church were not to be questioned under any circumstances. The government's policies were regarded as the policies of God and consequently any failure to obey them meant defying God and all the consequences thereof. The result was that according to the principles of the Christian National Education ideology, Whites were destined by God to benefit from the richness of the fruitful land, while non-Whites were damned by God to serve them. These principles controlled all aspects of life in Apartheid South Africa.

With the Afrikaner national party winning the 1948 election and apartheid becoming national law, Christian National Education guided the policy of *baasskap*, [26] which in turn dictated the educational practices in all schools and tertiary institutions. The informal racial policies of the past had now become the official policies of the country. *Baasskap* was devised by politicians who, according to Tabata (1959), had studied in Nazi Germany, and consequently were influenced by the Nazi ideology of the master Aryan race and the inferior races which existed to serve them. *Baasskap* education was seen by apartheid politicians as "training in blind obedience" (Tabata, 1959, p. 33). It was a method for establishing and enforcing the supremacy of Whites over non-Whites in all matters of life. This resulted in the exercise of complete control and elimination of any free form of scrutiny that might question this policy. Nevertheless, the real purpose of this subjugation was economic in nature. It was designed to ensure the continuance of a supply of cheap 'native' labor force with the perpetual positioning of whites as sovereign. To ensure this economic benefit, the *baasskap* policy employed the classic

---

[26] Baasskap is Afrikaans for "boss-ship."

colonial "divide and conquer" tactic. It did this by breaking the Black population in South Africa into small tribal units, isolating them from each other, employing uneducated tribal chiefs to control the educated Blacks, and limiting movement both within the country and abroad. This idea was to foster a narrow and insulated tribal outlook and to prevent Blacks from coming into contact with ideas that were in conflict with the "master race" and with contradicted the governmental policies.

Baasskap was implemented into teaching policies and practices by the 1953 Bantu Education Act[27] which shifted control over the African schools from the hands of the missionaries to the government's newly established Department of Bantu Education. Soudien (2012) described "Bantu Education" as an "attempt to maintain and perpetuate the subordinate status of African people" (p. 106). The Bantu Education Act was designed for the non-Whites to "make sure that our children only learnt things that would make them good for what the government wanted: to work in the factories and so on; they must not learn properly at school like the white children" *(SAHO, 2013)*. The "Bantu Educational system" was designed to 'train and fit' Africans for their role in the newly evolving (post-1948) apartheid society. This role was one of laborer, worker, and servant only. Education was viewed as a part of the overall apartheid system which included 'homelands,' urban restrictions, pass laws,[28] and job reservation.

---

[27] The word "Bantu" is the IsiXhosa word for "people." The Europeans did not comprehend the tribal system in South Africa and the existence of many tribes in the geographical location of South Africa and called all native South Africans (the South African Blacks) "Bantu." The word itself is considered to be derogatory, but "Bantu Education" and the "Department of Bantu Education" are the technical and official terms given by the apartheid regime.

[28] The pass laws were a body of laws in operation in South Africa under apartheid, controlling and restricting the rights of black people in their residence and travel, and implemented by means of identity documents compulsorily carried.

One of the policies of "Bantu Education" was to control and degrade the black educators of the tribal schools. These policies were designed to avoid and combat the "threats and problems" of educated black South Africans who thought critically and dialectically for themselves and who possessed the "dangerous" ideas of equality. Under the system of "Bantu Education," the black teacher was employed by the school board or committee through a specific grant which was made available for a specific post by the Native Affairs Department. The teacher could be removed, without question or enquiry, if he or she dared to question *baasskap*. Furthermore, the policies of "Bantu Education" were designed to ensure that the knowledge of the Black educators of the subject that they taught was very limited. This is so that they would not have mastered sufficient knowledge of the subject to be able to answer their pupils' questions and have a proper class discussion. All they could do was to recite very limited text to their students. The schools were designed to objectify the children and avoid any possibility of free and independent thinking or critical skills equipping them to question the white supremacist policies of the regime. The atmosphere in these schools was depicted by Tabata (1959) as "precisely calculated to facilitate indoctrination in all the perversities of *Apartheid*, a positive Breeding ground for servile automatons" (p. 46).

Black South African students and faculty members have told me how their teachers and parents told them that asking them questions and talking back was disrespectful, a challenge to their dominance, and that they should therefore unquestioningly accept what they were told. Asking questions and talking in class were considered taboo and they were banned from doing so. All that was expected was for them to listen and obey.

Hence, there was a situation in which students were taught to unconditionally accept dubious information, were ill-trained; certainly by no means prepared for high school, tertiary education, nor any position requiring analysis or the understanding of science or mathematics – that is, if they were to somehow attain such position in a culture that did all it could to prevent them from getting there. Very few did. The result was that, when apartheid crumbled, the vast majority of the population had extremely poor training in analytic thinking, formulating, asking, and answering questions, and social, scientific, and mathematical theory.

Educated Blacks were considered as a particular source of danger and threat to the nation. Teachers underwent schooling for one, two, or three years to become primary school teachers, and five years of schooling to teach in the higher primary classes. Their wages were those of an unskilled laborer. They were taught and expected to do little more than supervise large classes of fifty bored pupils without any teaching materials (Tabata, 1959). Everything was done to damage their authority. Teachers were interrogated and searched in front of their pupils. In addition, farm schools that provided the White Afrikaner farmer with unpaid foremen and a body of child laborers were established. It provided the farmers with complete authority over the educators and pupils and compelled the teachers and pupils to work on the farm. The teachers were forced to supervise the children working in the fields during or after school hours as needed and were paid for their 24 hours of service – the same salary as blue collar menial farm laborers. Tabata (1959) noted how the teacher

> is not only robbed of status but of security of tenure and the proper practice of his calling…under Bantu Education, the position of a teacher with respect to his immediate employer is reduced to that of master and servant…He becomes in effect a personal servant who can be dismissed without any reason being given or a charge laid against him. The long list of regulations

governing his employment would be more appropriate to the control of a criminal than a teacher. (p. 41)

He also described how the teachers "are carefully screened, selected and indoctrinated before they are let loose on the children" (p. 42) and added that

> Under the *Boerenasie* republic the Non-Whites will be reduced to utter helotry. In preparation for this, the schools are no longer centres of education, but of indoctrination for the docile acceptance of this position... Bantu Education, which is already being put into practice, is calculated to serve as an instrument for creating and ensuring the continuance of a voteless, rightless and ignorant community whose main purpose in life, apart from reproducing their kind (for there is not yet a specific law against that aspect of their life) is to minister to the Whites...Bantu Education...is calculated to serve as an instrument for creating...community whose main purpose in life...is to minister to the Whites population of the Union...docile slaves contented with their lot. (p. 53)

Hence "Bantu Education" infantilized Blacks and treated them as children in need of parental supervision. The policies of "Bantu Education" were designed to teach Blacks "how to be good tribal natives" and to halt and reverse the development of first the Blacks, then the so-called "Indians,"[29] and then the

---

[29] The linguistic racial classification of South African "Indians" refers to Asians who were brought by the colonialist powers. According to SAHO (2013), South Africans of Indian origin comprise a heterogeneous community distinguished by different origins, languages, and religious beliefs. The first Indians arrived during the Dutch colonial era as slaves. They continued to be brought as slaves, and with the end of slavery in 1837, they were brought as laborers. English is spoken as a first language by most Indian South Africans, although a minority of the Indian South African population, especially the elders, still speak some Indian languages. In the 2001 census the number of South African Indians amounted to 2.5% of the country's population.

so-called "Coloureds"[30] "lest they become a dangerous threat to the European civilization, take over the country from the Whites and force the Whites to leave." In his preface to Tabata (1959), Patrick D. Ncube described the primary purpose of "Bantu Education" as

> not only to produce a docile black labor force, but also a labor force unable to perceive the social, political and economic contradictions...to defuse these contradictions, education for the blacks had to be retribalised...to disorganise the Black population and weaken their resistance to the system, cementing a horse/rider coexistence and promoting a 'culture of silence'

Hence, "Bantu Education" did the exact opposite of what I see as the principle purpose of education, which is to develop individuals' personal growth, knowledge, thinking, lives, and sense of selves (Sarles, 2013) and to turn them into productive members of their society (Dewey, 1897, 1902, 1916).

Tabata (1959) noted that the aim of Hendrik Frensch Verwoerd, the Minister of Native Affairs in the early 1950s,[31] was "to create...a completely rightless, voteless, defenceless community, segregated from 'European Society' and

---

[30] "Coloured" is the common South African term for what would be "mixed race" elsewhere, people of both black and white descent. The South Africans who fall under the separate racial or ethnic classification of "coloured South African" commonly speak Afrikaans as their native home language. This ethnic, or racial, classification is to be distinguished from the "Black South Africans" classification. The "Black South Africans" belong to tribes, speak their tribal languages and follow their tribal cultural customs. The similarity of the term "coloured" to its American use is purely linguistic. The meaning is completely different and is based on the very different history of the South Africa. The "coloured" make up 8.9% of the South African population. The "Black South Africans" form 79.2% of the population in South Africa. The "Whites" amount to 8.9% of the South African population.
[31] Later on, Hendrik Frensch Verwoerd became the prime minister of South Africa from 1958 until his assassination in 1966.

completely dominated by the chiefs who are employed and paid by him" (p. 16). Any possibilities for innovative thought or challenging of the status quo were rigorously eradicated. Tabata wrote that

> the old textbooks on science, history and even languages are declared taboo. New ones considered suitable for Bantu schools are being written by servants of the Native Affairs Department. A furious and lucrative industry has been set up. Hack writers and people who, judged by the standards of the Education Department, would be regarded as philistines, are manufacturing books for Bantu Schools. It is easily understood that existing libraries must come under the axe. The library of an old established college collected over a period of more than a century was put up for public auction. The minds of innocents must be protected from 'dangerous' ideas. (p. 39)

With such training, the non-Whites experienced great difficulty, and still do, as a culture of critical and dialectical thinking and analytic understanding of ideas needs to be acquired early in human development, during early childhood, lest the individual become accustomed to a culture of obedience and uncritical acceptance of ideas and theories and find it is hard to transform him- or herself from this constrained type of thinking. It is crucial to start the practice of testing and criticizing ideas and a dialogue between the child and the teacher as early as possible in order to embed it in the child's cognition as a natural thing.[32] "Bantu Education" did the exact opposite. With the fall of apartheid and the new

---

[32] It should be recalled that the predominant culture and traditions among all South African ethnic groups entail the ethos of respecting, following, and not questioning older people. Critically testing and challenging what is being taught and said by older individuals is considered to be ill-mannered and a challenge to the culture and tradition.

South African government encouraging and impelling Black students to enter higher education so as to improve the economy of the country and ensure the idea of a participatory democracy among all South Africans by offering subsidies and government bursaries, students have entered higher education from "Bantu Education." This meant that they were indoctrinated to follow and accept ideas unconditionally. This led to the majority of South African students entering universities without being provided with a formal training in analytic methods and critical thinking.

To make things worse, during apartheid *baasskap* extended to academic tertiary education. Whereas prior to apartheid, universities in South Africa were multi-racial and independent, the Extension of the University Education Act of 1959 created separate 'tribal colleges'[33] for Black university students that were under direct government control and in turn exercised *baasskap*. This Act halted any possibility for open enquiry, critical and free thinking in the university classroom and enforced a very poor quality of formal teaching and learning.[34] Tabata (1959) described the Apartheid university education as "not only... robbing non-Whites of education but [also]...turning a whole population back to barbarism" (p. 46), with the university staff "as subjected to almost unbelievable control and interference. Regulations governing their appointment show an obsession with 'misconduct'." Furthermore, he described the conditions in Black universities as "permeated by fear that grips professors and students alike...intellectual paralysis and stupefaction" (p. 46). This resulted in non-White academics (individuals with a university training) being given poor formal education and not being trained in analytical and critical thinking, such as how to

---

[33] The so-called 'bush' Universities such as Fort Hare, Vista, Venda, Western Cape were formed then.
[34] I am aware of fact the critical movements that took place outside the formal classroom in the form of liberal media and student revolts, for example. Here I address only formal teacher-student interactions in the classroom.

formulate and answer questions. After the collapse of apartheid, those non-Whites who attained higher education and went on to train new generations of university students did not possess essential skills to run a productive classroom.

Baaskap and the use of education to enforce it affected both non-Whites and Whites. Education was little more than indoctrinating children and young adults to unquestionably follow governmental policies and to do as instructed. Both Whites and non-Whites were indoctrinated to know and respect their place in the South African social fabric. Any extension of the required skills to serve this destined social role was considered counterproductive and even harmful and unfair. J. G. Erasmus, Regional Director of "Bantu Education," noted on October 17, 1974, that there was no point in teaching mathematics to black youth "when they cannot use it in practice" (Boddy-Evans, 2013).

Consequently, on the one hand, Blacks were merely taught to perform hard labor, menial tasks, or at most, semi-manual skills which were required to serve Whites. White children, youth, and young adults were taught mathematics and what were considered to be skills needed to run the country as a developed 20th century nation. The only conditions under which the level of education was improved for non-Whites was when their White employers demanded servants with higher skills, as the quality of their merchandise was affected by the poor quality of training received by the workers. On the other hand, White children were taught that they were the superior race and as such meant to be served. Whites were indoctrinated to take for granted the notion that there was no such thing as equality or fraternity among human beings and that humanity was divided into inferior races (some more inferior to others[35])

---

[35] First, the "Indians," or South Asians brought to South Africa by the Europeans; see footnote 5. Then the "Coloured"; see above in footnote 6. Third, the Blacks, or natives. In that order.

271

in contrast to the superior White race. The idea that all human beings are equal and should be respected as such was considered to be a heresy. South African Whites were indoctrinated to act upon the requirement that "one of their duties at all times is to 'put the Black man in his place.' Each petty clerk sees himself as a representative of the master-race, who must assert his superiority by insult" (Tabata, 1959, p. 48). How can one dialogue with another human being when one's thinking and belief system are dominated and led by such ideology? Apartheid was an ongoing process of segregation and dehumanization that took the British and pro-British colonization a step forward towards greater oppression, dehumanization and enslavement for the benefit of white economic and societal prosperity. The segregation and dehumanization was a linear process and got worse and worse as the years went by, until global efforts (through economic sanctions) and physical resistance by non-Whites, who increasingly had less and less to lose and became more exasperated in their increased and lengthy oppression, led the Whites to give up and seek negotiations with the non-Whites to include them in the governing of the country. The most known illustration is the forced removal of the non-Whites in the early 1970s, some three decades into apartheid, from district six in Cape Town and South End in Port Elizabeth and the bulldozing of the houses in order to move the multi-ethnic districts into White-only ones. The worst acts of violence were committed in the mid-1970s with the infamous Soweto Uprising of June 1976, where hundreds of high school students who protested in Soweto against the introduction of Afrikaans as the medium of instruction in local schools lost their lives and in the 1980s upon the introduction of emergency laws. As time went by, some White South Africans began to understand that apartheid could not work and sustain itself over a long time and to understand its evil implications regarding mass dehumanization and oppression.

Hence, one can see the autocracy at play in the dehumanization, objectification, and degradation of the people of South Africa by apartheid. It is imperative to acknowledge and include this type of oppressive autocratic anti-education in our attempts to transform democracy and education in the new South Africa. It is important to reflect on and comprehend how the non-white inhabitants of South Africa had no rights whatsoever as human beings and citizens of a country. They could not determine the rulers of the country as they could neither vote nor participate in unions nor any political power base. It is also important to reflect on and understand how the white minority in South Africa were deprived of the ability to engage critically in matters concerning the equality and dignity of all South Africans. They were forced to reduce human beings to color and absurd racial classifications. This led to a human being, with all his or her qualities as an individual person, being reduced to racial and ethnic affiliation and disregarded as a person apart from the color of his or her skin. Despite the absurdity of these racial categories, the post-apartheid government still uses them to examine remedial progress and to use reverse discrimination in order to make amends for the past. With the burden of anti-education, even after South Africans encountered the eventual collapse of apartheid and the rise of a new era of liberal democracy, the transformation of South Africa for all its people in dignity, humanity, and equality has been hindered. A transformation into a non-racial society was endorsed by South Africans like Neville Alexander and Steven Biko and remains continuously debated.

South African Attempts at Transforming and Democratizing its Education

Where are the education practices and policies of South Africa today? The apartheid regime collapsed in the late 1980s and early 1990s. The first democratic elections of all

South Africans took place in April 1994. Yet SAHO (2013) noted that

> the legacy of decades of inferior education (underdevelopment, poor self-image, economic depression, unemployment, crime, etc.) has lasted far beyond the introduction of a single educational system in 1994 with the first democratic elections, and the creation of the Government of National Unity.

This is hardly surprising as *baasskap* policymakers were extremely efficient and ruthless in fulfilling their task of destroying equality, dignity and humanity. Part of being a dignified human being is being able to enquire critically into one's world and development through dialogue with other people as equals (Freire, 1996, 1973; Sarles, 2013). Trust, hope, and tolerance are necessary for a genuine dialogue.

At first, the euphoria reigned as some of the worst perpetrators of the apartheid regime took part in Archbishop Tutu's Truth and Reconciliation Process (Tutu, 1999) and repented and washed the feet of their victims while the country managed to avoid the feared bloodshed and chaotic division. Most South Africans were aware of the task at hand and how huge and painstaking the undertaking of rectifying the damage caused by apartheid would be:

> Nobody expects that this will happen overnight. The struggle for a non-racist, non-sexist and democratic South Africa will take generations rather than decades. The political and cultural leadership of our country, those people who are the role models for the youth, have a heavy responsibility to help to create the conditions for realising these goals. (Alexander, 2012, p. 207)

The leadership, policymakers, and practitioners of the new South Africa came up with noble policies and intentions as they were faced with the task of amending the unjust policies and practices of both apartheid and colonialism. For example, present governmental policy is led by the idea of "Inclusive Education" and ensures the wellbeing, agency, learning, and personal growth and development for all as free human beings. It has clear policies and guidelines for the meanings of "Inclusive Education" that it seeks to implement.

In its website, the Thutong, South African Education Portal (2013), defines Inclusive Education (IE) as "a process of addressing the diverse needs of all learners by reducing barriers to, and within the learning environment." For its part, the South African governmental Department of Basic Education (2013) expresses its commitment towards

> the building of an Inclusive Education system at all levels as outlined in Education White Paper 6: Building an Inclusive Education System, 2001 which will facilitate the inclusion of vulnerable learners and reduce the barriers to learning, through targeted support structures and mechanisms that will improve the retention of learners in the education system, particularly learners who are prone to dropping out.

In their paper "What Counts as Inclusion," Walton and Nell (2012) consider "the question of what counts as inclusion as important in this juncture in South Africa's development of an education system that realises constitutional values of equality, freedom from discrimination and human dignity" (p. 4) and which follows the guidelines of "tracking individual progress, consulting with parents and helping teachers to develop Individual Support Plans (ISPs)" (p. 13). The provision of individually relevant instructions, extra lessons, language support, and assistive devices are also regarded as important in order "to ensure that individual learners receive the support

275

that they require." They also identified the criteria for IE as composed of the utilization of cooperative learning strategies, teaching to accommodate preferred learning styles, and multi-level teaching and curriculum differentiation (Bornman & Rose, 2010; DoE, 2009; Sapon-Shevin, 2007; Shaddock, Giorcelli & Smith, 2007; Tomlinson, Brimijoin & Narvaez, 2008). These are part of "a range of teaching strategies" which are "conducive to inclusive education." In addition, they also stressed the importance of integrating various departments, fields and both private and public enterprises and agencies for IE.

These are marvelous intentions and linguistic propositions. However, their meanings and implementations have to be tested in real-world situations and not merely on a discursive level. IE was imposed by policymakers on teachers and educational practitioners and was constructed by theorists, most of whom are American and European and detached from the reality of many South African schools. The policies and methods of teaching need to be reformulated to comply with the reality of the current situation – ranging from no electrical connectivity to overcrowded classrooms – in South African schools and universities.

As such, policies need to be embodied and tested in relation to the realities of the South African educational environment. This should be done with the purpose of qualitatively transforming and humanizing democracy for all in South Africa. How do we improve the quality of life, wellbeing and growth of all South Africans in equality, dignity and humanity? And how do we transform the tragic legacy of South Africa and rectify the dehumanization of the majority of South Africans in the past?

There is much frustration and despair among many South Africans, in general, and South African educators, in particular, about the failure of 'Inclusive Education' due to very poor resources and lack of funding. These educators have posed to me a number of pertinent questions. For example, how could the good intentions, words and principles of "Inclusive Education" work when teachers are not paid, books do not arrive, classrooms do not have electricity and running water, there are no assistant teachers, classes are still too large, and teachers are still poorly trained? And, how could poorly taught pupils do well at tertiary education and get the qualifications that the country desperately needs? It does take a long time to completely transform hundreds of years of poor education.

In contrast, the practices of direct critical reflection and dialogue are carried out in the field. They need to be adapted to the situation in the field and the resources available. They are embodied within the practices of teachers and are carried out within the context of such deprived schools, poor resources and poorly trained teachers and the culture of the past. My approach enables politicians, theorists, academics, special advisers to policy-makers, community activists, and practitioners to meet up in the field, critically reflect and dialogue together on how to interrelate the noble intentions and ideologies with the reality of poor infrastructures, over-crowded schools and poorly trained teachers in order to work out ways of improving the education system. They bring, interrelate, and incorporate various perspectives and ideas, and construct and test innovative ways of doing this.

Increasingly, as the social problems remain intact, and the unity of the non-Whites in their struggle for liberation descend into individual struggles, many South Africans lose their initial hope and enthusiasm about the move to democracy. Many become disillusioned about the meaning and costs of the struggle for majority rule. As Alexander (2012) wrote,

Fewer and fewer people, more specifically in the middle classes to whom the notion was most appealing in the early 1990s, now believe that a sense of national unity and 'social cohesion' is attainable in the prevailing circumstances of extreme social inequality, high unemployment, predominantly and continuing 'black' poverty, widespread violent crime and social insecurity, the ravages of the HIV/AIDS pandemic, as well as the ever-present threat of xenophobia....economic growth...and...genuinely creative and constructive future...will remain vain hopes unless fundamental changes are made in economic, social and even in cultural policy. (p. 199)

There is no point in adapting abstract educational theories and methods that have been formulated outside the context of the deprived schools with their long history of dehumanization. Transforming South Africa from its past entails and perhaps even requires constant experimentation by trial and error and challenges to the traditional propositional ways of theorizing and theory validation.

Transforming South African Education into a Participatory Democracy

I arrived in South Africa during its post-apartheid struggles with the aim of working toward reversing the oppression and dehumanization of the past and building a prosperous liberal democracy. As a theorist, I had virtually no experience of working with people. I had ideas, ideals, and theories that I wanted to test out and critically reflect on. I was appalled by the townships and the living conditions and striking poverty of the majority of the population and by the socioeconomic inequality between the areas in which Whites and Blacks and non-Whites lived.

Seeking to introduce a culture of critically and dialectically testing ideas and theories, I introduced the students and staff at Nelson Mandela Metropolitan University to the following crucial citation from Popper (1963) on a scientific way of testing and validating theories and ideas:

> It is most characteristic of the scientific method that scientists will spare no pains to criticize and test the theory in question. Criticizing and testing go hand in hand; the theory is criticized from very many different sides in order to bring out those points which may be vulnerable. And the testing of the theory proceeds by exposing these vulnerable points to severe an examination as possible....Theories are put forward tentatively and tried out.[36] (Popper, 1963, p. 313)

I placed this citation on an overhead projector before giving the class a twenty-minute introduction to a theory and then asking them to spend the rest of the three hours in class applying Popper's method of theory validation and working as a group orally dialoguing together with me in class and attempting to find flaws in my theory and invalidate it. The intention of this exercise was to help them to build the discursive skills and confidence necessary to participate in scholarly debate and to refute a carefully prepared lecture on a theory by a theorist. The first reaction to this activity was one of shock. The predominant culture of education in South Africa entails an authority figure (an elderly, a teacher, a parent) lecturing to an audience that listens uninterruptedly and accepts the assertions of the lecturer. Interrupting and asking an authoritative figure questions is considered to be an ill-mannered act. Most classes, even at university levels, are comprised of the teacher or lecturer reciting the course syllabus

---

[36] The idea is that if we dialectically use the tension of falsifying and criticizing theories in the construction of theories instead of eliminating the contradictions, then the theories can be further strengthened.

and the students taking notes and preparing for multiple choice examinations every few lessons. However, as I persisted with my method of eliciting the students' ideas and critiques, they relaxed, understood the idea, and began to engage, look for flaws, and ask questions. From what I saw and heard from the students themselves, this was a new and unusual practice for them that would take time and practice to master.

My next move was to post Popper's citation on my office door. Affording passersby an opportunity to critically reflect on and dialogically co-enquire with me has become an important part of my educational practices in South Africa (Serper 2012a, 2012b), following Freire's and Dewey's ideas of democratic education outside the university's lecture halls. It enables all to express their thinking and share what they feel, experience, and value and collaborate on ways of solving community problems and improving their lives as members of a community. I would ask about the most immediate and crucial problems in post-apartheid South Africa and what could be done to solve these problems. I would also ask about the successes of the new democracy. Likewise, I would ask what South Africa could teach the rest of the world about social transformation from injustice and moral corruption to justice and morality. I would also ask about their personal experiences of their cultures, their perception of their identity, about their objectives and ambitions. I very gently approached individuals whom I observed reading and engaging with the codifications on my door. I asked students and colleagues about what they thought of my mildly provocative door experiment.[37] I kept a log in which I wrote immediate reflections on my actions and intentions, including the feedback I received from my targeted passersby, fellow academicians, and practitioners. In this log I included detailed

---

[37] I described the door experiment in detail in Serper (2014) that focused on my reflection on and descriptions of my door experiment.

descriptions and analyses of my feelings and experiences regarding doing this work in South Africa in comparison to the other parts of the world in which I had resided and worked (Serper, 2014).

I have also utilized Freire's ideas and added to my office door posters that contain slogans about the need for change and autonomous thinking. I wanted the passersby to learn to engage in free and autonomous thinking (Dewey, 1897, 1902, 1916). In doing this I have followed Freire's idea of the method of "codification" and his explanation in Chapter Three of *Pedagogy of the Oppressed* that "codifications are not slogans; they are cognisable objects, challenges towards which the critical reflection of the decoders should be directed." This is in addition to his explanation in his book *Education for Critical Consciousness* that his method of transforming naïve thinking into critical thinking lies in "the use of *techniques* like thematic "breakdown" and "codification" (Freire, 1996, p. 40). Moreover, Freire (1996) contended that "the codifications reflecting an existential situation must objectively constitute a totality. Its elements must interact in the makeup of the whole" (p. 96).

Freire (1996) perceived dialogue as "a fundamental precondition for…true humanization" in the course of which human beings "meet in order to "name" the world" (p. 37), advising educators that "our role is…to dialogue with the people about their views and ours" (p. 77) and differentiating between a dialogical theory of education where "subjects meet in cooperation in order to transform the world" (p. 37) and an anti-dialogical theory of education where "a Subject…conquers another person and transforms her or him into a "thing." He stressed that education and educational relationships "cannot be reduced to the act of one person's "depositing" ideas in another, nor can it become a simple exchange of ideas to be "consumed by the discussants" and that "it is in speaking their word that people, by naming the word, transform it" and subsequently dialogue imposes itself as a way by which "they achieve significance as human beings." Freire (1973) contended that:

> Knowledge is not *extended* from those who consider that they know to those who consider that they do not know. Knowledge is built up in the relation between human beings and the world, relations of transformation, and perfects itself in the critical problematization of these relations. (p. 109)

Like Freire, Dewey objected to education being a form of passive obedience training in which information and knowledge is placed in learners by teachers. Dewey believed in individuals taking responsibility for their own learning through critical reflection and dialogue and in educators creating conditions for this learning and educational, epistemological, and ontological transformation through critical reflection and dialogical co-enquiring. He saw education as the process of learning how to think for oneself and to participate constructively, actively, and meaningfully in one's community and thereby to become a significant and contributing member of one's community. Dewey's theory of education talks about children learning through "participation...in the social consciousness of the race" (Dewey, 1897, p. 77). Like Freire, he advocated re-humanization and democratization of education through freedom and independence of thought and critical thinking. He also promoted the active "hands-on" and experiential educational approaches in which individuals actively interact with real objects, and critically reflect on their experiences of doing so. This type of humanizing and democratizing education is the exact opposite of South Africa's apartheid education, which requires a complete transformation of what was so skilfully embedded in the collective psychology of South Africans.

Freire's method of teaching a language and literacy to people who have been deprived of education involved the learners cognitively, epistemologically, and emotionally participating in their own learning. It aimed at eliciting critical consciousness among them in regard to their lives and their environment, and sought to enable their active participation in the analytic understanding of their lives. This was done with an intention to improve their lives and experiences of human dignity and autonomy. It was implemented by ensuring that the learning is relevant to and is embodied within the social and moral context of the learners' lives. In the original field of teaching literacy to adult illiterates, Freire's work was based on the facilitator's presenting words to the learners that were already known to the learners and which are emotionally laden and contextualized within their lives. This was followed by group discussions in relation to these words about problems that they faced and shared in their community. These problems were named, defined, and discussed together in terms of how to solve them and improve their lives. After mastering the presented words, the words were then broken into fragments that were used in the learning of other words, from which sentences and expressions could be constructed.

In carefully selecting and posting provocative ephemera to my office door I experimented with Dewey's and Freire's ideas. Some of the items were familiar to residents of the South African province of the Eastern Cape. In addition to those mentioned, included were slogans advocating critical and autonomous thinking and education as a means of fighting ignorance and indoctrination. My first codifications were photographs of the *Strelitzia* flowers, also known as the "bird of paradise" or "crane flowers" that grow just outside my office. *Strelitzia* is South Africa's national flower, alongside the Protea flower. The *Strelitzia* is native to the Eastern Cape. My reasoning for using it was that it is likely to rouse feelings of national and community identification. To maximize the potential of this codification to stimulate reflection and co-enquiry I attached the thought-provoking poetic verse from R. D. Laing's (1967) *The Bird of Paradise*, which I saw as an invitation for self-reflection and as evoking profound ontological questions as to what it means to be human. The citation reads:

> I have seen the Bird of Paradise, she has spread herself before me, and I shall never be the same again. There is nothing to be afraid of. Nothing. Exactly. The Life I am trying to grasp is the me that is trying to grasp it.

This text appeared alongside the photos. Similarly I placed a few political posters on my office door that protested against globalization, neo-liberalism, capitalism, and government cuts, and that encouraged strikes and union action for better pay and working conditions. My aim was to encourage reflection, enquiry, and dialogue from South Africans from different walks of life. I made sure that the codifications that I attached to my office door were relevant and applicable to current national affairs, debates, and discussions. These also included codifications on social justice, socio-economic oppression, human dignity, pro-corporate propaganda, corporate oppression of the workers, liberation of the oppressed, humanizing education, critical and free thinking, and the scientific validation of theories and ideas (Serper, 2012a, 2012b). Many came from the "Occupy" movement and progressive and democratic education websites.[38] I reflectively observed individual passersby or groups of students gathering hesitantly next to the door, as if doing something wrong by discussing the codifications and co-enquiring into their

---

[38] I have used the Occupy Wall Street Facebook page at https://www.facebook.com/#!/OccupyWallSt.
I have also used the Facebook page of *Debunking Glenn Beck* at https://www.facebook.com/#!/pages/Debunking-Glenn-Beck/108099032602065 and its resources. I have also used the Nimukata – Promoting Science, Freethought and Secular Humanism in India webpages at: http://nirmukta.net. I also wrote my own slogans.

meanings. Everyday passersby have continued to critically reflect and co-enquire with me into the suggested current affairs and national questions. Some of them had much to say on these issues. They were passionate and emotional about what they were saying as they were given an opportunity to discuss matters that they long wanted to discuss but were never given the circumstances in which to do so. They seemed to open up and to be cathartically relieved of heavy burdens.

Like Sarles (2013), I also want students to share and manage their education, become autodidactic and "discover their own, usual, favorite paths of diagnosis and (self-) explanation" (p. 87). Similarly, I want them to go about their own social analysis and commitments to the promotion of social justice and the general welfare, and turn themselves into autonomous critical thinkers. In particular, I hope that the following questions might be raised to instigate heated discussions and answers that could transform the participants' thinking: What does this codification mean? Why does this "Dr A Serper" have them on his door? What does this mean for us and our life? What are we to do to improve our lives, ourselves and our and the world? How are we to do this?

However, I was somewhat disappointed that the usual responses that I received from passersby to my question of their views on the ideas posted to my office door were along the bland lines of "It is nice" or an idle promise to contact me about it later. I was disappointed that the door did not evoke heated debates on where the country is going or other issues I had hoped the passersby would mention. Similar experiments that I have conducted in Israel, the U.K., the U.S., and France and in the course of which I had elicited discussions among passersby prompted much more reaction and many more passionate and hectic debates and discussions. For instance, providing Israeli students with an opportunity to discuss the situation in the occupied territories, the relationship between Arabs and Jews, the peace process, Zionism in the 21st century, the Oslo Accord, and a retreat to the pre-1967 Green Line is guaranteed to fire up impassioned and emotional outbursts. Similarly, a discussion of university fees, privatization, the NHS, the British relationship with Europe, and government cuts would equally provoke a hectic discussion in the U.K. Discussion of current affairs items such as foreign policies, military interventions, immigration, globalization, and corporations in the U.S. would also lead to emotional discussion. Yet in South Africa, passersby looked at me as if they had done something wrong when I asked them their impressions of the door and seemed compelled to please me by noting that they liked it. This caused me to entertain the possibility that South Africa still fosters a culture of suspicion, distrust, isolation, and silence that are the characteristics of the oppressed. Overcoming anti-education will require time and drastic political and socio-economic changes. Without such changes, dialectics and dialogue may be of limited success.

Fifteen months into my postdoctoral fellowship, I wish to conclude this paper by reflecting on where I am now insofar as my educational and epistemological development, and realizations about my practice as a humanistic researcher and intentions and theories are concerned.

In the course of my elicitation experiment, I noticed some transformation very quickly. I saw how the students and passersby who engaged with reflection and dialogue on the codifications began to realize their powers as epistemological actors and gain more and more confidence to act on and fulfil these powers. In turn, upon practice, their ability to do this increased as well. Nevertheless, I also became aware of how the practice of trying out hypothetical assumptions, ideas, and intentions on people in real-life situations differs from the practice of working out these ideas in isolation as verbal possibilities. I often felt humbled and overwhelmed as I tried out ideas and abstractions that appeared so clear and significant in theory and in books and articles. I felt confused and insecure in regard to what I should do and how. I realized how much I still had to learn about working with people, and about post-colonialist pedagogy and oppression. I am currently working out an action plan thereby to resolve this problem.

The fifteen months I have spent in South Africa so far have shown me what happens in a place where any possibility for critical and dialectical thinking and dialectical co-enquiry of equals in humanity, dignity, and equality were officially[39] halted by the autocratic regime that saw democratic practice as a threat to its own existence. Most of all I have seen how arduous are the genuine attempts and practices to transform South Africa. Investing in material as well as human resources is crucial to transformation.

Likewise, my belief that everything must be done to ensure that critical and dialectical thinking and continuous questioning of the status quo and the past are encouraged has been affirmed. There is a need for a genuine dialogue within which people do not try to "out-argue the other person, but that one really considers the weight of the other's opinion" (Gadamer, 1975, p. 333). The only way to succeed in this transformation of theorized ideas to life-changing practices is to let go of the construction of verbal theories, intentions, and jargon in isolation, step aside, and allow for self-reflection and an open, authentic, and free dialogue that encourages and interrelates different perspectives and opinions. This is so much more difficult than it seems. It is contextual and culturally laden. It transcends good intentions. In a place where nothing is as it seems, and where everything is utterly complex, ambiguous, and self-contradicting, the foreigner who is trying to make sense of it is destabilized. The work is just too big for

---

[39] I am saying officially to acknowledge and stress that there was a strong clandestine culture of protest, criticism, dialogue, enquiring, and liberal media and that people risked their lives to protest again the policies of the regime.

the individual. It requires systemic and systematic political, sociological, and psychological changes. This is before individuals can make any social, political, and cultural difference. Collaborations, political actions, and protests en masse are required.

South Africa is also an excellent example of how social inequality is undemocratic. Alexander (2012) stressed that

> unless the economic basis of social inequality, justified by means of racial ideology (race thinking), is tackled, the racial order is simply reproduced...[and]...unless a radical redistribution of material resources is realised within the lifetime of this generation and the next, all the glib rhetoric about social transformation, national democratic revolution and an African renaissance will return to mock their authors and exponents. The late Reverend Beyers Naudé once said that 'true reconciliation' was only possible 'when we bridge the economic gulf, for you can't build a society of justice on the increasing gap between rich and poor.' He went on to say that only if the government moves towards an equitable distribution of wealth, land, property and income could the political 'miracle' begin to uproot the evil of racism which is 'deeply rooted in South Africa.' (p. 208)

This socioeconomic inequality was repeatedly mentioned in the conversations I had with those who lingered to engage in discussion outside my office door. It became evident to me that this is what the vast majority of them identified as the aspect of life in contemporary South Africa that most disappoints and frustrates them. I was deeply shocked and completely shaken when I witnessed the appalling physical conditions in which the majority of the population of South Africa live in contrast to the luxurious lifestyle that the minority enjoy. In general, Whites still enjoy a far superior quality of accommodation and infrastructure than non-Whites. Private hospitals offer a much higher quality of healthcare than state hospitals. Those who can afford expensive medical insurance enjoy far better treatment than those who cannot. The welfare system in South Africa is nonexistent. As an illustration, free state hospitals provide nothing but cheap painkillers to patients who suffer from acute mouth and tooth decay as well as other seriously degenerative illnesses such as cancer. Those who want to diagnose and treat the causes of their pain and avoid degeneration require costly private treatment that they cannot afford. The same applies to schooling and education. These issues require deep analysis and social solutions on a national scale.

I agree with Neville Alexander that a democracy, by definition, entails socioeconomic and sociopolitical equality and a just and dignified distribution and control of the democracy's resources, land, and wealth (Serper, 2013b). In a true democracy, there cannot be a huge gap between the very wealthy and the very poor (Rogers, 2011). Such a state is more aptly considered an autocracy (Serper, 2013b); Rogers (2011) terms it as a plutocracy.

Until we decrease the socioeconomic gap and the unjust distribution of wealth and resources, democracy and true dialogue cannot exist in South Africa. Rogers (2011) has shown how pro-corporate media use propaganda to indoctrinate audiences to follow corporate and neo-liberal ideologies that allow, if not encourage, the exploitation and oppression of the majority of the population who spend their lives ensuring the prosperity of the corporate world. Social equality and democracy go together just as neo-liberal corporate economy and pro-corporate media complement each other and tend towards fascism (Rogers, 2011; Serper,

2013a, 2013b).[40] Working to attain equality cannot be achieved merely through reflexivity and reflective accounts.

South Africans must gather all their patience together and work tirelessly and continuously to breach sociopolitical and socioeconomic inequality and create a true participatory democracy for all.[41] Otherwise, South Africans will witness more xenophobic attacks, strikes, violent crimes, and harsh police actions.[42] Collective action is needed that is grounded within dialectics and dialogue.

---

[40] Rogers (2011) discussed a situation in which multinational corporations, supported by pro-corporate media, work to control the education, employment, health care, housing, and transportation of the citizens of the countries where they are located. They seek to invest as little as possible in these essential human services and to use these services to increase their profits and to get the most out of their employees whilst spending as little as possible on them. For instance, similarly to apartheid education, the education the corporations provide is training how to best serve the corporation. Similarly, the housing they provide is low quality, company-owned residences next to the premises of the corporations. Likewise, the health care services provided by the corporations follow the intention of the private health insurance companies to increase their profits. Hence, these essential services are provided not in order to cater for the wellbeing of the majority of the people but to increase the wealth of the few shareholders of the companies and to get the most out of the employees.

[41] This means that one-hundred percent of the 53 million South Africans would benefit from the same quality of life and prosperity that the thirteen percent of the privilege Whites did in the past. This is a formidable task that will take many years, if at all, to achieve but when or if it is achieved South Africa will enjoy the prosperity and massive growth it deserves.

[42] The August 16, 2012 Marikana massacre in which 44 protesting miners were killed by the security forces of the new South Africa deeply affected me. It immensely disappointed, infuriated, sickened, shocked, depressed and discouraged me two-and-a-half months after I arrived to South Africa with a great passion and belief in the new post-apartheid democracy. Same goes with the continuous xenophobic violent attacks against poor African refugees and immigrants in the townships and the horrendous crimes against women and children. Still, as a dialectician I include and fuse these counterproductive feelings in my desire and work to contribute to South Africa and its transformations.

References

Alexander, N. (2012). The unresolved national question in South Africa. In N. Jeenah (Ed.), *Pretending democracy: Israel, an ethnocratic state* (pp. 199-216). Johannesburg, South Africa: Afro-Middle East Centre.

Boddy-Evans, A. (2013). *Apartheid quotes – Bantu education: A selection of quotes from apartheid era South Africa.* Retrieved from http://africanhistory.about.com/od/apartheid/qt/ApartheidQts1.htm

Bornman, J., & Rose, J. (2010). *Believe that all can achieve.* Pretoria, South Africa: Van Schaik.

Collingwood, R. G. (1939). *Autobiography.* Oxford, UK: Oxford University Press.

de Wit, M. (2013, August 2-7). Plenty of room at the bottom. *Getting Ahead: Supplement to the Mail & Guardian,* pp. 1-2. Retrieved from http://mg.co.za/section/education/

Department of Education (DoE). (2009). *Guidelines for full-service/inclusive schools.* Pretoria, South Africa: Department of Education.

Dewey, J. (1897). My pedagogic creed. *School Journal, 54,* 77-80.

Dewey, J. (1902). *The child and the curriculum, or, the school and society.* Chicago, IL: The University of Chicago Press.

Dewey, J. (1916). *Democracy and education: An introduction to the philosophy of education.* New York, NY: MacMillan.

Freire, P. (1973). *Education for critical consciousness.* London, UK: Sheed and Ward.

Freire, P. (1996). *Pedagogy of the oppressed.* London, UK: Penguin Books.

Gadamer, H. D. (1975). *Truth and method.* London, UK: Sheed and Ward.

Greenberg, L. S., Rice, L. N., & Elliott, R. (1993). *Facilitating emotional change: The moment-by-moment process.* New York, NY: Guilford Press.

Kahle, L. R., Liu, R. R., Rose, G. M., & Kim, W.-S. (2000). Dialectical thinking in consumer decision-making. *Journal of Consumer Psychology, 9,* 53-58.

Laing, R. D. (1967). *The politics of experience and the bird of paradise.* Harmondsworth, Middlesex, UK: Penguin.

Landsman, M. (2002). Across the lines: The phenomenology of cooperation between an Israeli psychologist and Palestinian mental health professionals. *Radical Psychology, 3*(1). Retrieved from http://www.radicalpsychology.org/vol3-1/

Lerner, R. M. (2002). *Concepts and theories of human development* (3rd ed.). Mahwah, NJ: Lawrence Erlbaum Associates.

Lewin, K. (1946). Action research and minority problems. *Journal of Social Issues 2*(4), 34-46.

Moustakas, C. (1981). Heuristic research. In P. Reason & J. Rowan (Eds.), *Human inquiry: A sourcebook of new paradigm research* (pp. 207-217). New York, NY: John Wiley & Sons.

Moustakas, C. (1990). *Heuristic research: Design, methodology and applications.* Newbury Park, CA: Sage Publications.

Moustakas, C. (1994). *Phenomenological research methods.* Thousand Oaks, CA: Sage Publications.

Popper, K. (1963). *Conjectures and refutations: The growth of scientific knowledge.* Oxford, UK: Oxford University Press.

Riegel, K. F. (1979). *Foundations of dialectical psychology.* New York, NY: Academic Press.

Rogers, K. (2011). *Debunking Glenn Beck: How to save America from media pundits and propagandists.* Santa Barbara, CA: Praeger.

SAHO. (2013). *South Africa history online: Towards a people's history.* Retrieved from www.sahistory.org.za/

Sapon-Shevin, M. (2007). *Widening the circle: The power of inclusive classrooms.* Boston, MA: Beacon.

Sarles, H. (2013). *Teaching as dialogue: A teacher's study.* Los Angeles, CA: Trébol Press.

Schön, D. A. (1983). *The reflective practitioner: How professionals think in action.* London, UK: Temple Smith.

Schön, D. A. (1987). *Educating the reflective practitioner.* New York, NY: Harvester.

Schön, D. A. (Ed.). (1991). *The reflective turn: Case studies in and on educational practice.* New York, NY: Teachers College Press.

Schön, D. A. (1995). The new scholarship requires a new epistemology. *Change, 27*(6), 27-34.

Serper, A. (1999). *A study of the conceptualisation of the human subject in empirical psychology by using textual analysis.* (Unpublished master's thesis). Hebrew University, Jerusalem, Israel.

Serper, A. (2010). *An analytical critique, deconstruction, and dialectical transformation and development of the living educational theory approach.* (Unpublished doctoral disseration). University of Bath, UK.

Serper, A. (2012, October). *Doing dialectical and dialogical education in South Africa.* Paper presented at the South African Comparative and History of Education Society International Conference, Port Elizabeth.

Serper, A. (2013a). Democratic reform of corporate media in America. *Continuum: Journal of Media & Cultural Studies, 27*(2), 326-328.

Serper, A. (2013b, July). *Anthropological, phenomenological reflections of a foreign educator for a participatory democracy for all on the South African culture, values, identity and life.* Paper presented at the Neville Alexander Commemorative Conference, Nelson Mandela Metropolitan University, Port Elizabeth, South Africa.

Serper, A. (2014). *Reflective narrative enquiry on evoking critical reflection and dialogue for change in South Africa.* Paper presented at the Proceedings of the South African Comparative and History of Education Society International Conference, Port Elizabeth, South Africa.

Shaddock, A., Giorcelli, L. & Smith, S. (2007). *Students with disabilities in mainstream classrooms: A resource for teachers.* Commonwealth of Australia.

Soudien, C. (2012). *Realising the dream: Unlearning the logic of race in the South African school.* Cape Town, South Africa: HSRC Press.

South African Governmental Department of Basic Education. (2013). Retrieved from http://www.education.gov.za/Programmes/Inclusive Education/tabid/436/Default.asx

South African Government Information. (2013). *Constitution of the Republic of South Africa*, 1996. Retrieved from http://www.info.gov.za/documents/constitution/19 96/index.htm

Tabata, I. B. (1959/1980). *Education for barbarism: Bantu (apartheid) education in South Africa.* Lusaka, Zambia: Unity Movement of South Africa.

Thutong – South African Education Portal. (2013). *Inclusive Education.* Retrieved from www.thutong.doe.gov.za/Default.aspx?alias=www.th utong.doe.gov.za/inclusiveeducatin

Tomlinson, C., Brimijoin, K., & Narvaez, L. (2008). *The differentiated school.* Alexandria, VA: Association for Supervision and Curriculum Development.

Tutu, D. (1999). *No future without forgiveness.* New York, NY: Doubleday.

Van Manen, M. (1990). *Researching lived experience: Human science for an action sensitive pedagogy.* Ontario, Canada: State University of New York Press.

Walton, E., & Nell, N. (2012). What counts as inclusion? *Africa Education Review, 9*(1), 2-16.

Winter, R. (1989). *Learning From experience: Principles and practices in action-research.* London, UK, New York, NY, and Philadelphia, PA: The Falmer Press.

Whole Systems Classroom Practices

John Warner
Whole Systems Agriculture

Abstract

This paper describes the whole systems method of teaching secondary students as evolved over 30 years of classroom practice. The practices revolve around key concepts of inclusion, active student participation, and individual creativity and expression in a mutually supportive and dynamic learning environment. The teacher turns classroom management, including the writing of tests, over to the students themselves to inculcate a sense of social responsibility within the learning environment. Students' ability to understand and analyze material is emphasized over rote learning and memorization. The whole systems student-centered classroom emphasizes the integral importance of each student's contributions, and as such is modeled on the world itself as an organic whole.

Keywords: whole systems education, classroom practice, dynamic learning environment, student-centered education

In a field
I am the absence
of field.
This is
always the case.
Wherever I am
I is what I'm missing.

When I walk
I part the air
and always

the air moves in
to fill the spaces
where my body has been.

We all have reasons
for moving.
I move to keep things whole.

Mark Strand
Poet Laureate of the U.S.,
1990-1991

I started teaching in the 1960s using the regular methods I learned in teacher training and, from there, over the course of my career of over 30 years teaching in secondary classrooms, developed a number of changes that made my work far more rewarding and effective. Learning increased dramatically and classroom management became much easier. For the most part these changes were cobbled together intuitively or by chance or circumstance but in the end I have been able to put them together into a comprehensive whole system backed by solid scientific models and research.

Importantly, I modeled my classroom on living systems as these systems are understood by biologists, ecologists, and social scientists. I found conventional practices to be extremely linear, top-down, undemocratic approaches that make classrooms look very much like filling stations where students get filled with facts just as automobiles are filled with gasoline.

I started off making lots of worksheets, which my students universally hated, and came to replace them with colorful student-written and hand-drawn lessons that, in many cases, were works of art that students wanted to show their parents and keep for a while after the semester was completed. (Worksheets, be they made by teacher or publisher, justifiably end up in the trash.) I call these "whole student lessons" because students are encouraged to think, to create, to compare and to use the higher orders of thinking that Bloom described in his famous *Taxonomy of Educational Objectives* [*Handbook II, Affective Domain*] and other more recent taxonomies (Bloom *et al.*, 1956). The content of the taxonomies is taught directly to the students by the teacher rather than simply being listed as goals in a lesson plan. The teacher refers to keyword lists posted more or less permanently in the classroom and referred to regularly. A poster high on the classroom wall may read thus:

Create
Evaluate
Analyze
Apply
Understand
Remember

This list works like this: Almost everybody can *remember* facts such as the year the pilgrims arrived in America but it takes more to get an *understanding* of why they came here in the first place and more still to *analyze* the alternatives they may have had before they left England. Then, stretching intellect still further, a person might want to *evaluate* the coming of Europeans to America and the impact these people had on the land and the indigenous populations. Finally she may *create* a piece of art or a piece of writing or an impassioned speech that communicates her point of view about this historical period.

The teacher explains that the list is read from the bottom up in order of increasing educational merit. She would explain that students should work their way up the list and demonstrate the higher orders of thinking. Remembering would be worth roughly the mark of "C." Marks "A" and "B" go to work done at the higher levels. Marks "D" and "F" go to students that don't show up for class or don't do their work.

A radically bold teacher such as myself might guarantee everyone with good attendance a passing mark provided all the lessons were completed (both sides of a sheet of 8.5 by 11-inch college ruled notebook paper, no less than eight words per line, colorful icons in the left margins, nice and neat, two lessons per week), regardless of whatever nonsense the student may write. The teacher might confess how he was fooled in a previous class by a student that wrote mostly Beatles lyrics and got away with it for weeks before he was caught. "But he still got one of the better marks. He was an artist type and *created*. . . [teacher pauses, points to wall chart with yardstick] . . . good icons and thereby demonstrated the highest . . . [points finger skyward] . . . orders of thinking."

Such an introduction will make it easier for students to participate in the great amount of oral work that they will be asked to do in both reading aloud from the text and commenting on the readings in self-generated language. Each student is invited to read aloud and comment each day. An axiom of the Whole System Classroom method is *"the success of a single student is a credit to everyone in class."* "Repeat with me please . . . *a credit to everyone in class* [three times]." This sets the tone for a responsible social ethic.

What are icons? They are small drawings, ten per lesson, that relate to the keyword pairs taken from the text. What are keyword pairs? They constitute the teacher's lesson plan. The teacher takes them from the textbook and most of them will be related in one way or another. For example, one of the words may be a cause and the other an effect; one may be a part and the other the whole. They may be related in time or space or not at all. The students are challenged to find a relationship, and write about it in the appropriate space. Example of a keyword pair: "Pericles & city states."

The lesson paper is sheet of 8.5 by 11 inch college-ruled notebook paper. Students count the available writing spaces, divide by five, and line off the spaces with a ruler or book edge in such a way that the spaces are close to equal size. There is one space per keyword pair, five spaces per day. One sheet of paper provides spaces for two days of lessons, perhaps Monday and Tuesday. A fresh lesson would be prepared for Wednesday and Thursday. Friday might be used as a catch-up day, another activity, student readings from their work, or the sharing of icons on the board.

Tests are similarly different from the norm. Students are obligated to demonstrate their mastery of subject matter by making a list of keywords from the text and writing about a sampling of them, perhaps 10 out of a list of one or two hundred items. They write a paragraph about each of the selections and, after the test is marked, students are called upon to respond orally to an item or two on their list. Students at the end of the semester are responsible for all the subject matter going back to the very first day of class. Keywords that students use on their lists are, for the most part, grouped by chapter, making it easy to check for content.

Perhaps the most radical departure from traditional schooling is that the teacher, after holding forth for no more than ten minutes or so, turns class management over to a student leader who introduces students and invites them to read and share. The teacher can then work at her desk, mark papers, observe the goings-on and communicate approval with subtle glances, gestures, nods, and smiles.

I started my teaching at a beautiful, brand new school in Woodland Hills, Hale Junior High School. Every student in the attendance area lived in a single family home. For the most part, they came from professional families, were highly motivated, courteous, and respectful and the problems were few. While there I changed the usual auditorium style of seating of my classroom into a rectangular arrangement where most of the students faced each other. This afforded a decidedly greater sense of community and eliminated back of the room corners where students could hide and easily slip off task. In working with the class I favored using one of the student seats rather than sitting at my desk.

While at Hale I developed the student-made test described above. I had advanced horticulture students who took my class for multiple semesters and I required them to prepare a test for themselves that included at least 200 keyword items for each semester in class (roughly two items for each day in class). Some tests exceeded 1000 items where, in this case the student would respond to every hundredth item starting with… [a piece of money is drawn and the last two digits of the serial number determined]…"22." Some of these students have gone into horticulture professionally and have become wonderfully successful.

I read William Glasser's book, *Schools Without Failure*, which made a strong impression on me and has colored my work with children ever since (Glasser, 1969). Dr. Glasser was doing some work at Los Angeles's largest elementary school, Miramonte Elementary in South Central, where my brother was principal at the time. My brother would fill me in on what Dr. Glasser was doing so I felt a kind of personal connection with Glasser's work. I cannot, however, endorse some of his later work – specifically his "Choice Theory" which posits that students who don't do well in school do so because they make poor choices. No fair blaming students for the poor job we are doing in schools. It's time for us to step up, make some changes that really matter and *compel* more students to succeed with *evidence-based* changes in classroom management.

Is there any question of the fact that environment strongly effects all the organisms in its realm? All the organisms I know of depend one-hundred percent on their environment for every need and every detail of their lives. Human beings are organisms and are therefore subject to the laws of nature. Young human beings go to schools where they sit in classrooms with other young human beings. It is widely recognized that young human beings (and old ones too) strongly influence each other. The teacher is responsible for creating a mutually supportive learning environment and she would do well to read widely in psychology with an eye toward furthering a mutually supportive learning environment.

This may be a good time for me to hold forth on the evils of tracking. I am talking about grouping students by "ability" or, under one label or another, into "highs" and "lows." A fact of psychology is that people, particularly young ones, live out the expectations society has for them. When students are tracked "high" there is a risk of making them snooty and distant from those tracked "low." If tracked "low" they are at risk of falling irreversibly into the underclass and a future much worse than just being snooty. The Whole System Classroom accommodates the full range of human ability or close to it. It fosters respect, empathy, compassion, responsibility and a number of other desirable social qualities. The Whole System Classroom is democratic in that everyone in the class gets the same floor time, gets the same name recognition, and turns in lessons similar in every way on the surface. Students learn from each other and those who speak mostly in grunts and exclamations get to learn good English from text and from the more articulate students. Most of all, everyone gets the same respect.

When will we wake up and stop trying to teach young human beings one by one? Any seating arrangement that has all the seats pointed in one direction, toward the teacher, reveals a *de facto* attempt to teach young human beings individually. And frankly, it's a fool's dream. Why not fill the room with young human beings who have a variety of talents and abilities in such a way that they can see each other, hear each other, know each other's voices, and the subtle details of their personalities? Then, the best and the brightest of this group can lead the way to mastery for everyone by their example and their support. It is mostly just a matter of setting up appropriate rules and procedures that lead to desired outcomes.

When I got to Webster Junior High School in West Los Angeles I found that the school had embraced behavior modification as a school wide policy. Posters were up in every classroom. The faculty was instructed on behaviorist strategies in meetings and workshops. I mention this because I believe that teachers, even whole schools, should have strategies for student success that rest on solid scientific ground. The behaviorist school of psychology can provide this.

At Webster the principal was very dynamic man with a prosthetic leg that was said to have replaced a leg he had lost in war. He was known informally as "Iron Mike" and he called sports events on radio and television. It would follow that most people would experience pleasure in having the attention of such an important person even if it was only momentary. I would speculate that the principal recognized this and, as the presumed initiator of the behavior modification model set up at the school, recognized his potential role as a reinforcer of desirable student behavior. Almost every morning the principal could be found greeting and giving messages of encouragement to students as they got off the several buses that came in from Central Los Angeles and other parts of the city. Mike was reinforcing the behaviors he was looking for in accordance with the principles of behaviorism.

After teaching a year in West Los Angeles I transferred to North Hollywood High School where I taught classes in agriculture, science, and the state-mandated health classes, which included units in family and sex education. It was at this time that I read physicist-philosopher Fritjof Capra's book *The Turning Point: Science, Society and the Rising Culture* and as a result was able to put some order to my grab bag of classroom tricks (Capra, 1983). Specifically, I was able to see how these tricks fit together into a comprehensive whole. I was able to define and refine the concept of leveraging learning with social dynamics.

The thirty-nine pages of Chapter 9, *The Systems View of Life*, struck me as if I had found the Holy Grail. This view of life went beyond the classroom to color and influence my life and work ever since. The chapter compares dynamic, living systems with simple linear systems such as machines and assembly lines. I used the material there to identify the concepts I needed to set up the Whole System Classroom and for the farm and business I set up after I retired, Whole Systems Agriculture. In checking Capra's website[43] I see that he has been working on a book with the same title as the chapter discussed here, *The Systems View of Life*. Presumably this will be an expansion of chapter nine.[44]

At this point it might be appropriate to mention that I am not an advocate of teaching systems theory in schools. That proposal would have to get in line with other subjects in school curricula such as history and algebra. What we are doing here is *using* systems theory to organize learning in the classroom and the students do not need to know a thing about systems to do that. Here the students *become* the system whether they are consciously aware of it or not.

---

[43] See: *www.fritjofcapra.net*

[44] Editor's note: Capra's book, *The Systems View of Life: A Unifying Vision*, co-authored with Pier Luigi Luisi, is published in English by Cambridge University Press with a release date of April 30, 2014.

Just a few days ago I received an invitation to a "Systems Thinking & Dynamic Modeling Conference for K-12 Education" being held in June 2014. In moving through their website[45] I was impressed that real systems heavyweights like Jay Forrester, Peter Senge, and Dennis Meadows would be participating in the conference as speakers and session leaders. This is all very laudable but has little relationship to what I am advocating in this paper. The conference seemed mostly about how to create lessons that integrate systems content into the existing curriculum and reflects in other ways regular teaching practice. To continue with the filling station metaphor I used earlier, it changes the grade of fuel from regular to premium.

Here the classroom with its students and teacher and the content of the room *is* the system. Living systems have inputs and outputs. Inputs are the subject matter in the textbook or other printed materials (or even material read aloud off laptops or tablets) as well as the verbal inputs of students and teacher. Outputs are the beautiful lessons the students create and the students who, at the conclusion of the class, leave with enhanced self-worth, confidence, knowledge of subject matter, and a sense of place in the world.

Here are some ways a classroom of students can become part of a dynamic living system such as we find in nature. These are in stark contrast with the assembly line model found so frequently in schools:

Circular, face-to-face seating as best as can be managed with the available furniture and classroom dimensions. Where seating is tight this may take the form of two or three rows of desks facing each other from opposite sides of the room with a wide isle between them. Students need to take the same seats every day because they are invited to read and comment by a

[45] See: *www.clexchange.org*

student leader who works from a list that corresponds to the seating arrangement. A simple way to do this is to seat students alphabetically, which also facilitates roll taking and mark recording.

Every day a fresh reading leader is chosen from a show of hands. The leader introduces and invites class members one by one to read aloud from the textbook and thanks them by name when they are done. This works in order of seating so class members can make a good estimate of when their turn will come and be prepared. The reader is mindful of the goal that stipulates that everyone participate every day and adjusts the time she uses accordingly. Then the reader is thanked by name for reading and asked if she has any thoughts to share and is again thanked by name. (The goal of having students read and speak every day adds a sense of urgency that keeps business flowing.)

A reader of this paper may be thinking, "This guy has been criticizing regular schooling as being overly mechanical but now he's describing a reading leader who acts a lot like a machine." I would reply that much in nature is mechanical such as the structure of skeletons and the apparent movements of the heavens. Here the leader is mimicking the regular cycles of day and night and the changing of the seasons. This repetitive structure gives order to the classroom just as day and night give order to our lives.

Name recognition is a strong tool we can use for developing classroom community. Everybody loves the sound of his own name. Therefore, the reading leader is asked to introduce students by name in a loud, strong voice with intonations that suggest that the new reader is a person of great importance. At the conclusion of the reading the leader thanks the participant by name and invites her to share any thoughts she might have. Perhaps it was in Carey McWilliams' book, *North From Mexico,* in which I read about the importance of names in Hispanic culture (McWilliams, 1949). There one's name is one's honor and if one lends his name to something that turns out not to be true, it is a terrible disgrace. But this idea surely applies to cultures everywhere to greater or lesser degree.

An axiom of the whole system concept is to *leverage learning with social dynamics*. It is universally believed that small classes are better than large classes because students in small classes get more teacher attention. I would posit the opposite: large classes are better than small ones (within limits) because students in large classes get more *social* attention and in this way teachers can leverage learning with the stronger social dynamic of a larger class.

In tribal times people probably spoke and listened in roughly equal ratios and although we have the same genetically driven needs as people did in times past, we now live in a culture where one speaks while thousands listen (even millions when presidents, pop stars, and popes are speaking). People in our times need to do more talking; orating if you will, if we are to honor our evolutionary and preindustrial heritage.

The agricultural branch of our whole system organization sells plants, flowers, and vegetables at a farmers' market. An astute philosopher who was visiting us observed that customers are more interested in giving information than receiving it. This has set us to musing about how we might improve our sales by planting intentional listeners at our booth to engage people in conversation and then just shut up and listen to them. Eddie Bernays, "father of public relations" and Freud's favorite nephew, might be proud to see how far his influence has reached into the corners and crannies of industrial society.

I would like to mention a once-famous school that was founded in Alabama in 1907 by Marietta Johnson that had no exams, no homework, and no possibility of failure. She called her school *The School of Organic Education*. In 1913 John Dewey visited and was impressed enough to make it the subject of a whole chapter in his book, *Schools of Tomorrow* (Dewey, 1962).

Mrs. Johnson was likely influenced by her contemporary, Rudolph Steiner, founder of the Waldorf School. While I was at North Hollywood, a physicist I knew, an anthroposophist,[46] suggested I visit the open house a Waldorf school in the North San Fernando Valley was holding. This was one the schools to which the high-profile Hollywood people sent their children. I was very impressed. By contrast with the regular model of teaching, students there did far more speaking, much of it in acting out plays. Also they did much more creative art. It was from this experience I came to emphasize reading aloud to the whole class, speaking to the whole class and drawing icons on lesson papers and sharing the content of their icons from time to time.

Another axiom of whole system classroom practice is *context trumps content*. Content is soon forgotten. (How much coursework can you recall?) But our *experiences* at school are long remembered. Many of these experiences get tucked away in the unconscious but continue to influence our lives for good or for ill.

How would a teacher go about introducing whole system procedures in her classroom? The answer to this question is an easy one – just do it. Everything suggested here rests within the professional prerogative of a credentialed teacher to initiate. School administrators are busy people. For the most part they do not have the time or even much interest

---

[46] See: *www.waldorfanswers.com/Anthroposophy.htm*

in discussing pedagogical theories. They have work to do and problems to solve and you can be sure they will appreciate it when the problems that come from your classroom are few. Students love it. Parents love it. When families come in for open house and see your students' work displayed, some find it hard to believe that children at that grade level can do such fine work. When favorable feedback gets to the office administrators have no problem understanding it.

But the greatest benefit goes to your students who become more skilled in language and expression, more self-confident, and more intrinsically motivated. Also, I am sure, they will score higher on those abominable state and nationwide subject matter tests to a marked degree.

The reader may note that the method described here is very much student-centered. A fair measure of student or teacher centeredness would be a measure of who is doing the talking. Here the guideline is 80% student and 20% teacher talk. In a nominal 60-minute hour, the teacher gets 12 minutes and the students get 48 but since secondary schools usually have the classroom hour reduced for passing, the teacher ends up with about 10.

John Dewey, the "learn-by-doing" philosopher, very much favored the student-centered approach. Students in a whole system classroom read, write, speak, listen, think, question, and plan all at the same time. This mimics an ecological community, such as a woodland, where the sun shines, the birds chirp, the leaves photosynthesize, the mice munch, and the raptors circle in search of a meal. I call this "*manifold, simultaneous transaction*" and count it among the axioms of the whole system learning concept. This is obviously more efficient than everybody doing things in sequential order, one at a time, which is the usual practice in teacher-directed classrooms.

Dewey was a champion of democracy. I would think, if he were with us today, he would appreciate the inclusiveness of the whole system classroom. Everyone is introduced and thanked by name every day for their contributions. An atmosphere of mutual respect is cultivated and, ideally, the most academically able sit and work in the same room and do the same things that students mainstreamed in from special education classes do. The quality of the work may differ widely but, just as we all share the same world, we all share the same classroom. Here, the world and the classroom are metaphors for each other.

References

Bloom, B. S., Krathwohl, D. R., & Masia, B. B. (1956). *Taxonomy of Educational Objectives, Handbook II: Affective Domain (The Classification of Educational Goals).* Philadelphia, PA: David McKay.

Capra, F. (1983). *The turning point: Science, society and the rising culture.* New York, NY: Bantam.

Dewey, J., & Dewey, E. (1962). *Schools for tomorrow.* Boston, MA: E. P. Dutton & Company.

Glasser, W. (1969). *Schools without failure.* New York, NY: Harper.

McWilliams, C. (1949). *North From Mexico: The Spanish-Speaking People of the United States.* Philadelphia, PA: Lippincott.

A Vision: The Idea of a University in the Present Age

Harvey Sarles
The John Dewey Center For Democracy and Education
University of Minnesota

Abstract

My vision for the future university acknowledges the facts of rapid change in the world. It attempts to conserve the idea of the university as structures and process by centering the university on a study of changes as they are redefining knowledge. As vision, it asks that faculties join in Centers for the Study of the Present Age to discuss, teach, and attempt to shape the futures of Science and Technology and their ramifications.

Keywords: future university, new vision, re-center the university, study of present age

The vision: When I speak and think of the university, I have in mind the largest institution, and the greatest number of students at all levels, professional as much as academic, graduate and postgraduate, as well as undergraduate. The curriculum is at its maximum: some 150 subjects/disciplines in which one can garner a Ph.D. I have in mind, then, the largest public research universities, especially those which (also) educate their students to serve their states in the traditions of the Land Grant University: including agriculture and the mechanical arts.

While there are ample reasons to describe a private (research) university of fame or privilege as *the* descriptor of the university – say, the top of the pyramid of American universities, an Oxbridge or a Berlin – I think it important for our understanding of the present toward the future to consider the university serving the interests of the widest public or publics. In this setting, I intend to focus on the structure-processes of the institution; particularly on how the idea of the university will intersect with, even help to define, the nature of the future.

I will therefore use the institution I know best – the University of Minnesota located in that urban cultural oasis of Minneapolis and St. Paul (the Twin Cities) – as an example and a metaphor. I will propose a new vision in the development of a truly important University of Minnesota: The Study of the Present Age (Kierkegaard, 1940).[47]

Whether this vision might apply to privately endowed universities, we shall see. Whether more than one university will survive, this we shall also see. Whether Minnesota is metaphor or reality, time will tell. We all find ourselves afloat in a sea of market-driven forces in this era of hype and the reality of online institutions, such as Phoenix University et al., MOOCS, and the recently globalized university where the very *idea* of a university is constructed as a new product for whatever its markets will turn out to be. I oppose the idea that the market alone will determine the nature of the university.

This vision is simple in its statement. The present University of Minnesota will expand to include and center itself about the Study of the Present Age. A number of Centers will be created that will literally study, discuss, and publish in the contexts of the most important issues of these times. Minnesota will be the place where the changing and continuing world is studied, criticized, and shaped.

---

[47] Kierkegaard's principal critique is of the rise of bureaucratic thought and thinking. In this context I have crafted an analysis of the University: "Idea of the University in the Present Age."

Primary will be the Center of the Study of Science and Technology as these domains are developing and changing the very ways in which we operate and think about being: new products, new ideas, even moving our ideas of reality from the world or from texts to whatever "virtual" will mean: media, and so on. Other Centers will include the Study of a Sustainable World; Life in the World's Cities; the Changing Nature of Work; Curing and Teaching; Globalization; the Crisis in Meaning; Aging and Sage-ing; Integrative Studies. There may be other suggestions.

There will be a Provost or Vice-President who leads this Center for the Study of the Present Age; and there will be an intellectual leader or coordinator as well. All the present faculty of the university will be included within it for perhaps 10 to 20 percent of their time; to join it at different points, and for varying lengths of time.[48]

The curriculum of the university as it exists at present, especially in the Liberal Arts and Sciences, will thus be preserved. Undergraduate students will be broadly educated in the Liberal Arts and Sciences. But they will also be educated to be able to join in discussions in several of the Centers for the Study of the Present Age at an advanced critical and intellectual level. To enable this, I propose a pedagogical-dialogic interactive approach to critical thinking.[49]

With the university centered around the Center for the Study of the Present Age, the current core values, central ideas, and primary disciplines of the university will be essentially preserved. Otherwise the idea of the university will drift with

[48] The faculty will also be asked to develop their own – new or renewed – plans for their future work: one-, two-, five-, or 10-year projections within disciplines and/or across disciplines.
[49] My own thought and work in teaching has been interactive, toward the Deweyan idea of becoming a self-thinker; an autodidact. See Sarles, H. (2013). *Teaching as Dialogue*. Los Angeles, CA: Trébol Press.

the winds and currents of money, politics, and possibly, religion: the worries of the permeability of integrity and academic freedom so carefully pondered by Hofstadter and Metzger (1955).

Our students – or, as they now say, consumers – will be quite capable in the context of (what I call) an unscripted time,[50] as they will be broadly educated, with an emphasis on critical and creative thinking; able to approach the world as it happens, and to perform within it at fairly advanced levels. Otherwise, the temptation in a time of great change is to derogate the history of the idea of the university, and to train rather than to educate students for a changing and clamoring market. The Study of the Present Age can both preserve the sense of the larger curriculum and provide for futurity and, to the extent that we develop an important University of Minnesota, it will also do much to shape that futurity.

The idea of a University in the Present Age should likely occur in an urban context that can accommodate and attract the kinds of enterprises and businesses that these Centers will spawn; more than, say, Amherst, Madison, or Ithaca. The moment seems ripe for the development of this vision. There is a large pool of older faculty-thinkers-wise persons from around the world who could contribute to such an idea: many of the more creative minds have been forced to be quite narrow in their work, and would welcome the

---

[50] By "an unscripted time" I mean that the future looms without much certitude about potential or real vocations or careers for which the university qua university can train them. In a world in which 'temps' are a leading career at present, and even some professions (e.g., medicine) are changing almost daily, it is unclear that the largely historical university can train students and retain any sense of its integrity or reason for being. Much of this discussion hinges on the perception of the pace and depth of changes which we are presently experiencing. I presume that we must educate students to be able to deal with their futurities, irrespective of the university's particularities.

challenge of broader critical thinking.[51] Many of them receive fairly nice pensions, would require less compensation, and could contract to develop, lead, and contribute to such a global enterprise. They also would be attracted to a cultural center such as the Twin Cities. Many of them could also attract funding and followings in the context of an important University of Minnesota. Similarly, a number of commercial enterprises would find it important to partake in these critical discussions with us. As we will attract many of the best critics, say, of biotechnology and virtual reality, so various businesses will find it most advantageous to discuss the development of pertinent issues in the areas of our Centers' concentrations, with more reasons to be located in an urban setting.

Early Brief Courses could be presented to entering students: An Introduction to the University; Culture and Technology; a Brief Course on America in company with entering International Students (a specialty of mine).[52] Education would be directly, perhaps primarily, aimed toward the students being able to enter into discussion in the various Centers at a thoughtful level. As the Centers both reflect and intersect the changing world, the criterion of students participating in the conversations would be a good measure of educational quality and utility, enhancing their ability to enter the world as educated and critically thoughtful persons.

The University of Minnesota is sufficiently large to accommodate the Study of the Present Age, and is quite possibly geared for a large change as it seems to find itself at a moment of declining resources and reputation, with the sense

---

[51] I do not mean that this envisioned university should be a mere retirement haven for ex-academics. Rather, it will draw the very limited number of older persons whom we can think of as master teachers or sages in the contexts of other traditions in the world that have highly respectful wisdom traditions of aging.

[52] I taught such a course for several years to incoming international Fulbright graduate students from all over the world, and propose it as a good introduction both to our own history and to global thinking. See Sarles, 1998.

that its future likely will witness its decline from a formerly great university to merely a 'pretty good' one. So, on to the Vision!

Context and Setting: Gradual Changes Since the 1950s

As the world is enmeshed in torrents of change, the very idea of the university is also much in flux. Newman's 'winds from the North' (Newman, 1976) – from industrial England of the 19th century – invade both our thinking and the funding of the institutions which until fairly recently seemed somewhat removed from the currents of ordinary life: the Ivory Tower now overgrown with weeds, hanging vines; exposed to the elements.

But it is not only money that offers – or threatens – to alter the university. There is a much larger set of changes that challenge the very idea of a university as it has endured with some centrality and continuity of purpose from Plato's Academy to the present time. I am thus cautious about the ideas of the university that we all bring to this discussion. Some of these changes have occurred fairly gradually, if profoundly. As an example, I take it for granted that the university consists primarily in its faculties and curricula. But most people seem to locate the idea of the university in its organization or administration. And many of the changes of the past generation seem to remain outside our thinking as they characterize the university as most of us have actually experienced it. Which and whose idea of the university are we attempting to preserve or reinvent? Below is a brief analysis of changes that have already occurred by the time most of us got to experience the university.

The very nature of work is undergoing a change – literally – as great as the Industrial Revolution and the technological developments of the 19th century. The rising power of the sciences and engineering; more recently biology, the decline of the liberal arts, as well as the sense of the importance of a university degree in order to find mostly monetary success in the working world . . . all this has backgrounded ideas of a good, contemplative, educated life, or of the education of the good citizen (which has almost vanished from the modern secular university). Perhaps this is driven much by the fading of the very idea of the nation-state with such vast sums of money passing through the world each day (Readings, 1996).

In the context of work and education, the numbers of students who attended university increased radically during the period of the maturation of the baby boomers in the late 1950s and early 1960s. The student population of Minnesota, for example, increased from about 17,000 to 35,000 in just four years between 1958 and 1962. The idea of university leadership was radically altered by the necessity of managing such multitudes. Federal and foundation funds increased after World War II, but especially after Sputnik in 1957, paralleling and driving the vast increase in enrollment. Any *community of scholars* as it may have existed prior to that moment in Newman's sense (Newman, 1953) splintered into those areas that had external funding and those that had none. The Institute of Technology at the Minnesota literally *stole* the hard sciences from Science and Liberal Arts in the late 1950s, and biology went its own ways to affiliate with medicine or agriculture. The two-culture split between the sciences and the humanities, noted by C. P. Snow already by 1959 (Snow, 1964), persists to this day. Faculties went their own ways. The only common interest or issue, already by 1963, was that of finding parking spaces (Kerr, 1963).

In the 1960s, the rise of grantsmanship further splintered faculty into individuated entrepreneurs, as careerism gradually replaced vocationalism. And in the early 1970s, when the expanded and newly created institutions slowed down their expansions, administration consolidated its hold on the university.[53] It was during this period that the structural idea of departments overtook the more conceptual notion of disciplines. Whereas disciplines developed and largely remain the outcome of particular questions, problems, or issues, departments are collectivities whose identity has become largely bureaucratic; places to house faculty whose power and importance are directly related to the size of its budget, more than to any intellectual import of its disciplined thinking. Whenever, perhaps especially now, the society (government, foundations, especially corporations) wants new or other questions addressed, the *department* has often been found to be intransigent and closed-in. The obvious solution has been to direct research across or among multi-disciplines. But the actuality of multi- or interdisciplinary work often disregards or loses the centrality of disciplined thinking, as it often directs itself to externally generated problematics. Current pressures on the idea of a university, then, seem to be largely integrative: trying to construct an administrative soul for a very loose collectivity in which department backgrounds discipline.

While much of this seems obvious and productive, there is often a loss of history and reason for differently disciplined thinking, at least some of which seems to be at the heart of the Liberal Arts. The question of the future of the university surely involves questions of the importance or integrity of disciplined thinking across a vast curriculum. As an example, much of botany and zoology have literally been replaced or overtaken by microbiology, the biology of the cell; a form of chemistry that is certainly both important and yielding of monies. But many important questions about humanity and life have simply disappeared, unasked: morphology, taxonomy. Geography, physiology, and philosophy seem about to fade as well.

---

[53] I note with dismay that there are very few if any current university presidents who have national intellectual stature.

During the 1960s and 1970s, the very nature of administration changed in what Bruce Wilshire (1990) characterized as the *moral collapse of the university* when administrators began shuffling paper more than judging the quality of their faculties, or asking questions about knowledge and the meaning of the university. During this time, there was also a democratization of the university: first, ethnic Europeans (primarily male Catholics and Jews), then (mostly white, younger) women, and not so many persons of color. While this was a wonderful occurrence, I think that these events took notice away from the administrative and bureaucratic changes that were also occurring. One result was that there was very little criticism of the idea of the university during this period. Another was the training of most administrators to think of the university as effectively without much sense of purpose: to judge one's own institution with respect to others, more than with respect to some idea of what a university *ought to be and do.*

Another aspect of the democratization was the vast increase in the numbers of students who came to the university, also contributing to its bureaucratization. The notion of a credential gradually began to replace the idea of an education (Kerr, 1991). A degree – any degree – replaced most of the deeper questions about the meaning of an education. As a result, the institution became increasingly opaque to the multitudes of students (parents and community, as well) as the faculty gradually disappeared into their productive modes.[54] The sense of isolation in universities markedly increased among students – perhaps more particularly for faculty.

---

[54] My metaphor continues to be the curriculum handbook of the University of Wisconsin at Madison when our son went there in the early 1980s: 135 pages of majors and courses and not a single mention of any faculty. Not one!

Visibility and image – as in the media – overtook the harder work of personal judgment. University presidents began to look at other places a bit better – a bit worse – to see where their institutions (and careers) were situated (Cohen & March, 1974). This established and continues to confirm the current pyramid of universities in which reputation largely determines quality, while actual work is done for like-minded colleagues in other places. Little occurs in one's home department or university of any institutional value. Visibility and celebrity have overtaken authority…one could go on.

Related is the rise of the knowledge society in which our Colleges of Education see information, access, and use of knowledge as keys to a good education. Teachers who might purvey wisdom have become managers and facilitators as the importance of education as a profession has dwindled. John Dewey's School of Education at the University of Chicago was phased out fairly recently – placing an apostrophe on an era when we might have had a dialogical interchange with a sage. This is to say that information and knowledge have overtaken education as wisdom has faded from our ideas of the course of a long life: something about the technologicalization and bureaucratization of life.

All this analysis affirms that the current wonderings about the future of knowledge and the university are set within an institution that has not thought too much about questions of its meaning since at least the early 1970s. My concern is that we are asking questions about futurity within a model of the university and knowledge that has been running as much on inertia as substance for quite a while.

The Recent Past

None of this analysis of the depth of change should be understood as a downgrading of any current sense of crisis and sudden change that have been occurring within the university. To return briefly to the vision of the Present Age, it is the pace and directions of change which have moved me to suggest that the central function of the *important* University of Minnesota will be to seriously study the changing nature of these times.

Where to begin? This crisis in meaning (Sarles, 2001), first noted by Nietzsche well over a century ago as the rise in 'European nihilism' (Nietzsche, 1968), has deepened. Television and advertising are prime examples in which authority has been replaced by celebrity. The pursuit of truth, and that faculty and universities can certify it as such, has weakened considerably. Techniques of revisionism such as *spin* and *PR* are by now so common as to be cliché. Fame and becoming a *star professor* is the current measure of competitive *quality*. A much longer story, but central to our concerns. Here the Internet and email have opened up opportunities for us to communicate easily and rapidly. No paper necessary to communicate all across the world – to develop conferences, to arrange…whatever. The downside is that questions of truth and authority are increasingly in flux.

The idea that the world is driven by politics or economics (in either order) – and nothing else – also seems increasingly attractive, and awaits (new?) theories of global governance whenever an apparently insatiable capitalism must eventually overstep itself. This, too, is a developing current of postmodernism, in which most left-leaning *neo-neo-Marxists* are searching against, but also for, new directions. Within the context of the meaning of the university, however, the notion that all is politics/economics tends to be undermining.[55]

---

[55] I usually agree with postmodernists that politics are involved in almost everything, but think that, with ongoing awareness and cultural critique, much of the politics can be overcome; cf., this essay.

As I often taught the Sciences and the Humanities course at Minnesota, and as I have that on my mind: whatever 'postmodernism' may mean or convey, the rifts between science and humanities have deepened a good deal. I characterize the differences being between the *World-as-Text* and the *Text-as-World*. As technology continues to rise with amazing power, science recedes into the background and the notion of narrative – that everything is *talk about*, but any actual reality is located in texts – seems very attractive. The rise of religious fundamentalism is related – as such thinkers are actually scholars of religious texts, which they use to determine the ongoing reality: thus, the Text-as-World. None of this can be overestimated in its possible powers. The intellectual impact of this is to replace ideas from history and linear development of our being with concepts derived from prophets whose sayings may overtake all of thinking.

The Future

It has not helped that science (thus rationality, and the politics of liberalism and democracy) is increasingly seen as self-serving: scientists working for corporations that fund research at universities more cheaply than they could do it. Isn't everyone for sale? (Philip Regal, personal communication, ca. 1980s[56]) Aren't our deans all urging us to apply for grants, never mind questions of integrity? Who can judge quality, anyway? And endowed professorships seem fairly open to those who can pay the prevailing price: professorial stars, or ideologues?

An increasing sense of globality has entered our thinking and actualities. Movements of vast sums of money each day and night have helped blur the conceptual boundaries

---

[56] Philip Regal is a now-retired ecologist from the University of Minnesota, and a close colleague and friend. He was at one time the lead scientist in a lawsuit directed against the FDA to require the government to label all genetically altered foods.

that we have called nation-states. Bill Readings (1996) wondered poignantly if the Kantian idea of the rational university that would teach the citizen about the rational state is now passé, and its meaning adrift. Where, then, may the idea of a university locate itself?

Relations between structures of economic and social life now rise into contestation, as transnational corporations operate between and around the concepts of nationhood and law. This further destabilizes or blurs our positioning in the world. Within the recent rise of cosmology, the sense of our being has diminished radically. After a few centuries of forms of humanism that urged us to center our being upon our lives and our experience, we find ourselves in the vast universes of sci-fi and more blurring of boundaries: in these contexts, between life and death, and the questioning of the meaning of life being determined outside of our very existence.[57]

One more arena of great change in the academy that has reflexes of a cycle from the late 19th century is the amazing concentration upon money as the measure of the quality of life, the developments that drove the 'Re-Organizing Knowledge' conference (where an earlier version of this essay was published) had led in the 19th century to the kinds of biology, evolutionary psychology, and neurology of determinism now increasing in vogue: then they called it eugenics. Here again, the temptation to ask questions about the meaning of our lives and of the university are obscured by the excitement the idea that we are close to finally solving the problem of the human by means of the brain MRI (magnetic resonance imaging). Evolutionary psychology – by any name – is very similar to the Social Darwinism that accompanied the Gilded Age and Robber Barons of the 19th century. Much of it seems like

---

[57] In a recent course, I taught 'philosophy' to a group of middle-school children. I observed that these arenas (stories, movies, videos, games) pervade their thinking, most of it remaining floating and uninterpreted (Minneapolis Metropolitan School).

politics in the name of science, especially if one takes seriously the political applications of eugenics theories in Hitler's realms. As a greater portion of our being is being seen as predetermined by our genes, the nature of our actual experience recedes into the background and is unimportant, or uninteresting…or not-psychology or not-biology. As money replaces meaning, and the game goes to the most competitive, the notion that these aspects of our being are particularly hereditary becomes first interesting, then compelling. Education is directed toward success; success determined by the opportunities and fads of the day.

If the experience of the early 20th century parallels the excesses of the current love affair with money, here at least there is some direction: some form of retrieve or return to a progressive pragmatism along the lines of thought of John Dewey et al. (Hofstadter, 1992).[58] What this presages is an increasing concern with experience and doing, replacing the sense that how we got here is more determinative than how we experience and live our lives. And we have to re-earn some of the authority that has so diminished in this era of celebrity and consumerism.

The Study of the Present Age

Much of this analysis of the university and the contexts in which it finds itself, our wondering about the future of knowledge and of the idea of a university, seem to be as much in flux as one can imagine. It is primarily for this reason that my vision of the Study of the Present Age seems like a good path for solution to the future university. In this essay, I have taken the position that the *Idea of the University* remains an important one, both in developing and preserving. I assume, believe, and trust, as well, that there must remain some deep

---

[58] See: Hofstadter, 1992, Chapter 7, "The Current of Pragmatism," pp. 123-142.

sense of integrity to the institution; that we can and must pursue the truth. I do not mind the polemics or arguments – at least most of them. The split between the sciences and the humanities, the curses or cries of joy of postmodernism, rifts like those between the notions of rationality that abound in economics, psychiatry, philosophy, and law, seem to me really interesting. I try to study and discuss them. Except – they get very little public discussion and less awareness. We have tended to retreat into our protective and protected spaces, rather than explore and confront those who are different from us, or those who disagree with us. The politics of academe are not always pretty. But the differences and depths of disciplined thinking remain very important in the human condition. And I remain somewhat confident that disagreements or passings-by can be brokered, understood, sometimes reconciled; but not within the currents of isolation that presently make the university easier to administer or to compete with others.

There are, in fact, several universities within the one that is the University of Minnesota. For example, many of the disciplines promote thinking that depends on case studies and abstracts to generalities later (law, medicine, anthropology, engineering, and in some ways the humanities, which often use texts as cases), while others begin abstractly and come to specifics much later (math, physics, much of biology). In this context, the notion of theory is often used as a bludgeon, a bit of politics attempting to raise the import of certain studies, persons, or claims, while the theorists often relegate the case studiers to lesser status. It is similar with those who tend toward the analytic and reductionistic *talking past* their colleagues who are more holistic. In this context, there are palpable cycles whose patron saint may be likened to Humpty Dumpty. Here, philosophy is presently seen as coming to an analytic impasse, with a call back to a renewed *American Pragmatism.*[59]

We have also been creating institutional distance and disparity between research and teaching, stemming from the 1960s, but continuing. In our recent attempts to distinguish the university from (apparently) competing private and public colleges, we have been playing games with teaching, making it burden more than joy. In the Center for the Study of the Present Age, students will want to study with the best thinkers, not merely seek the easiest or most convenient credentials. Lecturing with Power Point is most often *telling* much more than it is *teaching*.

I have to think that good management can enable us to get beyond the social definitions of whose teaching, thinking, knowledge is more important, simply by virtue of their belonging to a field that is currently prestigious or "hot." All of this tends toward the bureaucratic, neither attractive nor intelligible. Vast differences in pay scales represent image and visibility and the incursions of markets, and continue to erode the institution. And this has also contributed to the notion that credentials are more important than education. This will not be the case at an important University of Minnesota. The Study of the Present Age admits and commits to the idea that the world is changing very rapidly and in ways that we cannot fully understand or penetrate in any moment. The Present Age is a concept that may enable us to grasp the present, and to move it toward the futurity of its students (what parents, community, legislators, and businesses really desire – they are running scared for their children's futures!). In an unscripted world, the university has to become and remain some sort of anchor. It is necessary to be the important University of Minnesota because

---

[59] Donald Davidson, a leading analytic philosopher, made just this point in a series of lectures at the University of Minnesota in 1998: 'The Resurrection of Truth' pointed back to the work of Pragmatists, particularly John Dewey.

we have to have (earn and assert) sufficient authority to continue to claim to be persons who profess and pursue truth. It seems okay not to know everything at once…if we can show that we possess and continue to pursue the wisdom(s) of this time and of all of time.

The Center for the Study of the Present Age is a concept (soon, we hope, to be a reality) that will study, monitor, critique, and interact with these times. It will engage the entire faculty in a joint enterprise and regain in us the sense that we are a community of scholars: in it the distinction between research-scholarship, teaching, and service will meld into a singular pursuit. The university must remain open to various communities, inviting them to participate and join us on occasion. Here, I include the global community, perhaps especially those persons of wisdom from the entire world who wish to continue their pursuits in conjoint contexts. Leadership will be paramount. A central commitment – of the president or chancellor – is crucial because she or he will have to have sufficient *nerve* to take Minnesota away from the secure comforts of pyramidal location, and to take or support us as we go our own way. Similarly, parents, students, citizens, and legislators will have to swallow deeply as we relocate ourselves globally, then locally. And we have to adjust to the conceptual sense that Internet, email, and virtual reality *are* us. We will have to rethink our ideas of aging, aging faculty, and the aging of the developed world with some study of the traditions in which teacher-as-sage is the direction and path of a very good life (Peterson, 1999). All of this will be done with the integrative sense that disciplined thinking can be done within the contexts of particular ideas, problems, and histories. It is paramount that some of us can explore, broker, and explain the nature of knowledge and the broad curriculum with and to one another.

The Study of the Present Age will preserve the idea of a university by entering the world at a level and in senses where we can do what it is *important* to do, as much in our own terms as possible: call it the pursuit of wisdom in changing times. We do this by studying and critiquing the world as it is occurring: carefully, well, thoughtfully, continually. We will need constructive criticism from the global community – and hope that they will join us frequently in our deliberations. In this way, we will also be able to preserve, conserve, and continue the liberal arts and sciences as they pursue knowledge in their variously disciplined modes and manners. The curriculum is vast, often competitive, and whether it serves the futures of our students is at much risk in the momentariness of vogues, fads, and ready markets. I hope that having a Center that pulls everyone together some of the time will enable us to know and to study one another, and to stop much of the division and miscommunication that have characterized the bureaucratization of the university in the past few decades.

Careers belong to the ephemeral world and political economies, so we have to reinvent the pursuit of character and of vocation, which will help us to be models for and inspirers of our students. It is we, the thinkers, the teachers, those of us who attempt to be *real professors* who can attempt to guarantee or underwrite the sense that students' futures can remain hopeful and doable. It is the idea of a University in the Present Age that is the vision for this coming reality.

References

Cohen, M. D., & March, J. G. (1974). *Leadership and ambiguity: The American college president.* New York, NY: McGraw-Hill.

Hofstadter, R., & Metzger, W. (1955). *The development of academic freedom in the United States.* New York, NY: Columbia University Press.

Hofstadter, R. (1992). *Social Darwinism in American thought*. Boston, MA: Beacon Press.

Kerr, C. (1963). *The uses of the university*. New York, NY: Harper & Row.

Kerr, C. (1991). *The great transformation in higher education: 1960– 1980*. Albany, NY: SUNY Press

Kierkegaard, S. (1940). *The present age and two minor ethico-religious treatises*. (A. Dru & W. Lowrie, Trans.). London, UK: Oxford University Press.

Newman, J. H. (1953). *University Sketches*. Dublin, Ireland: Browne & Nolan.

Newman, J. H. (1976). *The idea of a university: Defined and illustrated*. Oxford, UK: Clarendon Press.

Nietzsche, F. (1968). *The will to power*. New York, NY: Vintage.

Peterson, P. G. (1999). *Gray dawn: How the coming age wave will transform America – and the world*. New York, NY: Times Books.

Readings, B. (1996). *The university in ruins*. Cambridge, MA: Harvard University Press.

Sarles, H. B. (1998). Explaining ourselves through others. Cultural visions: A mini course on America. In J. A. Mestenhauser & B. J. Ellingboe (Eds.), *Reforming the Higher Education Curriculum: Internationalizing the Campus* (pp. 135-149). Phoenix, AZ: American Council on Education/Oryx Press.

Sarles, H. B. (2001). *Nietzsche's prophecy: The crisis in meaning*.

Buffalo, NY: Humanity Press.

Sarles, H. B. (2010). *Prediction! or Prophecy?* Unpublished manuscript.

Sarles, H. B. (2013). *Teaching as dialogue: A teacher's study.* Los Angeles, CA: Trébol Press.

Snow, C. P. (1964). The two cultures and a second look: An expanded version of the two cultures and the scientific revolution. Cambridge, UK: Cambridge University Press.

Wilshire, B. (1990). *The moral collapse of the university: Professionalism, purity, and alienation.* Albany, NY: SUNY Press.

Contributing Author Biographies

Alethea de Villiers, *Nelson Mandela Metropolitan University, Port Elizabeth, South Africa*

Alethea de Villiers lectures Music Education at the Nelson Mandela Metropolitan University, South Africa, and serves on the teaching and learning committee in the Faculty of Arts. She is passionate about adult education and developed and manages an accredited qualification program for the arts for in-service teachers as funded by the Provincial Department of Education. She has extensive experience in developing materials and presenting workshops in the creative arts. Before joining academia, she was a senior education specialist for the arts and served on the Provincial Learning Area Committee. She is a Commissioner for ISME for the Commission on Music Policy: Cultural, Educational and Mass Media for the period 2012-2018. She is the Treasurer for the SASMT Port Elizabeth branch. Her research interests include creative arts, democratic citizenship education, multicultural education and continued professional development.

Giridhari Lal Pandit, *Institute for Social and Economic Change, Bangalore, India; University of Delhi South Campus, New Delhi, India; Institut für Theoretische Physik, Universität Heidelberg*

Born and educated in Kashmir, Giridhari Lal Pandit works in the fields of the methodology of science, epistemology, the philosophy of science, ecological economics, Umweltrealismus, international political economy of the environment, human rights, and ethics in the public domain. His publications include *The Frontiers of Theory Development in*

Physics: A Methodological Study in its Dynamical Complexity (2013, Trébol Press), *The Structure and Growth of Scientific Knowledge: A Study in the Methodology of Epistemic Appraisal* (1982), *Methodological Variance: Essays in Epistemological Ontology and the Methodology of Science* (1991), and *Von der Oekologie des Bewusstseins zum Umweltrealismus* (1995), among over 80 peer-reviewed published articles.

Karl Rogers, *Universidad de Belgrano, Buenos Aires; University of Buenos Aires; John Dewey Center for the Study of Democracy and Education*

Karl Rogers is Co-founder and Director of the John Dewey Center for Democracy and Education, Professor of Philosophy at the University of Buenos Aires, Visiting Lecturer at Universidad de Belgrano, Buenos Aires, and remains an Honorary Research Fellow with Columbia University, New York and at the University of Bath, United Kingdom. Professor Rogers's publications include *Occupy Media! Propaganda and the Free Press*; *Debunking Glenn Beck: How to Save America from Media Pundits and Propagandists*; *Participatory Democracy, Science and Technology*; *Modern Science and the Capriciousness of Nature*; *On the Metaphysics of Experimental Physics*, and other titles.

Harvey Sarles, *University of Minnesota*

Harvey Sarles is a cultural critic who attempts to study, analyze, and critique the world, thence the university within it. He was trained at the University of Chicago as an anthropologist-linguist in the pragmatist, symbolic-interactionist tradition of G. H. Mead, and John Dewey, receiving his PhD in 1966. He sees himself as "an anthropologist of the ordinary." His re-envisioning the university is an aspect or outgrowth of his book *Nietzsche's Prophecy: the Crisis in Meaning* (Humanity Press: 2001). He has also written about language as an aspect of interaction (*Language and Human Nature*, University of Minnesota Press, 1985), and about teaching as a dialogue (*Teaching as Dialogue: A Teacher's Study*, University Press of America, 1993; Trébol Press, 2013). In 2001, he was awarded the College of Liberal Arts, Arthur "Red" Motley prize for excellence in teaching, U. of Minnesota. For more information on publications and his blog, see: harveysarles.com/

Francis J. Schweigert, *Metropolitan State University, Minneapolis, Minnesota*

Francis J. Schweigert is Associate Professor and Director of the Master of Public and Nonprofit Administration program in the College of Management at Metropolitan State University in Minneapolis, Minnesota. His primary areas of instruction and research are nonprofit management, public ethics, and evaluation. He has twenty-five years of experience in nonprofit management and has served as a mediator and circle keeper in restorative justice since 1996. He earned his doctorate in Educational Policy and Administration from the University of Minnesota in 1997, with a focus on the social and philosophical foundations of education.

Alon Serper, *Nelson Mandela Metropolitan University, Port Elizabeth, South Africa*

Alon Serper received his PhD from the University of Bath, United Kingdom. The PhD was on a theoretical model of an applied dialectical method for the theorization and study of human beings and human existence through individuals learning to self-empower. He is empirically testing and developing this model and interested in using his method becoming a tool for the improvement of human dignity and equality. His Individual Graduate Programme (at the Hebrew University of Jerusalem) criticized propositional logic and argued that the dialectical logic is more suitable for the study of humanity and societies.

Laurel Cadwallader Stolte, *Harvard Graduate School of Education*

Laurel Cadwallader Stolte is currently a doctoral student at the Harvard Graduate School of Education and an English as a Second Language teacher and coordinator of a dual language program in Durham (NC) Public Schools. She has also taught social studies and Spanish and worked with service learning and action civics programs. As a practitioner, researcher, and parent, she is interested in educational approaches that promote civic engagement and cross-cultural interaction in diverse communities.

Austin Volz, *Harvard Graduate School of Education*

Austin Volz, born in Colorado, received his Bachelor's from St. John's College in Santa Fe, NM and his Master's in Education in International Education Policy from the Harvard Graduate School of Education. His international work experience includes teaching in Greece, a Fulbright in Germany, and running team building programs at international schools in China with the JUMP! Foundation. Now a visiting scholar at Fudan University in Shanghai he is researching students' perceptions of the value of non-specialized (or liberal arts) education in Chinese universities.

John Warner, *Whole Systems Agriculture*

John Warner is a former LAUSD high school teacher who operates *Whole Systems Agriculture* and *Whole Systems Education* foundation from his nursery and garden in Madera County, California, where he grows flowers and food for family, friends, and visitors. Visit his website
http://www.netptc.net/flowermanoat/WSAgHTM/Pages/

About the Editor

Viktoria Byczkiewicz is a lecturer in the American Language Institute at the University of Southern California. She is the Chief Copyeditor and Associate Editor for Trébol Press. She is the author of *Blaming, Shaming, and Framing the Immigrant as Other in U.S.-Mexico Borderlands Cinema.*

Call for Papers: Democracy & Education 2015

The John Dewey Center for Democracy and Education of the University of Minnesota seeks to publish a *second collection* of peer-reviewed papers continuing on the primary theme of "Democracy and Education."

The second in the series, to be titled "Democracy & Education 2015: Language, Communication, and Discourse," is slated to be published in **Spring 2015**.

The peer-reviewed 2015 collection will focus on matters pertaining to language teaching and discursive, critical, or analytical approaches to issues or phenomena connected to democracy, communication, and education. We welcome contributions that critically reflect upon or describe any aspect of language in relation to democracy and education. Works may address a broad spectrum of issues pertaining to language or communication in democracy and education, or how language relates to public discourse, social media, or discourse *in* teaching.

Required length: Minimum of 5,000 to a maximum of 12,000 words.

Style Requirements: APA style – Sixth Edition of the Publication Manual of the American Psychological Association. Contributors are responsible for conforming reference lists and in-text citations. (See the Trébol Press website www.trebolpress.com. Resources and advice can also be obtained via the editor.)

Deadline for abstracts: July 30, 2014
Deadline for submissions: October 31, 2014

Send submissions and queries to: byczkiew@usc.edu and/or to editor@trebolpress.com

Edited by Viktoria Byczkiewicz (University of Southern California).

To be published by Trébol Press, Los Angeles, CA.

www.ingramcontent.com/pod-product-compliance
Lightning Source LLC
Chambersburg PA
CBHW052119270326
41930CB00012B/2688